Secrets
of Successful
Speakers

Secrets of Successful Speakers

How You Can Motivate,
Captivate, and Persuade

Lilly Walters

With Forewords by

Norman Vincent Peale

and

Stew Leonard, Jr.

McGraw-Hill, Inc.

New York   San Francisco   Washington, D.C.   Auckland   Bogotá
Caracas   Lisbon   London   Madrid   Mexico City
Milan   Montreal   New Delhi   San Juan
Singapore   Sydney   Tokyo   Toronto

Library of Congress Cataloging-in-Publication Data

Walters, Lillet.
    Secrets of successful speakers : how you can motivate, captivate, and
persuade / Lilly Walters.
        p.   cm.
    Includes index.
    ISBN 0-07-068033-7 (hc) :   —ISBN 0-07-068034-5 (pbk.) :
    1. Public speaking.   I. Title.
    PN4121.W327   1993
    808.5′1—dc20   92-46321
                                                                        CIP

        7 8 9 0   DOC/DOC   9 9 8 7 6

ISBN 0-07-068033-7 (hc)
ISBN 0-07-068034-5 (pbk)

*The sponsoring editor for this book was Betsy N. Brown, the editing supervisor
was Jane Palmieri, the designer was Susan Maksuta, and the production supervisor was Suzanne W. Babeuf. It was set in Palatino by McGraw-Hill's
Professional Book Group composition unit.*

Printed and bound by R. R. Donnelley & Sons Company.

 This book is printed on recycled, acid-free paper containing a
minimum of 50% recycled de-inked fiber.

To Mom, who pushed me to "do,"
to Dad, who loved me even when I didn't,
and to Melodie, who for 30 years has given
me unconditional friendship and love

Contents

Step 1

SET OBJECTIVES THAT MAKE A FABULOUS SPEECH
Select the Seed   1

Step 2

DEVELOP THE RIGHT TALK FOR THE RIGHT AUDIENCE—CUSTOMIZATION
Find Fertile Soil   11

Step 3

CONQUER STAGE FRIGHT AND YOUR FEAR OF MAKING CHANGES
Plant the Seed in the Ground   31

Step 4

BE CREDIBLE—BE AN EXPERT
Sink Your Roots Down Deep   45

Step 5

THE KEY TO A MEMORABLE PRESENTATION— DEVELOP A THEME
A Solid Trunk   51

Step 6

FINDING AND ORGANIZING MATERIAL IN A MEMORABLE MANNER
Grow Strong, Sturdy Boughs   **57**

Step 7

EDITING THE MATERIAL FOR ITS BEST EFFECT
Prune the Deadwood   **92**

Step 8

YOUR IMAGE FROM THE PLATFORM
Leaves of Brilliant Color   **101**

Step 9

MOTIVATING AN AUDIENCE
Call Them to Pick the Fruit   **121**

Step 10

TOOLS TO DELIVER THE SPEECH AND BUILD RAPPORT WITH YOUR AUDIENCE
Till the Soil   **135**

Step 11
AVOIDING THE PROBLEMS AND PITFALLS OF THE PLATFORM
Protect It All from Wilt   169

YOUR PRESENTATION WORKSHEET   193

CHECKLIST TO SAVE YOUR PRESENTATION FROM DISASTER   195

THE 10 PERCENT I HOPE YOU WILL REMEMBER ABOUT MY BOOK   203

CURTAIN CALL BY LILLY WALTERS   205

Who's Who of
the Celebrity Speakers

Steve Allen is a comedian on radio and television and an actor both in Hollywood and on Broadway for over four decades. Among his numerous accomplishments are creating NBC's *Tonight* show and the award-winning PBS series *Meeting of Minds*. He is the author of many books, including *How to Make a Speech* and *How to Be Funny*.

Jack Anderson is a Pulitzer-winning investigative columnist, radio talk show host, television personality, Washington editor of *Parade* magazine, and editor of *The National Forum, American Satire*, and *The National Gallery of Cartoon*. He is founder and chairman of the million-member Young Astronaut Program, chairman of the International Platform Association, and cochairman with industrialist J. Peter Grac of Citizens against Government Waste.

Ralph Archbold, CPAE[1], has addressed over 7000 groups through his portrayal of Benjamin Franklin. His realistic portrayal and stimulating performances have brought him many awards and much recognition. He is considered the leading Franklin portrayer in the United States, and he delights thousands each year at corporate meetings, conventions, and special events.

Letitia Baldrige began her government career at the American Embassy in Paris, then in Rome. She was Tiffany & Co.'s first woman executive and first director of public relations. During John F. Kennedy's administration, she was chief of staff for Mrs. Kennedy and social secretary to the White House. She has served as adviser to four subsequent first ladies.

---

[1]The CPAE is an award for the National Speakers Association; CPAE stands for Council of Peers Award of Excellence. Each year five speakers are selected. A small committee within NSA picks the new CPAEs. This award is exclusive to the membership of NSA.

Arden Bercovitz, Ph.D., is a very unique presenter. He is a part of Walters International Speakers Bureau's Dead Speakers Society. "Einstein by Bercovitz" offers a fascinating, authentic, respectful inspirational interpretation of Albert Einstein, adapted to the theme and purpose of the meeting.

Dr. Kenneth Blanchard is the chairman of the board of Blanchard Training and Development and codeveloper of the One-Minute Manager and Situational Leadership and Professor of Leadership and Organizational Behavior at the University of Massachusetts, Amherst. He coauthored, with Paul Hersey, *Management of Organizational Behavior: Utilizing Human Resources*; coauthored, with Spencer Johnson, the best-seller *The One-Minute Manager*; and coauthored, with Robert Lorber, Ph.D., *Putting the One-Minute Manager to Work*.

Dianna Booher, M.A., is a prolific author and business communications consultant to many *Fortune* 500 corporations. Ms. Booher is the author of 25 commercially published books, 4 audios, and 4 videos. She is also the founder and president of Booher Consultants, Inc., a business communications training company.

Roger Burgraff, Ph.D., has spent over 20 years in healthcare and is the author of five audio album packages, including *Powerful Leadership Secrets, Management by Assertiveness*, and *Persuasive Power Skills*. Burgraff does keynotes and seminars on "Power Communication Skills to Influence and Inspire" and "Communicating through the Gaps: Gender, Age, and Cultural Prejudice."

Dave Carey, Captain, USN (Ret.), is a sought-after professional speaker, consultant, and trainer. His background includes more than 20 years of executive-level leadership, management, and sales positions, as well as over 5 years as a POW in Vietnam. Dave works extensively in the areas of motivation, team building, leadership, and organizational development.

Nick Carter is vice president of communication research of Nightingale-Conant Corporation—the world leader in audiocassette and videocassette training systems. He has three books published and has produced many cassette albums for Nightingale-Conant.

Jim Cathcart is an international speaker, author, and expert on human behavior as applied to business. He has given over 1000 presentations worldwide. He is the author of six books, including *Relationship Selling*, and the creator of the seminar "The Art of Choosing Well."

Terry Cole-Whittaker is a speaker, workshop and seminar leader, best-selling author, teacher, counselor, futurist, star, executive producer of over 250 television shows, entertainer-singer, and ecologist.

Philip Crosby, an executive and author, has written eight books which have sold several million copies. He founded Philip Crosby Associates, Inc. (PCA), in 1979 to counsel corporations on quality management. Today PCA has 300 employees worldwide with annual revenues of over $80 million and is the largest in its industry. Today he is chairman of Career IV, Inc., a new company established for the purpose of helping executives to prepare for managing in the twenty-first century.

Jeff Dewar is an international author, speaker, and trainer who is famous for the set of statistics that say, "What Does 99.9 Percent Quality Mean to You? It means…" He is the author of *Competing for Quality* (audio tape); *Outdated Quality vs. the Total Quality Revolution* (booklet); *The Conquering Change Challenge* (audio tape); *How to Out-Participate Your Participative Manager* (book); and *Games Presenters Play* (video training program).

Harvey Diamond is an international speaker, author, lecturer, wellness pioneer, and coauthor of *Fit for Life*, written with his nutritionist wife Marilyn; the book has sold 8 million copies globally and has been published in 19 languages and printed in 33 countries. (Mr. Diamond's participation in this book was thoughtfully arranged by his exclusive agent, Gerry Taush, Speaker's Connection Bureau.)

John Patrick Dolan is a hard-charging trial attorney; his book, *Negotiate Like the Pros*, and his audio and video by the same title are best-sellers. Dolan has spoken about negotiations to audiences in Hong Kong, Singapore, Malaysia, Australia, New Zealand, Africa, the United Kingdom, Ireland, Canada, and all across the United States.

Tom Faranda is an international customer consultant with clients such as IBM, AT&T, 3M, Siemens S. Africa, Bayer German, and Prudential Singapore. He is a former president of the Hospital Corporation of Chicago and author of *Uncommon Sense: Leadership Principles to Grow Your Business Profitably*.

Ed Foreman was a self-made millionaire at 26, the only person in this century to be elected to the U.S. Congress from two different states (Texas and New Mexico). Foreman developed a financially successful business career in construction, transportation, and petroleum development and has been president or executive committee member of 12 successful, diversified corporations.

Patricia Fripp, CPAE, is the first woman president of the National Speakers Association. Author of *Get What You Want*, Patricia speaks on "Change," "Teamwork," "Customer Service," and "How to Position Yourself Ahead of the Crowd."

Bobbie Gee is president of Bobbie Gee Enterprises and the founder of Halitec, a high-tech research and development company. She is also a consultant, speaker, and author who travels worldwide, making 50 to 75 presentations yearly.

Bill Gove, CPAE, was the first president of the National Speakers Association in 1972. Gove is chairman of the Advisory Board of Wilson Learning Corporation, and his awards include "Speaker of the Year," Sales and Marketing Executives, 1988; and "Golden Gavel Award" winner,[2] Toastmasters International, 1991.

---

[2]The Golden Gavel is the most prestigious award offered by Toastmasters International. It is presented annually to individuals who have distinguished themselves in the fields of communication and leadership. Recent recipients include Dr. Ken Blanchard, Tom Peters, Rear Admiral Grace Hopper, and Dr. Robert Schuller.

Colonel Gene Harrison (ret.) is president of Quest Management Consultants. A draftee, he rose from private to full colonel in the U.S. Marine Corps. A full-time speaker, executive coach, and management trainer for over 100 companies worldwide, his topics include leadership, team building, and total quality.

Ira Hayes, CPAE, is "The Ambassador of Enthusiasm." Hayes has crisscrossed the world for 37 years with his program, *Keeping Pace with Tomorrow*. A corporate executive with NCR Corporation and past president of the National Speakers Association, Hayes has written two best-selling books: *Yak, Yak, Yak* and *Success—Go for It*. He has been seen—live or on video—by more than 10 million people.

Christopher Hegarty is a businessman, author, journalist, and speaker. He has done programs for more than 400 groups. Elected to the Speakers Hall of Fame of the National Speakers Association, he is president of a foundation devoted to finding health and human competence breakthroughs.

Hattie Hill-Storks is president of Hattie Hill-Storks & Associates. Hattie has been around the world as a speaker and consultant combining people, information, and energy to provide universal change. Her personal story of triumph over poverty and racial prejudice has made her an inspiration to thousands.

Hermine Hilton, known as "America's Memory Motivator," is author of *The Executive Memory Guide* (considered to be one of the best "how-to" books for anyone's memory) and of the award-winning cassette *A Head Start to a Better Memory*. Hilton is the author and creator of the "NAMEMONIKS," the *N* word for the sound habit of remembering names.

Marcy Huber has 35 years of experience working with foreign-born people whose first language is not English. She gives seminars and workshops teaching American English accent reduction, idioms, and culture as well as working with Asian executives on American communication and presentation skills.

Suzie Humphreys is a speaker and wacky radio personality. A former TV talk show host, she now speaks around the world, often on the humorous topic, "Life Is What Happens While You Are Making Other Plans."

Dale Irvin is a comedy writer, stand-up comedian, humorous convention speaker, and a veteran of over 100 television appearances, including shows on MTV, Showtime, and A&E. He writes and publishes *Funny Business,* a comedy newsletter subscribed to by professional speakers, television and radio personalities, and corporate executives.

Danielle Kennedy, M.A., CPAE, is a celebrated author, lecturer, and inspirational speaker. She holds an honorary doctorate degree in the humanities from Clarke College. She is a member of the NSA Board of Directors and is in *Who's Who of America's Women*.

Al Lampkin has shared the stage with superstars Johnny Cash, Joan Rivers, Jerry Van Dyke, Henny Youngman, Crystal Gayle, the Pointer Sisters, Charlie

Pride, Reba McEntire, and many others. He has performed in 25 countries on 5 continents. He has appeared in over 100 movies and television shows.

Tom Leech, author of *How to Prepare, Stage, and Deliver Winning Presentations*, following a 20-year career in business development, engineering, and communication with General Dynamics, is today a full-time speaker coach. As a trainer, he's helped hundreds of businesspeople add to their presentation capability.

Stew Leonard, Jr. is the president of the original Stew Leonard's in Norwalk, Connecticut. This store serves 100,000 customers a week with sales in excess of $100 million a year—the most successful retail store in the world. Leonard is featured in Tom Peters' and Nancy Austin's *A Passion for Excellence*, where he is referred to as "the Disney of retail." He is currently one of the most sought · after speakers in the United States.

Candy Lightner's leadership, tenacity, and wonderful speaking skills enabled MADD (Mothers Against Drunk Drivers) to become an international corporation with over 377 chapters throughout the world. She is a popular campus and corporation speaker on such topics as "You Can Make a Difference" and "How You Can Succeed in Business Without Knowing What You Are Doing."

Florence Littauer, CPAE, is the author of 18 books that focus on areas of personal and spiritual growth. Her best-selling titles include *Personality Plus, Your Personality Tree, Personalities in Power, Silver Boxes*, and her most recent *Dare to Dream*. She is a graduate of the University of Massachusetts and the president of CLASS Speakers, Inc.

Dr. Layne Longfellow is a philosopher, a psychologist, a perceptive social commentator—and a musician with a quick wit. He has a talent for helping audiences connect aspects of life we all experience but don't quite understand. He speaks on ethics, the environment, generational values, and the cycle of life, addressing each with humor, compassion, and, above all, substance.

Doug Malouf is considered by his peers as the master of audience participation. He is the foundation vice president of the National Speakers Association of Australia. He has authored five books and two audiocassette albums and travels the globe showing audiences how to "Deliver a Presentation" that sells, in a fun and exciting way.

Dr. Albert Mehrabian received graduate degrees in engineering and psychology from MIT and Clark University and has been professor of psychology at UCLA since 1964. He is internationally recognized for his pioneering research in nonverbal communication, person and product names, emotions, temperament, and personality measurement. He has authored numerous books and scientific articles.

Dr. Michael H. Mescon is founder and chairman of the Mescon Group, Inc. (TMG). Chairman of the Management Department and Dean of the College of Business Administration at Georgia State University, he is the author or coauthor of over 200 articles and books, including *Business Today* (McGraw-Hill),

Management: Individual and Organizational Effectiveness, and *Showing Up for Work,* and Nightingale-Conant's audiocassette program, *Management Excellence: Leadership for the Future.*

Gerald C. Meyers, former chairman of the board and CEO of American Motors, is an industrialist, author, lecturer, and management consultant. He is also the Ford Distinguished Professor of Business at the Graduate School of Industrial Administration at Carnegie Mellon University. He wrote the highly acclaimed book, *When It Hits the Fan: Managing the Nine Crises of Business.*

Hope Mihalap is a humorist and accent specialist whose original wit and theories on good communication are based on her personal life as a Greek-American (from Virginia) married to a Russian. She has worked in the fields of journalism, radio, opera, and theater. In 1991 she received the International Platform Associations Mark Twain Award for humor, placing her in the company of such former recipients as Bob Hope, Danny Kaye, Erma Bombeck, and Art Buchwald.

Anita Cheek Milner, M.A., J.D.—known as the "Change-of-Life Attorney"— passed the California Bar Exams at the age of 50. She is a humorist and presents all over the United States. She often moonlights as a stand-up comic. She has appeared on TV, at the San Diego Improv, and on *America's Funniest People.*

Jeanine Walters Miranda has taught speech communication classes at Chaffey College for 20 years. She applies her communication skills helping high-risk teens to stay in school and graduate. She runs one of the most successful programs of its kind in California and has traveled to Canada and spoken to the Ministers of Education about her program.

W Mitchell has been called the "Man Who Won't Be Defeated." He delivers a message about mastering adversity from his wheelchair on how people can deal with setbacks and put themselves back in charge. Mitchell was hit by a drunk driver and suffered massive burns over his entire body, resulting in the loss of most of his hands, face, and feet. He fought through to become a millionaire. He went up in his private plane one day and crashed, becoming a paraplegic. Mitchell then went on into a new life again with tremendous success. Having overcome these two life-threatening—and life-changing—accidents, he talks to groups about the possibilities of the human mind and spirit.

Judi Moreo has been the CEO of Universal Convention and Trade Associates for 21 years. She is a motivational business speaker in the United States, Canada, Australia, Europe, Africa, Singapore, Indonesia, China, Malaysia, Thailand, and Mexico.

Tom Ogden brings over 15 years of performance experience as a comedian and magician to the lecture platform. His television appearances include dozens of talk shows from New York to Sydney, Australia. Ogden's magic skill has won top awards, including twice being voted "Magician of the Year" in the Parlor of Prestidigitation at Hollywood's Magic Castle.

Alan Parisse has 25 years of executive-level experience in one of the fastest-changing industries of all—investments. In the investment business, he is something of a legend. Today he advises a wide variety of organizations, including AT&T, IBM, Texaco, New York Telephone, Westinghouse, and Monsanto, as well as many major securities firms, banks, insurance companies, and real estate firms.

Dr. Terry Paulson, CPAE, is a licensed psychologist and author of the popular books *They Shoot Managers Don't They, Secrets of Life Every Teen Needs to Know,* and *Making Humor Work.* Dr. Paulson has conducted programs on "Making Changes Work" with ARCO, AMI, 3M, Hughes, IBM, Nissan, Texaco, TEC, TRW, YPO, and many universities, hospitals, and associations throughout the country. *Business Digest* has called him the "Will Rogers of business consultants."

Dr. Norman Vincent Peale is the author of 42 books, of which *The Power of Positive Thinking,* one of the most successful books ever published, has been translated into 42 languages, with a sale of over 15 million copies. The title has become part of many languages. His latest books are *My Favorite Quotations* and *The Power of Positive Living.* Messages by Dr. Peale are mailed to over one million people monthly from the Peale Center for Christian Living in New York. Over 31 million copies of his inspirational booklets are distributed yearly. Dr. Peale has received 22 honorary doctoral degrees.

Allan Pease is the head of Pease Training Corporation, which teaches sales and negotiation techniques. He is the creator of video and training films, audiocassette programs, and books that are used in over 100 countries in 29 languages. His best-selling books include *Body Language, Talk Language,* and *Write Language* (with Paul Dunn).

Rosita Perez, CPAE, is a former social worker and mental health administrator who uses music and a guitar to share substantive messages in an atmosphere of fun and camaraderie. Perez is noted for the dynamic way she brings people closer by addressing their roles apart from what they do on the job.

Gene Perret, a humorist and the head writer for Bob Hope, has written comedy for many of the greats, including Phyllis Diller, Bill Cosby, Tim Conway, and 25 years with Bob Hope. He has won three Emmys for his humor writing. Gene is an entertaining banquet speaker who preaches the value of a sense of humor for everyone. Perret has also written 14 books of or about humor.

Stephen C. Rafe is an international spokesperson and counselor who worked with such clients as Johnson & Johnson during the Tylenol Crisis, AT&T during divestiture, President Reagan's Committee on Strategic Forces for the MX missile, and NASA's administrators, flight directors, and astronauts for the space program. Rafe has written three books on presentations.

Reverend Bob Richards, CPAE, is a two-time Olympic Gold Medalist in the pole vault and was a national decathlon champion for three years. He won the Sullivan Award and the Helms World Trophy and is in seven halls of fame. As a speaker he has won the highest speaking awards given: The Golden Gavel from Toastmasters International and the Sales and Marketing Executives' International Speakers Hall of Fame.

Anthony Robbins, 32, is a nationally recognized authority in the field of human-development training. He has served as a peak-performance consultant to executives of such organizations as IBM, AT&T, American Express, McDonnell-Douglas, and the U.S. Army. He annually conducts more than 100 days of personal, professional, and corporate improvement seminars across North America, with attendance figures for the last eight years exceeding 400,000. In the last 2½ years alone he has distributed more than 10 million educational audiocassettes, and his *Personal Power* television show has reached 100 million nationwide. Mr. Robbins wrote the national best-sellers *Unlimited Power* and *Awaken the Giant Within*.

Cavett Robert is the founder and president emeritus of the National Speakers Association in the United States and a recipient of the Golden Gavel Award from Toastmasters. In 1973 he was selected by United Airlines and International Speakers Network as the Speaker of the Year from a canvass of over 10,000 associations, convention planners, and corporations. He has been honored many times as a top speaker and salesperson.

Wess Roberts, Ph.D., is a former executive with American Express, Fireman's Fund, Northrop Services, and Courseware, Inc., and the best-selling author of *Leadership Secrets of Attila the Hun, Straight A's Never Made Anybody Rich*, and *Victory Secrets of Attila the Hun*. As an adjunct professor, he has taught undergraduate and graduate courses in business, education, and psychology.

Mark Sanborn has spoken in 48 states, Canada, Europe, Asia, and Australia to audiences ranging in size from 12 to 22,000. He presents over 80 speeches and seminars a year on leadership, team building, and service and is the author of four audio and two video training programs. His book *Teambuild: Making Teamwork Work* is published by Master Media.

Jeff Slutsky, "The Streetfighter," specializes in teaching how to advertise, promote, market, and increase sales without spending money! Slutsky is the author of *Streetfighting: Street Smart Marketing* and *Street Smart Tele-Selling: How to Get Clients*. He has been featured in *The Wall Street Journal, USA Today*, and *Success*.

Dottie Walters is the president of Walters International Speakers Bureau. Dottie began her speaking career over 25 years ago when she wrote the first book ever written for saleswomen, by a woman, *Never Underestimate the Selling Power of a Woman*. Since then she has been one of the premier female sales motivators on the platform. She has spoken around the world and is publisher of *Sharing Ideas*, the largest publication in the world for professional speakers.

R. Michael Walters is an attorney, author, and speaker and one of the leading experts for mobile home park owners.

Somers White, CPAE, CSP, CMC, has presented programs to executives and sales personnel from 400 of *Fortune*'s list of 500 largest companies. He has spoken in all 50 states and every continent except Antarctica. His master's degree is from Harvard, and he started his business career on Wall Street with the Executive Training Program of Chase Manhattan Bank. A former Arizona state senator, he has been a member of the Arizona State University faculty, teaching the course in management and bank management.

Zig Ziglar is a motivational teacher and the author of nine books, seven of which have made best-seller lists. He is the chairman of the board of his own company, the Zig Ziglar Corporation, and is considered by many as the foremost sales speaker in the world.

Foreword

Lilly, you got me fired up today talking about speaking. Your mother, Dottie, has shared her enthusiasm with you! I remember when Dottie came around to meetings, she'd say, "Think of your speech as food for your audience. As a speaker you must fill people up! There are a good many discouraged people out there. They are coming to hear you speak. You must fill them up so when they go out into the world they can *solve* their problems."

I find inspiring speakers all around me. Listening to great speakers got me fired up to speak myself. I'm 94 now. I got started speaking in my youth when I was president of the Ohio Boys Congress. I went around to every county in the state making speeches. I must have been 17 years old then.

I was greatly inspired by Williams Jennings Bryan. He was enthusiastic, he was a believer—not a nonbeliever. He didn't talk about what he didn't believe, he talked about what he believed. The audience went away from a speech by Bryan convinced or not convinced—but at least they were thinking. I still admire him.

I was living in Brooklyn, New York, when Bryan came to speak in the old Academy of Music. He was a master at drawing the attention of his audience to some simple little thing. He had on the stage a table, a chair, a pitcher of water, and a glass. Nothing else. During his speech, when he wanted to let something soak into the minds of his audience, he'd pick up the pitcher. He'd lift it 2½, maybe 3 feet and pour a stream of water into the glass. He'd pour that water into that glass without dropping a single speck of it! Then without missing a single beat, the water went down the hatch! That is what endeared him to the public. He could take a little situation like that and make a real memory of it—one that I've remembered for 60 years.

When you get people to listen to what you believe, you get on fire yourself—big fires, little fires—that never do go out. I met Everett Dirkson in the airport in St. Louis, one of the greatest speakers of the day. He said, "You are a great speaker, I know, I've heard you."

"Where was it?" I asked.

"I forget the circumstances," he answered, "but you said the following . . . ," and he repeated what I had said verbatim. That is the greatest compliment you can have as a speaker. It lights a real fire in you.

I remember a young fellow who wanted me to advise him on how to be a good speaker! I told him,

> "Be interesting,
>
>   be enthusiastic...
>
>   and don't talk too much!"

Norman Vincent Peale

Foreword

Did I ever mention how I ended up getting into speaking? It was Sam Malone down at Milikin Textiles. He asked if I would come and give a speech to his management group. "Management group"—that's the way he said it. I said, "Wow! But I don't give speeches like *that*!" And he said, "Don't worry about the speech. I'll be your coach."

The night before my speech I walked into a ballroom where the meeting was to be the next morning. There were 400 chairs set up for this "little ol' management group." They had me set up to speak right in the middle of Buck Rogers, the retired senior vice president of IBM, and Joe Girard, who was in the *Guinness Book of World Records* as the world's number-one car salesman.

The guy who is the head of Jack Morton Productions was doing the whole big high-tech side of the show, and he said, "Where's your slides?" He took one of my slides out, looked at it, and said, "Who took these?" And I said, "Why, I took them all myself, right around the store." He looked at me and said, "These are the most *unprofessional* slides I've ever had to work with." See, they weren't glass-mounted. I didn't even know what a "glass mount" was.

So the next morning I give my speech. Well, I get all done, get off the stage, and the same production guy smiles and he shakes my hand. He says, "Stew, don't change a thing. Your slides match your speech perfectly."

So I come back to the store, I feel great. No more speeches, the whole thing was good and done. The next Saturday morning Tony D'Amelio from the Washington Speakers Bureau[1] came into the store and said,

---

[1] The Washington Speakers Bureau is one of the largest speakers bureaus in the world. Even speakers who have been speaking professionally for years would be honored to be called by the Washington Speakers Bureau.

"Stew, I just got reports back from Jack Morton Productions. They said, you have a fresh type of style. You're not polished, but you have a strong message. How would you like to do a few dates for us? Just a few speeches, I think we can get you six a year." I talked it over with my wife and finally figured, well, I can do *just* six....

The first one I did was Domino's Pizza for Frank Meeks, who's one of their top franchisers. I was as nervous as could be. But after I was done Frank and I sat and talked about our businesses. We each walked away with pages of notes to use to improve our business. Later I said to my wife, "Wow, what a lucky thing it was that I was able to go give a speech to this guy, I'd never have met him otherwise." So I got pretty excited about speaking and started going and meeting different people from all kinds of different companies. I started doing 20 talks a year, and now I do pretty much about one a week.

Some of the groups I talk to are big fancy productions—really million-dollar shows. People put on the teleprompters and all sorts of computers and video graphics. They even use speechwriters to write the speeches for the executives of their companies. Once, one of the former U.S. president's speechwriters was in my audience. I had met him before my talk, and I asked would he do me a favor and critique my talk. So he sits down after I'm done and gives me pages and pages and pages of notes. Do this—do that—don't put your hand in your pocket—don't scratch your head as you're talking—don't say "um."

Then I meet other speakers and consultants on presenting. I even hired one of them to help me with my speaking, 'cause everybody told me I wasn't professional enough. They tried to get me to use all these acts: when you make a major point stretch your arms out so that you appear twice as big and it will have more of an impact. Make sure there's a lot of voice intonation, use better words, etc. So anyway, by then I had got almost a whole file on how to improve my speaking, but I was still feeling confused and uncomfortable.

Every Christmas my father and I have lunch with Paul Newman. We sell his salad dressing, and he lives right in town here. So I'm sitting with him, and I say, "Could you do me a favor? I'm all confused with this speaking stuff." I tell him about all the things the experts told me to do—how to dress, how to walk, how to talk, how to do all of it.

The first thing he said was, "Stew, don't listen to any of them. Speak from the heart. Speak about something you love talking about. Get into what you're doing. Don't write a script out. Prepare for the talk—but speak from the heart."

I don't want to downplay the use of speech coaches because there is a fellow that we use—Ron Arden of California—but, Lilly, he tries to get me to do what you do in this book, to be *me* more.

The best compliment I get is, when I'm done, somebody from the audience comes up to me, shakes my hand, and says, "Even though you're not professional, you could go out and get paid to speak." I'm sitting there thinking I'm glad I give that image of being fresh. I still scratch my head and say "um," but I am doing 50 or more professional speeches a year and just speaking from the heart.

Lilly, tell the readers in this book of yours to find out about the rules of making a good speech, but after they do, put them way in the back of their minds and just speak right from the heart!

Stew Leonard, Jr.

Preface

Did you pick up this book because y ou want to be in the top 2 percent of presenters? No? You were hoping for *standard* suggestions for presentation improvement? You are only doing a simple informative speech, maybe once every two years? Well, there are a bunch of excellent books on that. Try the next book over on the shelf.

Do you give presentations repeatedly? Do you *want to be captivating, motivating, and persuasive on the platform*? In that secret spot in your heart have you wanted to be as good as that wonderful speaker you heard as a child? This book is for you.

What makes the difference between presenters that are paid $1000 to $25,000 for an hour's presentation, and those that are asked to speak at no fee, but only a smiling, "Of course we'd be glad to buy you dinner"? What makes presenters memorable, captivating, and motivating? This book is the answer.

As a speakers bureau and lecture agent that also speaks on secrets of successful speakers, I am giving you my own secrets. In fact, a speaker who "lives" in my mind—what I call my "alter ego"—is always asking me questions. I'm passing on these questions, which will appear in italics, as well as my answers. But because I wanted more for you than just *my* secrets, I went to over 60 top speakers—celebrities, entertainers, trainers, and keynoters—and asked them to help me write this book. Great orators and masters of the spoken word, such as Norman Vincent Peale, Steve Allen, Anthony Robbins, Ken Blanchard, Jack Anderson, and Coach John Wooden, offer you their advice and secrets to your success on the platform. There is a Who's Who of Celebrity Speakers in the front of the book if you want to know more about each speaker.

I noticed with great delight that often these masters will state their "secret" as a hard-and-fast rule, only to have the next master totally disagree!

These masters have all traveled different roads to arrive where they are today. Harvey Diamond, author, lecturer, and wellness pioneer, feels an excellent image from the platform is vital; Ken Blanchard doesn't think it matters much at all. Yet both are undisputed masters of the platform. Many of their opinions on the "right way" to present are in direct opposition to mine.

So, who is right?

As you read, some of the secrets will reach out and grab you. Those are the "right way" for you. These secrets will give you the tools and inspiration you need to achieve the success you are ready for today. Reread our advice in a year and someone else's ideas will suddenly illuminate a dreary spot in your presentation style. All the while, you will develop your *own* secrets on how to become a master of the spoken word.

Make This the Most Valuable Book on Presentations You Have Ever Read!

How many times have you read a book with great intentions of going back over those great ideas you highlighted? How many did you ever go back to? One out of 20, maybe?

Time is precious. Chances are, you are going to read this just once, and, good intentions or not, you'll be off to your next project. (My favorite fantasy is that you will pick up this book again and again and carry it with you, close to your heart! But all of us are busy. When you're done with this book, 20 more on the bookshelf will be crying out for your attention.)

Think back to those books you have read that have been the most valuable to you. You most likely appreciated those from which you gained three or four good ideas.

Only three or four?

Yes! Even after investing the time and money it takes to read a book, you are lucky if you get that many good, solid ideas you are really *ready to use*.

Think for a moment, what would make this book very valuable for you—right now, today? Why did you buy it in the first place? What would make it *worth all the money and time* you are spending with me by reading this book? What are your special needs and wants? This book will act as a catalyst to bring out solutions for special needs, especially **if you define those needs up front.**

Some of the great ideas you come up with may emerge because of the ideas you learn while reading. Some will be triggered from the vast knowledge you have already stored away, waiting for a trigger—such as this book—to bring them back into your working memory.

Grab the idea before it gets away. Research shows if you don't write it down, you are much less likely to act upon it. Get some scratch paper, use it as a bookmark. Keep a writing utensil handy. Write down only those ideas that you know you want to take action on. When you finish this book, hang your action items list where you can see it at work.

A Yale University study concluded that people lose 40 percent of what you say to them within 20 minutes of hearing your presentation. Within half a day, they lose 60 percent, and within one week, 90 percent of it is gone. Depressing, isn't it?

Don't despair. This book is about designing a presentation that increases retention and turns your listeners into doers, believers, and buyers.

Lilly Walters

Acknowledgments

I want to give special credit to my Mother, Dottie Walters. All my life I have heard my Mom use the "tree" analogy when describing the attributes of great speakers. Then a few years ago I heard Florence Littauer, a wonderful speaker, use the tree analogy in a 45-minute keynote.

Much of my outline was inspired from the speech I heard Florence give. Of course, isn't that the way with family? Your parents tell you one thing all your life, you hear someone else say much the same thing, and then, suddenly, it seems like great wisdom. As Shakespeare said, "My best is making old words new!"

But many of the stories I use and insights I have learned are from the vast experiences Mom has had on the platform. Even as a tiny child I can remember hearing her and many other great performers on the platform. As a family, even years later, we are still analyzing what made those speakers so wonderful.

Special thanks to Marcy Huber, Bob Vetter, Burt Siemens, Michael Kurland, Steve Gotleib, Jeff Dewar, Jim McJunkin, and Keith Piantkowski for reading this through and being honest in their feedback.

The whole issue of giving credit where it is due is important to me. I have literally sent out hundreds of faxes and letters all over the world trying to find the original sources of the material I have used in this book. But if you notice an omission, drop me a note!

We'll fix it in the next edition!

Step 1

Set Objectives That Make a Fabulous Speech

_____Select the Seed

There are many ways to teach and many ways to learn. One way to teach is to take the unfamiliar and hang it on the familiar. Jesus taught this way. He often taught in parables. He said such things as, "I am the bread of life." People didn't know who He was, but they understood "bread" and they understood "life."

I'm taking the familiar concept of a tree, and hanging on it all of the unfamiliar things I want you to learn:

First, we will help you **select the seed**—to decide what you really must achieve with your presentation.

Second, we will help you to **find fertile soil** for your seed—in other words, find the right audience for your topic. And when you can't, we'll help you customize your talk to that specific audience.

Third, we'll take your seed and actually **plant it in the ground**—you will learn how to overcome the obstacles that are stopping you from making necessary changes.

Fourth, no tree will be strong unless you **sink your roots down deep.** We will work on how you can be credible and how to be an expert on your topic.

Fifth, you'll develop **one major trunk,** a thought, a theme that will enable the listeners to retain your information.

Sixth, you need **strong, sturdy boughs,** organizing your material for the greatest impact—what material is effective, ethical, and legal to use.

Seventh, **prune the deadwood** from the tree constantly—how, when, and why to edit the presentation.

Eighth, we will help you grow **bright brilliant leaves**—ideas to enhance your image, your voice projection, the colors that you wear on the platform, and how to project—and protect—your reputation.

Ninth, you'll learn to **call them to pick the fruit**—how to motivate an audience to take home the information you're offering.

Tenth, when you **till the soil,** you'll learn to work the audience and build rapport with them.

Eleventh, you will develop strategies to **protect the tree from wilt**—how to ensure "war stories" don't happen in your presentation: what to do when the microphone breaks, the lights go out, and the building burns down around you!

The first thing to do to grow a tree is to **select the seed.**

The Mandatory Start to Grow a Fantastic Speech

When it's foggy in the pulpit...it's cloudy in the pew.
—CAVETT ROBERT, FOUNDER OF THE NATIONAL
SPEAKERS ASSOCIATION

It's so very easy to plunge into developing your talk with the attitude of "My purpose is to give *all* this wonderful information to you, my eager and expectant audience!" The problem is, no matter how eager and expectant every audience is (and unfortunately, unless you get *real* good, real *quick,* they *ain't* all that eager and expectant!), a week later they will remember only about 10 percent of what you said.

Instead of aiming at just giving them information, aim at changing their actions and attitudes. Focus on just how effective the audience needs to be at knowing, feeling, or doing—whatever your message is about—after they hear it.

To change listeners' actions and attitudes with depth and conviction, you need to start with *you*. What do you want to accomplish with this presentation?

I want them to think I did a great job.

Well, that's part of it. But it's not nearly enough. Except on a rather superficial level, the audience doesn't care much about you, they care about themselves. The success of your presentation will be judged not by the knowledge you send but by what the listener *receives*. Your success as a presenter is judged by the response that knowledge elicits from the audience after it's all over. Your presentation must leave *them* knowing, feeling, or doing something different from what they did before they heard you.

I heard a story about a young man who approached Leonard Bernstein, the famous composer. "I have a fantastic idea for a play," he exclaimed. Bernstein said, "I'd love to hear it. Write it on the back of your business card." The young man was incredulous, "I can't possibly put the whole idea in that small of a space!"

Bernstein replied, "Then you don't have a usable concept."

Before you worry about the *road* to get your results, figure out what you want those results to be. To make the presentation captivating and memorable, decide what your mission is.

Perhaps the mission is to leave the audience lighter of heart or to increase their understanding about "that new concept on parking lot maintenance" your management needs you to deliver. Whatever it is, use a piece of blank paper and write in one clear, concise sentence the mission (that is, purpose or objective) of your next important presentation. Pick just one of your presentations. We will follow it through from start to finish in this book.

Failure to prepare is preparing to fail.
—Coach John Wooden

There are so many messages and memos being hurled at today's business professionals, they are in information overload. It's like sipping through a fire hydrant. Don't unnecessarily add to the stream by including unnecessary fill, facts, and fluff. Volume and graphs will not have a lasting impression, having a focus will. Ask yourself early in the process: What do I want them to remember and do three months from now? If you can't succinctly

answer that question, cancel your presentation. After all, the greatest gift you can give any business person is to cancel an unnecessary meeting!
—TERRY L. PAULSON, PH.D., CSP, CPAE,
PSYCHOLOGIST AND PROFESSIONAL SPEAKER,
AUTHOR OF *THEY SHOOT MANAGERS,
DON'T THEY?*

Developing Your Presentation Mission Statement

If you want to be as good as the top 2 percent of professional speakers, invest this time in yourself:

1. Write out your mission statement in a clear concise sentence that says just what you want to accomplish.

2. Find a few of your friends who don't know the topic you are going to present.

3. Tell them it is very important that they listen carefully—no more than that. Do not add why.

4. Read your mission statement—only the one sentence—to your friends.

5. Totally change the subject. Get them to tell you about their day or anything else. After about 10 minutes, ask your friends to repeat to you that one sentence. *Do not correct them!* Instead, write down what they remembered and compare it to the mission of what you want to accomplish.

Did they remember what you wanted them to? Was it the 10 percent you had hoped they would remember? Was the portion they remembered something that would stay with them for years and help them change their actions and attitudes? No?

How did you know they were unclear about what I said?

Well, I start off each of my workshops on presentations with that same exercise—except I have them tell their objective to a small group of just four to six people. Then 10 minutes later we come back to it in that same group. Ninety-five percent of all the people are unclear about what the others said.

Think of your mission statement. What did you hope your friends would remember that would change their lives? Rewrite your mission statement with that in mind and try it again on new people.

When we do this exercise in my seminars, the results are always the same. A strong mission statement, delivered with focus and intense concentration on the audience, is remembered. Mediocre mission statements have mediocre results.

Lilly, you don't understand! My friends were preoccupied. They didn't really understand that this was going to be important; otherwise, they would have listened more carefully.

Yes. Just like every audience you will ever address.

Barriers to Your Audience's Learning

That simple exercise, in the last section, will give you some first-hand experience on barriers to learning. Why didn't people remember what you told them? Only one sentence, and they didn't even remember that very well after only 10 minutes. Imagine what is happening to your one-hour message after a full week!

Why didn't your friends remember with clarity? One barrier to learning may be the presenter's use of unfamiliar terminology. We like to use big words so people will think we're smart. Unfortunately, your listeners don't want you to know just how "unsmart" they are. They'll nod with a sage expression on their faces and a fog in their minds.

The main problem? They just weren't listening. They were thinking about their own troubles. It's called preoccupation. They didn't realize that what you have to say is important to them, even though you may say, several times, "This is going to be important!"

To get them on the path to learning you must break their preoccupation, and redirect their attention. Get it "occupied" on your topic. It's not enough to tell them it's important, find ways to show them that what you have to say is important.

I'd rather see a sermon than hear one any day;
I'd rather one should walk with me than merely tell the way.
The eye's a better pupil and more willing than the ear,
Fine counsel is confusing, but example's always clear.
　　　　　　　　　　　—EDGAR A. GUEST, *SERMONS WE SEE*,
　　　　　　　　　　　1881[1]

---

[1]Edgar A. Guest's *Sermons We See* illustrates so well what a successful, a great, a magnificent speaker strives to live up to, that I have included portions of this epic poem throughout the book.

To get your audience on the path to learning, you start by examining the objectives of the talk. What kind of a tree are you planning to grow?

Setting Smart Objectives

Now that I've got your heart in gear toward making this presentation magical, we can work on the specifics of how to set objectives for your presentation.

In Bob Pike's seminar, "Creative Training Techniques," he says objectives must be "smart": specific, measurable, achievable, relevant, and possible in your time allotted.

> **Specific.** First, is your mission/purpose statement specific? Not "Oh we want to do stuff better than we did before" or "We want to just feel better than we did before." When your objectives are that vague, it's very difficult to achieve them!

> **Measurable.** Can you redefine your mission so you can measure it? For the mission "to feel better"—how much better? How will we know it is "better"? Can you get them a test to measure it? Is it measurable at all? If not, consider changing the mission, it's too vague.

> **Achievable.** Is your mission/purpose statement actually achievable tomorrow? World peace tomorrow is a wonderful objective, but is it something that's achievable for your listeners tomorrow? Try something that's a little smaller. For instance, "Let's start an association that will work toward the goals of peace." Or, "On your way out of this room today, hand a check of no less than $20 to the person at the door." This objective is *achievable,* and not too far beyond what people are likely to do.

> **Relevant.** Is your mission/purpose statement actually relevant to what's going on with your listeners? "Ending job discrimination in Ethiopia" may be important for you (and Ethiopians), but if you can't find reasons why that should be relevant to your listeners, you will be talking to an empty room.

> **Time.** Finally, is it possible to accomplish the mission within the time limits that are allowed you in your presentation?

Assignment: Look at your mission statement. Test it against the list below and see if you can mold it and change it. This is actually a lifelong process, but take two or three minutes right now and see if you can make your mission statement smarter and more effective.

The speaker's objectives are like the writer's thesis statement. What are you trying to say? Accomplish? What is the purpose of the speech? Its mission statement? If you don't know, should the audience guess?
　　　　　　—DANIELLE KENNEDY, M.A., PROFESSIONAL
　　　　　　SPEAKER, AUTHOR OF *SELLING THE DANIELLE*
　　　　　　KENNEDY WAY

The precision you use in identifying and establishing clear and valuable objectives will determine the precision and relevancy of your presentation.
　　　　　　—CHRISTOPHER HEGARTY, AWARD-WINNING
　　　　　　PUBLIC SPEAKER

The Three Aspects of "Step 1— Selecting the Seed"—Needed to Motivate, Captivate, and Persuade an Audience

Seeds are not as simple as they first appear. To develop this very special and superior seed, the kind that will grow something wonderful and unique, your seeds need to be comprised of three aspects.

1. What is the mission and *purpose?*
2. What catches your emotions? To influence your audience's effectiveness, you need to have a *passion* for the topic.
3. What are you *compassionate* about?

That sounds so basic, I've been presenting for quite awhile, let's get on to the good stuff. Let's talk about the overheads.

You will be trying to grow this tree with an infertile seed if you don't include all three aspects. I have helped presenters go from being free speakers to $5000-a-talk speakers. The ones who can motivate, captivate, and persuade the best all have these three common aspects to their "seed": passion and compassion with a purpose.

Purpose. Clarifying and simplifying the mission of your presentation.

If you can't write your message in a sentence, you can't say it in an hour.
　　　　　　—DIANNA BOOHER, AUTHOR/SPEAKER

Passion for your topic. It doesn't matter if you're on the platform or at home late in the evening when you should be tired, ask you about your topic and you come alive!

Passion is the genesis of genius.
—ANTHONY ROBBINS, AUTHOR OF *UNLIMITED
POWER* AND CHAIRMAN OF THE BOARD,
ROBBINS RESEARCH INTERNATIONAL, INC.

Compassion. I receive almost a hundred phone calls and inquiries a month, sometimes more, from people who would like to be professional presenters. All want me to start booking them. I always start with, "What's your topic?" That often stops the conversation cold. Sometimes they come back with, "I can present on anything! Give me a topic and I can get an audience to follow me around like sheep! Like Mary with those little lambs."

I don't think so. I've never met a successful presenter who can make that work for very long. Perhaps "some of the people, some of the time...." You know the nursery rhyme, "Mary had a little lamb..."? Bruce Barton (of Barton, Barton, Hutson, & Swab, the largest advertising company in the United States in the 1940s) used to say in his sales seminar that salespeople should pay heed to the last verse in that rhyme:

Why doth the lamb love Mary so,
the eager children cried?
Because Mary loved the lamb, you know,
the teacher doth reply.

Perhaps the most important is this third aspect of this seed—a compassion for your audiences.

They don't care how much you know, until they know how much you care.
—CAVETT ROBERT

If I have prophetic powers, and understand all mysteries and all knowledge, and if I have all faith, so as to remove mountains, but have not love, I am nothing.
—PAUL THE APOSTLE, IN HIS LETTER TO THE
CORINTHIANS (I CORINTHIANS 13:2)

MORE SECRETS ABOUT STEP 1: SET OBJECTIVES THAT MAKE A FABULOUS SPEECH (SELECTING THE SEED)

Select a seed in which you clearly communicate passion and compassion, with a purpose, and you will be ready to become the kind of presenter who can motivate, captivate, persuade, and change lives.

The secret of successful speakers? Passion and compassion...with a purpose!
—LILLY WALTERS, SPEAKERS BUREAU AND
LECTURE AGENT

Anyone can cut an apple open and count the number of seeds. But, who can look at a single seed and count the trees and apples?
—DOTTIE WALTERS, FOUNDER AND PRESIDENT,
WALTERS INTERNATIONAL SPEAKERS BUREAU

Never give a speech on something unless it is something you like yourself.
—STEW LEONARD, JR.

If you are not excited by your message, how can you expect your audience to be excited by it?"
—RALPH ARCHBOLD, CPAE, AS BENJAMIN
FRANKLIN

If you don't aim at the audience, they may take aim at you.
—ALAN J. PARISSE, SALES AND SECURITIES
INDUSTRY SPEAKER

Setting goals is the first step in turning the invisible into the visible—the foundation for all success in life.
—ANTHONY ROBBINS

If you don't know what you wish to achieve in your presentation, your audience never will.
—HARVEY DIAMOND, AUTHOR OF *FIT FOR LIFE*,
LECTURER, WELLNESS PIONEER

As said to Alice in Wonderland, "If you have no idea where you are going, how will you know when you get there?"
—JEFF DEWAR, PRESIDENT, DEWAR INTERNATIONAL

"The shortest distance between two points is a straight line." Know WHAT your message is, WHY it's important, WHERE you're going with it, and HOW best to get there!
—HERMINE HILTON, EXPERT ON MEMORY

If you don't have objectives for your presentation, you will probably present a talk you didn't intend to. Objectives are a security blanket to protect you from rambling.
—WESS ROBERTS, PH.D., AUTHOR OF *LEADERSHIP
SECRETS OF ATTILA THE HUN*

A good speaker says what he or she has to say and then sits down. So it's wise to know what you are going to say so you know when you've said it.
—GENE PERRET, HUMORIST AND HEAD WRITER FOR
BOB HOPE

With objectives, you assure your audience of receiving something. Without objectives, you assure your audience of receiving nothing.
—JUDI MOREO, MOTIVATIONAL KEYNOTE SPEAKER

The audience only pays attention as long as you know where you are going.
—PHILIP CROSBY, ONE OF THE LEADING QUALITY
EXPERTS IN THE WORLD

Careful planning beats careless presentations.
—DOUG MALOUF, AUSTRALIAN AUTHOR AND PRE-
SENTATION SKILLS EXPERT

There is no "secret" to being a successful communicator—just prepare, know your subject and care.
—LEO BUSCAGLIA, AUTHOR, LECTURER, TEACHER

Step 2
Develop the Right Talk for the Right Audience— Customization
_____*Find Fertile Soil*

If your themes are broad enough, customization is not necessary. But! *Customization transforms an excellent talk into a memorable one.*
—Dr. Layne Longfellow

Of those 200 new presenters that call me every month, many are "marching to the beat of a different drummer." One call was from a lady who speaks on orangutan cultures in Borneo. She does pretty well on developing the right kind of seed. She is passionate. (Truly passionate. She crawls around the jungles of Borneo on her hands and knees collecting Orangutan feces. This is real passion!) She has great compassion for her audience. She certainly has a clear and well-defined purpose. But she doesn't do so well with the next step, which is to find **fertile** soil.

You see, my Speakers Bureau is not the soil that her "seed" will take root in. I work with business and management speakers. She needs to find the audiences who want to hear about what she has to say.[1] Or, she needs to fix her talk so it will be fertile in the soil she is trying to plant it in—in other words, customize her talk.

Who wants to hear about what you have to say? Find the right market for your talk—**find fertile soil.**

What the People Who Invite You Want to Know First

In deciding what the most fertile soil will be for your talk, first evaluate the cost to all the people involved in the talk. The formula that Meeting Planners International (MPI), one of the major education and advancement associations for professional meeting planners, located in Dallas, Texas, developed is:

Total number of people attending	_____
Average hourly wage of attendees*	_____
Number of hours in the meeting	_____
Total	_____
	_____ × 2
Total cost in people hours	

*Virginia Johnson of the 3M Meeting Management Institute states the figures in Table 1-1 will help you to evaluate the hourly cost of bringing people into a meeting. The 3M Meeting Management Institute is an excellent source for information on audiovisual resources.

So, if you have 10 people in the meeting, and they're all making $100,000 per year, the cost to the person footing the bill will be $1000 an hour. Let's say they're going to be in the meeting for 2 hours, that's $2000. In addition, consider other costs: traveling; transport; the work they're not going to get done while they're in your audience; materials, such as workbooks; accommodations; conference facility; speakers fee; etc.

To make your seed *grow* in this soil, you must be able to show the people holding the event that, "If you spend this money to send your people to my presentation, you'll receive this much value, this much return on investment (ROI)."

---

[1]Dottie Walters (my mother) and I wrote an entire book, *Speak and Grow Rich* (Prentice Hall), about getting into the right market.

Table 1-1. Hourly Cost of a Meeting

Annual salary	Number of people in meeting						
	2	4	6	8	10	15	20
$100,000	$200	$400	$600	$800	$1000	$1500	$2000
$80,000	160	320	480	640	800	1200	1600
$60,000	120	240	360	480	600	900	1200
$40,000	80	160	240	320	400	600	800
$20,000	40	80	120	160	200	300	400

SOURCE: From the June–July 1989 issue of *Global Meeting*, a publication of the International Society of Meeting Planners, located in Scottsdale, Arizona, another educational and networking organization for professional meeting planners.

One of the best ways to tell if you have the right talk for the right audience is to find out which audiences gain the most from hearing you speak. Whenever you are preparing a talk, ask yourself how you can make your presentation have more tangible monetary value, that is, more return on investment to the people hosting your talk.

Do this by asking yourself, "Who cares?" Who cares about what you have to say? That's the group you try to deliver your talk to.

Find a problem, then look for a solution. Don't develop a solution, then spend your life searching for a problem for it. Pull through an idea from the market place, don't push it through from inception towards some intangible market.
—JACK RYAN, INVENTOR[2]

Don't try to sell alarm clocks to people without jobs.
—AL LAMPKIN, COMEDY ENTERTAINER

The Right Talk for the Right Audience

There is no such thing as an all-purpose good presentation. What goes over well with one audience may receive a tepid response from another. Generally this is because the talk never grabs them by tuning into their backgrounds and interests.
—TOM LEECH, AUTHOR OF *HOW TO PREPARE, STAGE, AND DELIVER WINNING PRESENTATIONS*

[2]Jack Ryan was the inventor of the Barbie doll and the Hawk missiles and was called the "Marvel of Mattel" because he invented 90 percent of their toys. An amazing man, he had at his death more patents than any other person in the United States.

You can't just assume your group will qualify in the "who cares" category until you do some research. As the old adage says, "Prescription without examination is malpractice."

Once, my mother was giving a speech. The speaker before her, speaking on "Time and Money Management," gave some great tips to her audience. "Save all your containers and jars, don't throw them away. Don't waste your money on those expensive containers!" Good idea, but the client she was speaking for was the sales staff of one of the largest manufacturers of plastic containers in the world.

One visiting corporate executive looked out at his audience consisting of the executive staff at that division. He started by saying, "I'm so happy to be here, thank you all for coming. I'm honored so many of you took the trouble to bring your wives!" You got it—the spouses had not been invited. The "wives" were all female executives.

Either of the above situations might have involved me or you. But don't agonize—analyze! Don't prescribe your solutions for their problems until you examine their needs.

Good clues to know you've got the wrong audience:

1. *If they fall asleep*
2. *If they walk out*
3. *If they withhold the check*
4. *If the President's face begins to match his red power tie.*

> —TOM OGDEN, MASTER MAGICIAN AND
> COMEDIAN

Turn What You Want to Talk About into a Great Topic

You customize in order to connect with the audience. If I am speaking to a group of business people who sell widgets, I should become so familiar with widgets that the audience will think: "Maybe she is one of us. Maybe she secretly sells widgets." This is the highest compliment I could receive from the audience of widget salespeople.

That effect just doesn't happen by accident. The speaker creates that response by doing her homework weeks in advance. How do you do that? Prepare questionnaires or market information surveys and insist that you receive the information in plenty of time before the presentation. Talk to their staff, management, people in the field.
> —DANIELLE KENNEDY, M.A.

We started with what you are motivated to talk about—what has "passion and compassion with a purpose"—for you. Then we defined it and made it "smart." Now, see if considering the needs of all four groups involved in your talk will help you to customize your mission to a specific group. The four groups are (1) sayor, (2) payor, (3) sender, and (4) sendee (I adapted this from a phrase by Bob Pike of "Creative Training Techniques").

- **The sayor.** That's you! What are your needs, what is going to stir your passion? You already started to analyze this when you thought about what makes you passionate in Step 1.

A speech should not just be a sharing of information, but a sharing of yourself.
—RALPH ARCHBOLD

- **The payor.** The payor is the person footing the bill for the sendor to send a sendee to attend!

Doing a great job and not meeting the customer's objectives is as useless as doing a poor job within the customer's objectives.
—THOMAS FARANDA, PRESIDENT OF FARANDA &
ASSOCIATES, INC., A GLOBAL CUSTOMER
CONSULTING CORPORATION

- **The sendor.** The person who sends the people to sit in on your presentations. Often a supervisor or manager. Find out why the senders send an attendee to your presentation.

It is mandatory to appropriately customize each presentation. Do so by interviewing the chairperson of the meeting to get your "mission" clear. Also, interview a range of individuals from the group and within the company or association to get the direction and tone of your presentation. Name names, dates and places. How well you do this will determine the level of rapport and intimacy you establish with individuals and the audience as a whole.
—CHRISTOPHER HEGARTY

- **The sendee.** The sendee is the person sitting in your audience. Ask yourself what the sendees must (1) know, (2) feel, and (3) do differently when they leave you.

The more you know about the audience, the more likely you are to deliver material of value to them. The more they think you know about them, the more value they will perceive your material to have.
—JUDI MOREO

In many situations there is overlap. In a small business the payor may also be the person telling the sendee they need to attend. If you went to a personal development public seminar you would be the sendee, and sendor, and payor.

Assignment: Check your mission statement against the above list. How can you restructure your mission statement to better meet the needs of all four groups?

When You Can't Choose the Right Audience, Add Fertilizer!

But my boss says **do** *the presentation for* **this** *group. I don't have a* **choice** *about whom I'll present to!*

So the soil you must plant in isn't fertile? Add some fertilizer! But, to determine what kind of fertilizer to add, Tom Leech, author of *How to Prepare, Stage, and Deliver Winning Presentations* (AMACOM), says there are four things you need to analyze first about your audiences—their

1. Attitudes and interests
2. Needs
3. Wants
4. Capabilities

When the group is not just the "right" group to hear your topic, dividing your analysis into these four areas makes the customization of your presentation easier. It will help you adjust your topic so it can take root in this potentially unfertile soil.

Adjust to Their Attitude and Interest Level

What is their attitude likely to be?

Are they excited and happy about being in your audience? Perhaps especially chosen award winners or honor role types? Or did the "sender" imply to them they were inept at their jobs and in desperate need of your topic (which of course may or may not be true)?

Employees hearing about a new bonus plan and being paid time-and-a-half to do it have great attitudes! The same employees, if forced to hear about executive parking lot maintenance (on their own time), have rotten attitudes.

People's interest in a topic can affect their attitude. The home owners association of a housing project located next door to a proposed nuclear waste dump site may have a rotten attitude toward you if you're presenting in favor of the dump site. But they *will* have a very keen, even savage interest!

Adjust to a "Need" Level Where They Can Listen

Begin your presentation addressing people at their current need level. Otherwise, they just don't hear what you are saying. Their "need" is making them think of something else. Let's pretend your topic is about customer service. If they or their families are hungry or living in the street, they are not at a need level that matches your topic. So, they don't listen.

First analyze your audience's need level, then target your topic to meet it. In the case mentioned above you might change your topic to "How Improving Your Customer Service Will Put More Food on Your Table." (Then make darn good and sure you've got the answers to make that true for them!)

Many studies have focused on human nature in regards to needs analysis. Perhaps one of the most widely quoted is Abraham H. Maslow. Maslow, a psychologist, studied thousands of people at varying need levels. His work gives us one way to look at how people learn according to their needs. He decided people are always in one of the five needs levels below. You must satisfy the bottom level before you can go on to the next.

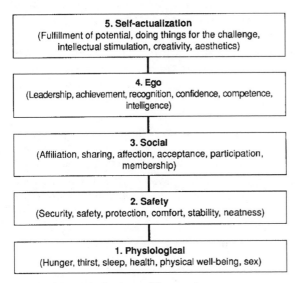

Figure 2-1. Maslow's need hierarchy.

When you give a presentation, you begin by addressing the audience members at their current need level. Then you pull them into one of the higher levels. They may already be at a higher level, but factors during your presentation may bring them down. For example, if a fire breaks out in your meeting room, the audience goes right back down to the lowest need level. How much tea or coffee audience members drank an hour ago can strongly affect their need level. You're up there, rattling away, and what are they thinking? Certainly not about what you are trying to persuade them to learn. They're thinking "I've got to get out of here." Are they smokers? If they have that urge, their minds are no longer with you.

The first level (at the bottom of the chart) is physiological. Imagine a person at this level thinking, "I want to live now." Like someone who is being chased by a bear.

The next level up is safety. People at this level might be thinking, "I want to live tomorrow." The bear has stopped chasing them, so now they think it's a pretty good idea to go find a cave. If you're presenting on a day when the newspapers are filled with predictions of an earthquake, it's hard to keep the audience's attention focused on statistics of company profits.

Third would be the social level, "I want to live tomorrow with friends." They found their cave, but they are thinking that having a few friends close by to talk or live with would be a good thing.

The next level is ego, "I want to live tomorrow with friends and be someone special." They want these other people living in the cave with them to think they are are special and important.

The final level is self-actualization, "I want to live tomorrow with friends and be someone special and important." Now our cave dwellers want to feel good about themselves.

A lot of work we do as presenters is attempting to bring our audiences up in the self-actualization level and keep them there. It's a level most people target but don't spend much time in. Life intrudes, and we spend time worrying about how we will make our house payments, get our relationships back on line, etc.

What is your listeners' need level? What level do they need to be at to get your point? Missionaries, whose topics were targeted at the higher levels of self-actualization (unless they used the hellfire-and-brimstone approach, and then it was focused at the physiological level), learned centuries ago they couldn't persuade anyone to their point of view until the listeners' lower-level needs, i.e., food, shelter, etc., were met first. Feed them first, then save their souls.

No, we're not ready to put in the right amount of fertilizer. We still need to do some examination. After you have examined and customized to meet the audience's "attitude," then their "needs"—above—you can start to concentrate on their "wants," which is our next point.

> *Be audience driven, organize each point starting with the audience's needs.*
> —SOMERS WHITE, AUTHOR, SPEAKER, FORMER
> ARIZONA STATE SENATOR

Adjust to the Audience's "Wants" Level

To make this ground even more fertile, find out what people want. A speaker friend of mine, Mona Moon, quotes a survey in her seminar, regarding what people really *want* out of life. She says they want professional and personal success; happiness; praise; recognition; respect; beauty; health; wealth; influence over other people and events; to conserve time, energy, and money; and to avoid embarrassment and pain. Which of your audience's needs and wants does your topic address?

> *I talk to them one on one ahead of my speech. Even 20 minutes' building awareness of who they are and what they are going through is a tremendous asset.*
> —W MITCHELL

Adjust to the Mode in Which They Are "Capable" of Listening

Many things affect your listener's capability to learn: age, schooling, socioeconomic level, IQ, etc. We repeatedly overlook that we often use a mode in which the listeners simply don't listen.

We speak in the mode we like to listen in. As the Golden Rule says, "Do unto others as you would have them do unto you." As "golden" as this rule is, we often confuse the exact translation with the spirit of the rule. I love food that is spicy and hot—very hot! If my makeup is still on when I'm done eating, I feel cheated. If the Golden Rule was literally true, I would serve all of my dinner guests jalapeño peppers and hot chili sauces.

Jim Cathcart and Tony Alessandra, in their cassette album *Relationship Strategies*,[3] by Nightingale-Conant, say the spirt of the Golden Rule is to "do unto others as *they would like* to be done unto."

When you present, don't do it just the way *you* would like to hear it. Add into the talk the things that make that specific personality type of audience listen. It's the only way your listeners will be able to learn. To

---

[3]*Relationship Strategies* is a very humorous and easily understandable approach to personality analysis. It brings the entire concept into an easily learned system.

discover that mode of listening, we must know the personality type of the majority of the audience.

Personality type? Like shy, friendly, bossy?

Yes. Over the millennia, sages have been trying to analyze people's personality types and categorize them. Most have found that people divide nicely into four distinct groups. One of the earliest personality studies was astrology. They divided all peoples into earth, wind, water, and fire. As science has advanced, many other studies emerged. Often they divided people into four groups.

The study of personalities and how they learn is fascinating. This following brief overview will give you some ideas on how to apply the concepts to customizing your talk to specific audiences.

It would be almost impossible to have the whole audience be of the same personality type. But often you will address people that are in a similar career area. People in similar careers often have some similarities in personality traits that you can play to.

Analytical, Thinker, Compliant Audiences

These personality types are often found in audiences whose careers are quality control, accounting, engineering, computer programming, architecture, systems analysis, dentistry—all the technical and hard science professions. Two extremes of this type would be Mr. Spock of *Star Trek* and Sherlock Holmes.

You're not going to persuade these people to do anything if you don't first give them a great wealth of information on *how* you researched your conclusions. They learn well by reading, so charts and graphs are great. They find it difficult to make decisions if you don't give them a detailed process to follow.

How about getting them to jump up and do some hugging exercises in the first five minutes of the presentation?

You'd likely find yourself talking to an empty room!

Relater, Feeler, Steady, Amiable Audiences

If people in your audience have careers such as counseling, teaching, social work, the ministry, psychology, nursing, or human resource development, they will have strong "relater" tendencies.

They enjoy and respond to those warm commercials on TV showing a family at a restaurant, the waitress gives a toy to the smiling child, the beaming happy group. These are the images this group is persuaded by. They like to feel that their families are warm, safe, and happy. Two examples of this type are Bill Cosby and Mary Tyler Moore.

This group doesn't learn as easily from graphs, charts, or long, involved discussions of statistics. Although everyone needs *some* logic to persuade them, this group doesn't need as much of the long process, as does, for example, the first type. A group participative exercise where everyone hugs each other works very nicely with these people.

Director, Dominant, Driver Audiences

Audiences with careers as stock brokers, independent consultants, corporate CEOs, or drill sergeants are typical directors. Two examples of this type of personality are past–Prime Minister Margaret Thatcher and Clint Eastwood.

Use lots of action in your talk to this group. Be concise. Give them quick, "one-minute manager" methods to get the job done now! Summarize and "bottom line" your points quickly.

Don't talk to this group about personal development. They don't appreciate your getting up close and personal. Suggest ideas for business strategies instead.

Don't use pointless humor. Make sure your humor makes a specific point that is important to the presentation.

They do not want to know the details of the long process you used to arrive at your conclusion. They want to know how much they are going to save or lose, and what they're supposed to do about it.

Sum up the talk (the quick talk) with a call for action—one that they can delegate to their staff!

Inspirational, Expressive, Socializer Audiences

You find these people in audiences whose careers are glamorous high-profile sorts of jobs—these folks need audiences. Careers such as sales, acting, public relations specialists, trial attorneys (not all attorneys. A group of estate attorneys—people who draw up wills—are almost accountants. Chances are they lean more toward the analytical personality. But the trial attorney gets to "perform" and is more likely to be this type.) Examples would be Robin Williams and Lucille Ball.

This group loves the opportunity to talk and perform. Give them exercises that get them talking. (It will take very little encouragement on your part. Actually, they will be most happy to come up and take your microphone.) Make sure to give them a time limit!

Straight lecture doesn't bear much fruit with these people. They don't want to listen to you, they want to listen to themselves. They don't want to hear long processes, detailed facts and figures.

A room full of this personality type tends to be a real problem—like trying to present at the Tower of Babel. If you've only *got* one within each one of your other discussion groups, they're bound to dominate the discussion. To keep group harmony, change the groups around.

> *You do not speak to a four-year-old child in the same way you speak to a forty-year-old adult. You do not address your boss with quite the same bantering tone with which you speak to your fellow employees. We speak one way to those we love, another to those we are not especially fond of. We speak in one style to friends and in a somewhat different manner to strangers. The same thing goes for different kinds of audiences.*
> —STEVE ALLEN, ©1986

How Far to Adjust Your Personal Teaching Style

With all the above types, we are talking about *tendencies*, not 100 percent traits. It is the degree to which they learn that is important. As a presenter you are responsible to "stretch" them. So using a hugging exercise for the director types might actually be a terrific learning experience for them—but don't start off your presentation with it! Start with those things with which each type is comfortable, then work on changing them.

Let's say you are an expressive personality. Your audience is all analyticals. So you only use the charts, graphs, and statistics, right?

Well, I did say that over the last several pages, but...

What, you were just kidding?

No, no. But, I don't want you to go crazy trying to turn yourself into someone you are not. Be who you are, but adjust the focus for each listener. Give more charts and graphs for that type, but don't pull yourself so far away from your roots that you freeze up there.

> *To change my style would rob audiences of seeing my "window to the world" at its best. I'd suggest going with your "strength" as your major*

impact style, but work at learning some way to touch listeners who are different. You don't need to change your style to reach them. You do need to allow them time to get used to how you deliver your message.
—TERRY PAULSON, PH.D.

Analyze Your Audience

It's all very well and good to say, "all right you need to analyze your audience's needs, wants, capacities, and attitudes." But how? Try a few of these ideas:

- Ask former attendees.
- Ask the current attendees.
- Ask some of the other presenters for this event.
- Ask former presenters to this same group.
- Ask whoever is planning the event.
- Ask whoever planned the event last time.

Preparing a preprogram questionnaire (see Figure 2-2) to send to some of these people may be a real time saver and facilitate getting answers.

Customization Secrets

I want to meet and shake hands with as many people as possible before the talk. That way I'm not surprised when the first three rows have English as their second or third language. Once you get on stage, major changes in the presentation are very difficult.
—TOM OGDEN

Research your audience then you can reinforce your material. Ask three people three questions:

1. *What would they like to know from you?*
2. *What is important to them?*
3. *What can they do with your information?*
—DOUG MALOUF

When I know there are children I make sure that nothing I say will miss them, nothing will go over their heads. I try to get their names ahead, I always try to incorporate them into the talk. I think the adults appreciate that I respect all of the audience.
—W MITCHELL

Figure 2-2. Sending out a preprogram questionnaire to key people can help you analyze your audience's needs, wants, capacities, and attitudes.

Preprogram Questionnaire

Dottie Walters is presenting to your group on _____.

We need your help! Dottie would like to specifically meet your needs with her presentation. Would you take a few moments to give us the answers we need?

    We have filled out the answers to the questions below to the best of our knowledge. Please double check our answers and make additions and corrections. Fill in the questions we left blank. We were uncertain of this information and thought it best for you to provide it for us.

PLEASE: Send us any printed information on your group that may help: corporate report, news publications, etc.

Return this questionnaire to: Dottie Walters, PO Box 1120, Glendora, CA 91740 no later than _____. If you have any questions call 818-335-8069.

Presentation title: _____ Date: _____

Time frame? _____ Start time: _____

End time: _____ Any breaks? _____

What happens just before Dottie speaks? _____

What happens right after she speaks? _____

Appropriate dress code for presentation? _____

Conference theme? _____

Specific purpose of this meeting (awards banquet, annual meeting, etc.)

_____

Specific objectives for Dottie's presentation? _____

_____

Sensitive issues that should be avoided? _____

Introducer's name? _____ Phone # _____

Is there any publicity work Dottie can do for you while she is at your event? Radio or TV?

Who are the other speakers on the program?

Speaker: _____ Topic: _____

Speaker: _____ Topic: _____

Speaker: _____ Topic: _____

Speaker: _____ Topic: _____

What speakers have you used in the past that covered topics related to the material Dottie will be doing for you? _____

_____

What did you like and/or dislike? (Without their names if you would like, but do comment on the material they used!) _____

_____

Three main Movers & Shakers of your group that will be in Dottie's audience. We would like to contact them for more research information on your group.

1. _____ Phone: _____

2. _____ Phone: _____

3. _____ Phone: _____

What would make Dottie's presentation meaningful for your group?

_____

_____

_____

ABOUT THE AUDIENCE

Number attending: _____ Percentage of male to female: _____

Spouses coming: _____ Average age: _____

Annual average income: _____ Income range: _____

Educational background: _____

Major job responsibilities of audience: _____

Problems? _____

(Continued)

Challenges? _____

Breakthroughs? _____

What separates your high-performance people from the others? _____

_____

TELL US ABOUT YOUR INDUSTRY

Problems? _____

Challenges? _____

Breakthroughs? _____

TELL US ABOUT YOUR ORGANIZATION

Problems? _____

Challenges? _____

Breakthroughs? _____

Significant events (mergers, relocations)? _____

_____

Will Dottie's presentation be taped? _____

If you wish Dottie to make her educational materials available to your audience so that they may continue the learning process at home, we can arrange this two ways. Please check the one that is the most appropriate for your group:

A. __ Group purchase in advance for each attendee, at wholesale.

B. __ Materials made available at the back of the room after the presentation.

If you checked "B," please make sure that

1. Nothing will be happening after her presentation for at least 20 minutes.
2. A table will be made available for her to place her materials by the exit door.
3. Someone from your group will assist with sales.

TRAVEL INFORMATION

Location of presentation, venue name: _____

Address: _____ Phone: _____

Location at the site, room rate, etc.: _____

Airport to arrive at: _____

How will Dottie be transported from the airport to your site?

Taxi?____ Car rental?_____ Pickup person?____

Pickup person's name: _____ Phone: _____

If an emergency occurs on the way to the site, who would an alternative contact be if you are unavailable?

Name: _____ Business phone: _____

Home phone: _____

You were invited to speak because you had something to say. Put it in words that are meaningful to the group...their world, time of the year (football, Christmas, etc.). You want the audience to say: The speaker was right with it...timely, on the ball.
—IRA HAYES

Nothing makes an audience feel more important than a speaker who takes the time to get to know the special needs, vocabulary, and history of their group. Small adjustments are appreciated and can often be done even moments before you speak.

Take the time to talk to those who come early to your presentation. Ask: What problems do you see on the horizon? What's working in your industry? What things is it wise for speakers to avoid with this group? Are there any things or people the group would enjoy me making fun of? What's unique about your group's common vocabulary that outsiders just don't understand?

Use what you learn and be prepared to watch the looks of amazement and the jump in enthusiasm for your message.
TERRY L. PAULSON, PH.D.

The simplest way to customize is to phone members of the audience in advance and ask them what they expect from your session and why they expect it. Then use their quotes throughout your presentation.
—ALLAN PEASE, AUSTRALIAN AUTHOR OF *BODY LANGUAGE*

Customizing by talking to several members of your audience in advance provides these benefits:

1. *It shows you've done you're homework,*

2. *Quoting a member of the group supports the point you are making and,*

3. *It gives you instant rapport with the people you've interviewed when you show up to speak.*

—MARK SANBORN, PROFESSIONAL SPEAKER AND
AUTHOR

Customization Isn't Always a Good Idea

But you said...

I know, but there are at least two sides to everything: When you interview as many people as I did to write this, you get almost too many sides of an issue to even try to keep count! Consider the following thoughts before you customize your next presentation.

Can you imagine someone inviting Neil Diamond or Pavorotti to sing at their annual meeting and saying "Here are the words to our company song, our company motto, and our sales brochures... please be sure to sing only these words and phrases, not those popular, meaningful songs you perform so well that have made you famous and inspired millions of people"?

The basics of my most popular speech are always the same. I carefully study the group to be addressed, their interests and challenges and carefully weave these into my basic presentation to make it "customized." Do an advanced study of your audience—know their interests, challenges, fears, desires—then, through your own experiences, tell 'em, show 'em, how you handled it in your own activities.

—ED FOREMAN, FORMER U.S. CONGRESSMAN
(TEXAS AND NEW MEXICO), CORPORATE CEO,
AND SPEAKER

If you customize too much from your known speech and image, you get into a real danger zone. Don't allow yourself to go into a situation where you are ill prepared. Besides, if you change your standard presentation too much you may build an Edsel.

—WESS ROBERTS, PH.D.

"Customizing" does not mean tailoring a complete talk for each assignment. It means drawing from one's wide repertoire of like experiences and using only those that fit.

—BILL GOVE, FIRST PRESIDENT OF NATIONAL
SPEAKERS ASSOCIATION

My basic message is always the same "It's not what happens to you, it's what you do about it," so I don't need to draft a new speech every time I stand up in front of an audience. By questionnaire and by meeting with the people before the event I find out what their needs and concerns are. I tell the story of my life, but weave their challenges in and out.
                    —W MITCHELL

I give the same mashed potatoes for each speech, I just change the gravy.
                    —DR. NORMAN VINCENT PEALE

MORE SECRETS ABOUT STEP 2: DEVELOP THE RIGHT TALK FOR THE RIGHT AUDIENCE (FIND FERTILE SOIL)

Most of the magic of great speakers actually comes from this section—finding fertile soil for your seed to take root or fixing the soil (your talk) so it will be fertile. Ask yourself, "Who cares about what I have to say?" then present to those groups. You will know your talk is fertile by analyzing the audience's attitudes, capacities, wants, and needs. Sometimes you have no choice, you must present in "the wrong soil." Fertilize the soil by speaking in the audience's listening mode.

Presentations are for the audience not for the speaker. The message embodied in the speech can be enhanced or destroyed by the inclusion or lack of audience analysis.
                    —JOHN PATRICK DOLAN, ATTORNEY

Nothing makes people happier than to feel you're interested in them. If you've customized, you're paying attention—and everyone loves attention.
                    —HOPE MIHALAP, HUMORIST

I've learned from a quarter of a century of customizing material for Bob Hope that the best material is the stuff that hits the audience right between the eyes. Audiences love to know that you're talking directly to them, and when they recognize that in a speaker or a performer, believe me, they'll reward you for it.
                    —GENE PERRET

You can't preset a "boiler-plate" speech and expect it to fit the audience any more than your parents can pick out your prom dress the day of your birth. Chances that it'll fit are infinitesimal.
                    —DIANNA BOOHER

One size does not fit all. Customizing shows that you care for that specific audience.

—Col. Gene Harrison, Ret., president, Quest
Management Consultants

Make love to your audience. Live their thoughts. See the world their way.

—Gerald C. Meyers, former chairman of the
board of American Motors

Every speech needs to be an original, even though the thoughts may be the same.

—Philip Crosby

There is nothing worse than having the right message for the wrong audience!

There is nothing better than having the right message for the right audience!

—Capt. Dave Carey

Step 3

Conquer Stage Fright and Your Fear of Making Changes

———Plant the Seed in the Ground

Take the seed that you are passionate and compassionate about and have a clearly defined purpose. You find fertile soil or you make the soil fertile. Now we concentrate on how to get over your very natural and human fears of the platform and of making change.

> *Everytime you change and improve, you have to dig in and learn something new. That involves all kinds of scary old feelings coming up to the surface again. Yet, the pros know the importance of staying green and growing for each new audience they encounter.*
> —DANIELLE KENNEDY, M.A.

> *Top presenters have total control of their fears. They make their fear their slave, not the master.*
> —DOUG MALOUF

> *I always turn every presentation over to the Lord before beginning. He isn't afraid of anything.*
> —PHILIP CROSBY

What Works Best to
Conquer Fear?

I once did an interview for our newsmagazine, *Sharing Ideas With Professional Speakers* (Royal Publishing, Glendora, California), with Steve Allen. He said, "Stage fright is a deceptive term. It implies you will be frightened the minute you get up on the stage, when of course it really happens the minute you accept the assignment!" (And gets progressively worse!)

I don't get stage fright anymore, I've been presenting for years.

Stage fright does not happen just when you first begin speaking in public. It also happens to seasoned veterans *every* time they decide to make a change of any kind. That's why it is so easy for even speaking pros to get into a rut and stay there.

> *A rut is a grave with no ends!*
> —AL LAMPKIN

Stage fright can be reduced by 75 percent through simple preparation and rehearsal. Deep breathing will take care of an additional 15 percent. Ten percent will be conquered through mental preparation. Let's explore these three strategies in more detail.

	Reduces stage fright by
Rehearsal and preparation	75%
Deep breathing	15%
Mental preparation	10%

Rehearsal and Preparation
Reduce Your Fear
by 75 Percent

Yes, but I want to get so good that I don't need days and days of rehearsal. I want to be like those fabulous entertainers who just come up with great stuff on the spur of the moment.

Those fabulous entertainers who seem to think of great one liners off the cuff often use those same lines over and over in every performance.

Mark Twain, one of the highest paid speakers of his era, said, "It takes me at least three weeks to prepare an impromptu speech." A friend of

Winston Churchill's, R. E. Smith, said, "Winston has spent the best years of his life writing impromptu speeches."[1] Another friend, Harold Nicholson, once congratulated Churchill upon a witty remark he seemed to improvise in a talk to a small audience. Churchill shot back, "Improvised be damned! I thought of it this morning in my bath and I wish now I hadn't wasted it on this little crowd."[2]

Churchill estimated it took him six to eight hours to prepare a 45-minute speech. Dr. Roger Burgraff, one of the speakers I often engage on the topic of "Advanced Communication Strategies," says it takes one hour of preparation for each minute of presentation time.

But, as the saying goes, "It's not practice that makes perfect. *Perfect* practice makes perfect." Practice effectively. That means do it out loud. Then, try your material out at parties, at home, or even with friends on the phone.

You're kidding?

No, I'm not. It's the way all professional speakers fine-tune their material. Your friends will think you've just come up with some witty one-liners, little realizing all the work and rehearsal you put into them!

When you are testing your material out on your friends and family, do not say, "I want to test out some new material on you." It spoils the impact. Just tell it naturally as if you just came up with it and see what kind of response you generate. (Important safety tip: Don't keep practicing the same material on the same people. Your life as a speaker will be short-lived as angry mobs of exasperated ex-friends chase you out of town.)

One of my friends, a fantastic presenter, Doug Malouf of Dougmal Training Systems in Wollongona, Australia (no kidding, Wollongona!), suggests you practice your speech, especially your opening, to a spot on the wall. He feels you are the most neurotic in those first few minutes when you get in front of an audience. So he says to memorize a dynamite opening *word for word*. Practice it while you are staring at a spot on the wall. He says you develop such fantastic confidence that it carries you through the rest of the speech.

I thought he was joking—"talk to a spot on the wall." What's so tough about that? I walked over to the wall, opened my mouth, closed my mouth and tried again, and again, and.... My own speech, I have given many times, and I couldn't think of what to say. What an amazing technique! Give it a try yourself.

---

[1] William Manchester, *The Last Lion—Winston Spencer Churchill*, Dell, 1983, p. 32.
[2] Ibid.

You never want to sound mechanical and overrehearsed. However, you will project that image when you are not comfortable with your material. You can only become comfortable through hours of preparation and rehearsal.

The following are some secrets of good rehearsal and preparation:

Trust yourself and your material. The best way to do that is with solid preparation.
—GENE PERRET

90% of how well the talk will go is determined before the speaker steps on the platform.
—SOMERS WHITE

If the speech is awkward for you, it will be awkward for the audience.
—W MITCHELL

Keep falling on your face—when the fall doesn't hurt anymore you're there!
—HATTIE HILL-STORKS

Best way to conquer stage fright is to know what you're talking about.
—MICHAEL H. MESCON, FOUNDER AND CHAIRMAN
OF THE MESCON GROUP, INC.

Don't open on Broadway. Work on parts of your presentation before small groups or in individual conversations to test the material and to fashion memorable quotes, phrases, challenges, etc.
—CHRISTOPHER HEGARTY

I do pretest major changes before local Toastmasters groups. They are a receptive audience that offers valuable feedback. Evaluations help to assess new material.
—ARDEN BERCOVITZ, PH.D. (PORTRAYS "EINSTEIN
BY BERCOVITZ")

What generates confidence is preparing well, practicing with astute colleagues or coaches and getting their feedback, making sure all the little details are taken care of, and speaking often.
—TOM LEECH

Both Tony Robbins, who wrote Unlimited Power, *and Chuck Hogan, one of the top mental experts in the field of golf, feel that if you want to learn to do something and overcome your fear in a specific area, you need to observe people who are good at doing it and find out what they do. They point to three things that can impact your performance in a desired skill: body language, routine and your belief system.*
—DR. KEN BLANCHARD[3]

---

[3]From the *Blanchard Management Report* by Dr. Ken Blanchard. Copyright 1990 by Authors Media Syndicate.

Be prepared, and be honest.
—Coach John Wooden

I only have stage fright when I did not adequately prepare. If I don't take into account everything that could go wrong, I'm afraid that they will go wrong!
—Tom Ogden

Speakers don't make big fees by ad-libbing. Besides, I've never known anybody in this business (professional speaking) who, under stress, could ad-lib a burp at a Hungarian picnic!
—Bill Gove

REHEARSING THE SPEECH
by Steve Allen*

Common sense can also dictate the forms your rehearsal might take. The following are some of the possibilities:

1. Read the speech over several times, silently.

2. Read the speech several times aloud.

3. Practice your delivery, including the entire address, standing in front of a mirror. This gives you the opportunity to observe not only your general attitude but also your gestures, posture, and facial expression.

4. Read the speech into a tape recorder and listen to the results. Then listen to them again. At this stage you will make an astounding discovery. Things begin to become apparent to you at a second listening (or, for that matter, a tenth) that had escaped your attention earlier.

5. If you have access to videotaping equipment, make a record of your performance in that way.

6. If you have cooperative family members, deliver the speech to them and ask for their honest comments. Don't make the mistake of welcoming only compliments and tuning out messages that are analytical or critical. If your spouse says something like "I think it's quite good but you were talking too fast," don't argue the point, whether or not your ego will permit you to agree at that moment. Just absorb the message and let it bounce around in your internal computer.

*From *How to Make a Speech* (McGraw-Hill) ©1986, material reproduced with permission of Steve Allen.

Seventy-five percent of your fear of making change will be reduced through "good" rehearsal.

To Reduce Your Fear by Another 15 Percent

For 10 years I taught a sport called "vaulting": gymnastics on the back of a moving horse (not the metal and leather thing they use in a gymnasium, the big furry animal that whinnies). The horse canters around in a circle while the kids, sometimes three at a time, do back flips over each other, and then off the horse to the ground. Definitely a *high stress* kind of activity, one that caused heavy stage fright. If you sat in on one of my coaching sessions, you would most often hear me yelling "Breathe!"

For some reason, we forget to breathe normally when we get nervous, which makes us more stressed, which makes us breathe less, which makes us more nervous, you get the idea. Suddenly a vaulter would be on the ground looking at the ceiling and wondering how she or he got there!

Control your breathing. Think, "Deep breath and hold, 1, 2, 3, 4, 5." (Add a "Mississippi" onto the end of each number—it's pretty tough to figure out how long a second is when your adrenaline is racing.) Tell yourself, "slow release, and inhale 1, 2..." etc.

> *If you are afraid, breathe slowly, feel your feelings and share them if you need to and then proceed to enrich the lives of others through your presentation.*
> —Terry Cole-Whittaker

Reduce That Final 10 Percent— Control Your Mind

Zig Ziglar[4] says that fear is an acronym[5] for *f*alse *e*vidence *a*ppearing *r*eal.

What kind of "false evidence" are you feeding yourself before you present? What words are you saying to yourself that make you feel so frightened?

(Mona Moon, a seminar leader, says another acronym for fear is *f*orget *e*verything *a*nd *r*un!)

---

[4]One of the most successful, highly paid sales speakers in the United States and the author of many books, including *See You at the Top*.

[5]Well, actually F-E-A-R is an *acrostic* for any word purists reading this. See the section on Acronyms and Acrostics in Step 4 if you want to know the difference.

For instance, do you say things to yourself like, "They're going to *hate* me." "It's going to be *awful*." "I'm going to look like a *fool*." "My boss is going to think I'm an *idiot*." "Everyone in my audience knows *more* about this topic than me!" "I'll look *fat*."

Have you ever gone to a presentation and really wanted the presenter to be terrible?[6] *Most* of the time you'd much rather have a good time than a bad time. The same is true for your audience. Most listeners are sitting there, ready and willing to make allowances for your mistakes. In fact, a few mistakes make you human and just that much more lovable.

Gregory Rapiort is an expert on Soviet mind control techniques. Gregory was also a leading Olympic sports coach in Russia before he defected to the United States many years ago. He says the human mind can only hold one thought at a time. So think thoughts of success while on the platform. Your one thought pushes out the other false evidence that tries to push in.

Albert Einstein said, "Imagination is more important than knowledge." Imagine the audience with beaming faces. Imagine their minds as hurting. Your message can touch and heal if you allow it to. Imagine the healing taking place.

Instead of letting negative thoughts—"They are going to hate me," or "They are not going to like me"—enter your mind, try things like "I know what I know." "I'm glad I'm here." "I'm glad they are here." "I can help." Give yourself positive affirmations that have importance to you. Those will give you power and confidence.

What are some of those self-talk statements you say to yourself now? What dreams of success can you replace them with?

> *Before you begin your talk, turn inward, remind yourself that you are there to serve, to be of service to these people. Ask for guidance and support in that purpose.*
> —DR. LAYNE LONGFELLOW

> *I still get nervous before I speak. When I feel that nervousness I say, "Ah that's good, that's good, that's good." I just keep saying it over and over. I take control with deep breaths.*
> —STEW LEONARD, JR.

> *Tell yourself how lucky you are to be doing this—today I get to go do what I love to do! I can't wait to have people hear it!*
> —SUZIE HUMPHREYS, SPEAKER AND RADIO PERSONALITY

[6]A CareerTrack (the famous seminar company) executive told me their statistics show that about 2 percent of every audience is looking for a reason to hate the presenter, no matter how good the presenter was! Two percent of every audience also loves the presenter, no matter how rotten he or she was.

Have you heard about some crazy people in California who go to seminars and walk on hot coals?

*Oh, **those** seminars!*

Those seminars are usually the work of Anthony Robbins, a psychologist and author of the book *Unlimited Power* and one of the most successful speakers in the world today. He is most famous for seminars where his attendees walk across hot coals. He talks about NLP, Neuro Linguistic Programming.

Most psychologists deal with "why" you got the way you are. They start you off with, "Let's go back to your childhood. You say your dog bit you?" Tony looks at people's fears and mental problems differently, with the use of NLP. In simple terms, NLP is about finding out what you would like to be and *acting* that way.

In his excellent tapes *Unlimited Power,* produced by Nightingale-Conant, Anthony Robbins tells the story of a woman who came into his office and whined about her depression.[7] She had been depressed for years and years and didn't know what to do.

He simply asked, "How did you create this?" She said she didn't understand what he meant.

He explained that when she became depressed, things happened to her body. He tried to get her to explain what those things were.

The body slumps into that position, the voice whines.

Then he said, "What are you *thinking* about when you're depressed?"

She said, "Well, I'm thinking about all the terrible things that have happened in my life!" When he got her to change her body posture and think about something happy, then she actually became happy! That's a simplistic version of Neuro Linguistic Programming.

Try it for yourself. Crunch your shoulders over, look down, and think of something really awful and depressing, and say "I am depressed." Do you feel wonderful at this point? Most likely not.

Sit up straight, smile, and take your arm and raise it above your head and shout, "I feel great!" (If you're in the middle of a restaurant and reading this, you may want to go into the restroom.) Done? You're smiling at this point aren't you? No doubt you're thinking "I can't believe I did that!" or "I can't believe she thinks I'm going to do that!"

Remember, the human mind can only hold one thought at a time. Program in thoughts of success!

Rehearse in your imagination how to handle any changes you can foresee might be necessary. Visualize how you can respond to a change you could

---

[7]The album is well worth listening to; you can hear the real version of the following story instead of my paraphrasing.

not plan for: Get experience and confidence by introducing changes in all of your presentations.
—CHRISTOPHER HEGARTY

Always visualize the end of the program with 5000 people standing up and applauding your ideas and presentation—it removes stage fright.
—THOMAS FARANDA

A MESSAGE FROM DOTTIE WALTERS ON STAGE FRIGHT*

If your knees are knocking, your heart pounding, and your mouth dry, don't feel lonely. The *Book of Lists* shows speaking in public as the number one fear in the world today. Dying is farther down the list!

My personal theory is that the reason we are afraid is because we are thinking of ourselves. We think, "If I am not perfect, will I be ridiculed?"

Even though we have done everything possible to look our best, be prepared, checked all the things we need to do to make the presentation perfect, we still have a black cloud hanging about over our heads tagged, "Not perfect. Not up to their standards." The stomach turns over, the knees knock. The mouth dries up and the heart beats a noisy tom-tom.

Replace fearful "Self" worries about hair, clothes, and petty details, with **audience benefits.** You will find an automatic take-over of your subconscious.

Controlling stage fright is like riding a bike, driving a car, or typing. You are so involved with the task at hand, you don't worry about your image or appearance at all.

Do all you possibly can about your preparation and your appearance, then release those worries from your mind. You are then free to give your best to your audience. Your personality and sincerity will shine.

The first time I spoke before an audience of 5,000 I was petrified. I thought my entire body was frozen to that stage. My lips were stuck, permanently, to my teeth.

Then, out of desperation I visualized the scene in my life when I felt most secure. I saw myself tucking my children into their beds with a big, soft, pink blanket. Our family called it a "comforter." So I mentally filled the whole auditorium with a pink "comforter." I turned to my left, tucked everybody in, looked up to the balcony, then moved to my right. I smiled and began.

---

*From "Speak and Grow Rich" by Dottie & Lilly Walters, an audio album published by Royal CBS Publishing, Glendora, California.

(Continued)

Afterwards, a woman came backstage and said, "How did you get that pink light into the auditorium? It was lovely." There was no pink light. It was the picture I projected from my mind to theirs. It really works.

Most speakers develop their own courage-strengthening technique to use just before they go on. Some do deep breathing. Others do exercises to escape the demon of fear.

As I wait off stage with my mental motor roaring, straining against the minutes before I can let my energy flow, I do mental visualization.

First I ask my Heavenly Father for help, using the words of Saint Francis of Assisi: "Lord, let me be a channel of Your love."

I visualize the people sitting in my audience. I see them coming from a long distance. They are hungry, tired, discouraged. My modules of material are platters of delicious, steaming, nourishing food. With all my heart I want to give these people this good food they are hungry for.

When I hear my introduction, I mentally "jump up in my mind" as I walk on stage. Instead of fear, I become full of anticipation, excitement, happiness. I leave all those "self" thoughts in the wings.

The sensation is like pushing up from the bottom of a swimming pool and breaking through the water into the sunshine. Albert Einstein called it the "leap of the mind."

I look out into my audience, searching for the faces of all those who are hungry, who need my nourishing ideas. My heart calls to them, "It is OK! I am the one you have been waiting for! I have what you need! Eat! Eat! Enjoy."

The truly amazing thing is that I constantly have people come up to me after my presentation to say, "I came a long way. I needed help badly. I am so grateful for what you gave me today. I thought you were speaking just for me."

My audiences have often given me this "just for me" thank you backstage after my program. No matter whether my audience was 100, 5,000 and even 14,000, they always thank me for individual personalization. But I know better. I was just the conduit.

Best Tip to Abolish Stage Fright: Focus on the Audience

Focus your mind on your audience and you won't have time to worry about yourself. When you visualize yourself rehearsing and performing, do you see yourself standing, poised, smiling, a glimmer and twinkle in your eyes, a laugh on your lips? Are you seeing *you*, or do you see *the audience?* What's the picture?

Rarely do we see the audience's faces, usually we see ourselves—a dramatic gesture here, a brilliant quip there. Adjust the picture in your mind when you are practicing, picture the faces of the people in the audience. See them saying, with their expressions, their eyes, their body language, "Oh yes, that's good! That's what I needed."

If you approach each audience with an attitude of generous love, there will be no room for fear.
—RALPH ARCHBOLD

Forget about stage fright! Think about all the problems your audience needs your solutions to.
—JEFF DEWAR

Concentrate on the message not on yourself.
—JOHN PATRICK DOLAN

I speak to an audience as if I am speaking to one person.
—TERRY COLE-WHITTAKER

You can only talk to one person at a time, move your eye contact through the audience looking and talking to one person at a time—the friendly ones!
—CAPT. DAVE CAREY

No matter how big the audience, they're like friends sitting at your dinner table.
—HOPE MIHALAP

You seldom prepare for conversations at parties, I doubt whether you even need note cards! Consider your next presentation as an expanded parlor conversation with the added advantage of preparation.
—TERRY L. PAULSON, PH.D.

Share from your heart, don't recite word for word. Who ever heard of having stage fright while talking to a friend?
—HERMINE HILTON

Dealing with Dry Mouth

I'm holding a great big juicy lemon. I take a knife and slice the lemon open. The juice rolls slowly all over my hand. Did you salivate? That's one way to deal with dry mouth—just think about lemons. Another is to actually keep a slice of lemon with you and lick it. You may be salivating right now just thinking about it.

What's wrong with water?

Dry mouth is a nervous reaction. You are not really thirsty. So, no matter how much water you drink, you'll still be thirsty. You will find this out the hard way when the two gallons of water you drank hits your bladder after your first 20 minutes on stage.

Other techniques to help with dry mouth are

- Very, *very* carefully bite the side of your tongue with your back teeth. Not so that you hurt yourself, but just with the tiniest bit of pressure.
- Press the top of your tongue into the top of your mouth until you salivate.
- Bite lightly on the inside of your cheek.
- Try a pinch of salt.

All the above may not work for you, but one or two should be helpful when you feel yourself go dry.

What to Do When You Are So Nervous You Can't Sleep the Night Before (or the Week Before!)

Of course, if you focus *intensely* on the audience, you won't have these sorts of problems. But, if you're human (and I'm not sure who else would be reading this anyway!), you are bound to have many a restless night. Give some of these stress relievers a try.

- *Warm Milk.* Yup, Grandma was right. Warm milk does put you to sleep. It needs to be warm, not cold. Cold stuff is stimulating, and we are trying to relax the body, not wake it up. Milk is high in calcium, which is a natural relaxant. Good for your body, nice and wholesome. One problem— have you ever tasted warm milk? Ick! I'm sure that's why we invented chocolate milk—to give warm milk some kind of flavor. Unfortunately, all the sugar in chocolate milk acts as a stimulant, and we are right back where we started from. If you just can't stand warm milk, like me, but you need it, try putting in a few tablespoons of your favorite liqueur. Please do this with discretion! Using alcohol to help settle your nerves is a rotten habit to get into. There are several vitamin supplements for milk that have no caffeine, but add taste.
- *Stretching Exercises.* Do some yoga exercises to get the body stretched out. It will give your mind something other than your problems to focus

on and make you feel great. Books, audiotapes, and videotapes are now available on "beginning yoga" at most bookstores.

- *Hot Shower.* The warmth relaxes your muscles. Often your mind then follows suit and slows down as well.
- *Self-hypnosis.* I have several tapes by my bedside that put me to sleep and fill me with positive affirmations on various topics. You'll find all kinds of these tapes in book and audio stores. Some speakers even make up their own self-hypnosis tapes using their own voices.
- *Eat Something Heavy.* Eat a heavy meal with lots of rice, potatoes, pasta, etc. Of course, I don't recommend this eating habit if you present often, but it does tend to put you to sleep!

MORE SECRETS ABOUT STEP 3: CONQUER STAGE FRIGHT AND YOUR FEAR OF MAKING CHANGE (PLANT THE SEED IN THE GROUND)

Your mind can only hold one thought at a time. Focus on your listeners, visualize yourself successfully *meeting their needs,* and you won't have time to worry about you.

> *Bob Orben talks about* stage fright. *He says, "It's not the stage that frightens me—it's the audience." Know exactly what you are going to say— memorize it—practice it—and get up and give it as often as possible.*
> —BILL GOVE

> *Successful speaking doesn't mean eliminating anxiety; it means controlling it. If you aren't a little nervous before you speak it could be a warning that you're overconfident or cocky. The trick is to channel nervous energy into passion and enthusiasm. This can be achieved only through the confidence that comes from being thoroughly prepared.*
> —MARK SANBORN

> *Do what you* know, *what you* live, *what you* believe. Doing *overcomes fear every time!*
> —ED FOREMAN

> *Before I talk, I make sure I get to talk to a couple people who will be in my audience, so I realize they are regular folks. I never sit at the corporate table with the President and all that stuff, I like to go out and sit with one of the dealers, or one of the salespeople—whoever the speech is for. It gives me a good feeling that I don't have to be too fancy, 'cause they're just regular plain old people like I am.*
> —STEW LEONARD, JR.

Honesty is the great enroller. If you are nervous, tell your audience! They will empathize and go out of their way to make you feel welcome and comfortable.
—HARVEY DIAMOND

Stage fright isn't all bad. It can give you an edge, make you more alert, and give you an energy that makes your presentation more dynamic.
—ANITA CHEEK MILNER

Always make sure your fly is zipped before you go on.
—AL LAMPKIN

Step 4
Be Credible—
Be an Expert
_____Sink Your Roots
Down Deep

Research and perception improve your reception.
—AUTHOR UNKNOWN

You started with your **seed of interest** that you are going to be passionate, compassionate, and defined about. You found **fertile soil** to put it in, or tailored what you have to say in such a way that it will grow where you are forced to plant it. You then found ways to encourage yourself to **plant the seed in the ground,** to overcome your fears of the platform and of making changes. Now, you need to **sink your roots deep,** so deep that no storm can blow you over. That means being an expert, a credible expert.

There are three crucial steps to ensure being taken seriously by your audience:

1. *Know your subject*
2. *Know your subject and most importantly*
3. *KNOW YOUR SUBJECT!!*
—HARVEY DIAMOND

Why Be "an Expert"?

If you realized that you needed brain surgery, would you look for a gynecologist? Or a proven expert in the world of brain surgery? (We're in big trouble if you're having trouble answering this.) When someone has a problem, they want *an expert*. Audiences and meeting planners are waiting for you to offer solutions to their problems; they want experts.

Although your audiences won't "care how much you know until they know how much you care" (Cavett Robert), your *eloquence* will grow as you become more comfortable on the platform. Benjamin Disraeli said, "Eloquence is the child of knowledge."

If you claim you can solve all of your listeners' problems, they tune you out. Audiences, right or wrong, follow the old adage, "A jack of all trades is a master at none."

There is a place in the Capitol building in Washington D.C., Statuary Hall. It has many of our U.S. heroes, mainly Presidents and great politicians, and one *simple* speaker. One of the greatest presenters of this century, a man called Will Rogers. At his death in the 1930s, Will was the highest-paid and most beloved speaker in the country. Will was famous for saying—in his simple country-boy style—"Well, *ah* only know what I read in the papers!"

Will gave the impression he was just a simple country boy who "don't hardly know 'bout newspapers." What most people didn't know was that Will Rogers had just about every major publication sent to him wherever he was on the road, every single day. As a political humorist he needed to be a leading expert on the political situation. Will did his homework.

Great presenters take all the common information that surrounds us all, but they study it, contemplate it, and absorb it more than the average presenter. The result is a great and unique speaker.

> *The greatness of art is not to find what is common, but what is unique.*
> —Isaac Bashevis Singer

As a speaker, it is horrifying to realize an audience knows more about the topic than you do. Even worse is being in an audience and realizing that the *presenter* is clueless! If you are an expert, you don't need to be a Winston Churchill. The audience wants your knowledge, so they forgive your presentation flaws.

> *Brain surgeons earn 10 times that of a general practitioner—it pays to be an expert.*
> —Allan Pease

> *Substance and sincerity are not just the pillars of a talk's strength, they're the only reasons for the talk. Sincerity follows from substance.*
> —Dr. Layne Longfellow

What Is a Credible Expert?

There are those that know that they know,
There are those that know that they don't know.
Then there are those that don't know that they don't know.
—FROM TONY KING, INVENTOR AND SPEAKER

Credibility comes from what you say (content), how you say it (delivery), and who you are (character). Who you are is the foundation for everything else. Prepare carefully, claim expertise only in those areas where you've earned it through experience, research or both, and be honest about what you don't know.
—MARK SANBORN

The true expert is the person who has a passion for the subject and a burning desire to share that passion. Who has given his or her heart and soul to the search for answers. One who does not just quote statistics, but one who relates the statistics in a meaningful way to the audience.
—RALPH ARCHBOLD

Secrets on How You Can Become an Expert

In my very first presentation, "Life's Higher Goals," I gave my "secret" for becoming the best: "You want to be a scholar, you want to be great in the athletic world, you want to be a great statesman, a doctor, a lawyer, anything in life—you want to be great in business, in selling—put 10,000 hours of work into it and see what happens in your life!
—BOB RICHARDS, OLYMPIC CHAMPION

One year I spoke at the National Conventions of the National Speakers Association, the International Platform Association, and Toastmasters International. A young speaker who attended all three said, "How can I be asked to do that too?" I said, "Write for 20 years for Bob Hope...." There is no shortcut to being an "expert" and anyone who tries to find one becomes an "amateur."
—GENE PERRET

Becoming an expert depends on each person's learning style. Some people are readers, they need to find everything they can to read on a topic. I learn by interviewing and talking to people. I go out and talk to everybody who knows anything about the topic.
—DR. KEN BLANCHARD

Read extensively, listen to audios, and view videos of established experts—then get yourself some experience in the field. It's important that you are not just a reporter but an expert.
—WESS ROBERTS, PH.D.

Start by being able to argue either side of the position.
—SOMERS WHITE

If you are an expert—say so. If you are not an expert, be a superb reporter giving full credit to those you quote. You will establish as much, or more, credibility by being a superb reporter than by attempting to prove you are an expert when you are not.
—CHRISTOPHER HEGARTY

Whatever you're talking about, you got to keep on doing it everyday. You've got to make sure you're immersing yourself in your topic regularly to stay up to date on it.
—STEW LEONARD, JR.

Deciding What Kind of Expert You Really Want to Be

Assignment: Take a few moments and describe to yourself the credentials of an expert in your topic area that you would be excited to travel a great distance to hear. You would actually even jump on a plane and fly across the country to hear this person—if she or he existed. Don't worry that you don't believe this sort of person, does, or could exist, just pretend. What credentials might this expert have? College degrees? What practical on-the-job experience does this person have? Other than the specific topic area, what other special study areas does this person have? (For example, your own specific topic area may be presentation skills. For you to really get excited about hearing someone else present on this topic, he or she may have studied acting skills, voice, camera protocol, etc.) How well read is the speaker on your topic? How many relevant books does the expert read a week, month, etc.?

Once you know what kind of presenter you would be excited to hear on your own topic, you will know where to start to build your own credibility. Look at your answers to the questions above. In order for you to be that person in five years, what would you need to do? What tiny steps could you do tomorrow that would be a start toward accomplishing those goals? For example, if you need a degree to become that person, could you order a catalog from a few schools that offer those classes? Buy a book? Go to the library to find out more information?

Once you decide what that credible expert looks like in your own mind, you can take those first tiny steps toward sinking your roots down deep! Is it time to put anything on your action plan list?

When to "Just Say No!"

It is easy to get caught up in the excitement, glitter, and glamor of being *the speaker!* Then, no matter what they ask you to present on, you say, "Sure! I'll do it; no problem!"

Your mind goes conveniently blank. You forget you spent all those months, maybe years, developing your expertise and talent—selecting a seed, planting your tree in the right soil, etc. You jump on the platform with zeal and this new topic and deliver the same sort of mediocre performances you used to give before you committed to all the steps we have already discussed!

If you're not an expert on the topic they request, and you're not planning to expand to that area of expertise as part of your long-range plan, then learn to *just say no.* Suggest someone else who is an expert on the topic they want. A *credible* expert is not an expert on everything!

Never profess you are an expert without the credentials to back it up. One day you will face an audience with a famous certified—bonafide—expert in your area and you had better know what you are talking about.
—BOBBIE GEE

Once a communication wire got crossed and I found out right before I went on that they expected a totally different event than I was expecting. I thought if I said "no" I would appear arrogant. So I went on. Big mistake. I should have re-scheduled. The audience and the client did not get the full benefit of what I could have done for them.
—WESS ROBERTS, PH.D.

Don't try to be an expert on their topic, just your own. It's a mistake to bring coals to Newcastle. I don't know much about coals, I do know about the backroom of Washington.
—JACK ANDERSON, COLUMNIST

I'm more concerned about getting asked back the second time, than taking a wrong speech the first time. If I'm not right for a talk, I just say "no."
—TOM OGDEN

Stick with what you know; pitch it to fit.
—GERALD C. MEYERS

REHEARSE...REHEARSE...REHEARSE. Stick to YOUR message. "Leave the banjo playing to the banjo player."
—IRA HAYES

Don't talk about golf if you don't know which caddy to hit the ball with.
—AL LAMPKIN

MORE SECRETS ABOUT STEP 4: BE CREDIBLE—BE AN EXPERT (SINK YOUR ROOTS IN DEEP)

Sink your roots in so deep that no winds can blow you down (like someone in the audience knowing more than you about the topic)! "Research and perception improve your reception." Don't get so excited with the thrill of the platform that you agree to speak on anything; learn when to just say no.

Speak only on those topics in which you have truly immersed yourself. No one follows an uncertain trumpet.
—Col. Gene Harrison, Ret.

The audience sizes you up quickly from several factors: your depth of knowledge, the experiences you speak from, the love you have for your area of expertise.
—Tom Leech

Give yourself a "padding" of extra knowledge and points to insulate you against surprises in the Q & A period.
—Hope Mihalap

Talk about what you know about. If you ain't done it, you can't teach it effectively!
—Ed Foreman

Don't pretend to be an expert—be one. Why would anyone set out to use the "second best" presenter? Immerse yourself in your subject—anything less would be frightening for you as well as the audience.
—Dianna Booher

Be honest.
—Coach John Wooden

You don't need to be an expert on your subject matter, but you do need to be honest. I was not an expert on drunk driving in the beginning, but I was certainly knowledgeable about being a victim of drunk driving.
—Candy Lightner, founder MADD

It's effective to quote experts, but don't overdo it. If you "over-quote" your audience may think you aren't knowledgeable enough to form your opinions and conclusions.
—Anita Cheek Milner

Strive to know so much about your subject that when writing your presentation, your biggest problem is what to cut out, not what you can use to fill your time.
—Jeff Dewar

Step 5

The Key to a Memorable Presentation —Develop a Theme

_____ *A Solid Trunk*

The Key to a Memorable Presentation

Who said this:

> We shall not flag or fail.
> We shall go on to the end
> We shall fight in France

We shall fight on the seas and oceans
We shall fight with growing confidence and growing strength in the air.
We shall defend our island,
Whatever the cost may be
We shall fight on the beaches
We shall fight on the landing grounds
We shall fight in the fields and in the streets,
We shall fight in the hills
We shall never surrender![1]

Winston Churchill. Were you even alive during World War II? Even if you weren't, there is very little chance that you have not heard reference to that particular speech. That message has been repeated since the 1940s. Why? That man gave thousands of talks—why that one? Let me break it down to the greatest "truism" you are going to receive from this book:

We have remembered at least a part of that particular Churchill speech for all this time *because we can.*

That's it?

Yup! That was the best part of the book. People will remember what you have to say if you just make it so *incredibly simple* that they *can* remember it.

A theme acts as a retention tool.

A Theme Is Like a Slogan—
A Rallying Call

You need a speech theme like a new product needs a slogan.
—DIANNA BOOHER

In spite of the fact that some people hate the simplicity of catchy themes, re-alize their value. Seeing it on signs and hearing it in meetings creates a memory hook that often unlocks key content, stories, and action commit-ments from a past presentation. By stating and restating your theme, you are making it more memorable in the minds of your listeners. You don't have to be original; be ready to lift themes that work for you in reinforcing the content of what you want to say. You may want to start a collection of themes and quotes as you find statements that work; the palest pencil mark is better than the best memory.
—TERRY L. PAULSON, PH.D.

[1]The Dean of Canterbury, the Reverend Hewlett Johnson, was quoted in the *Associated Press,* June 22, 1947, as having been present at that broadcast (the famous "We Shall Fight" speech), on June 4, 1940. He said, "Mr. Churchill put his hand over the microphone, and in an aside said to me with a smile: 'And we will hit them over the heads with beer bot-tles, which is all we have really got.'"

Many well-delivered and entertaining presentations are quickly forgotten because their messages are lost. Consider the theme your rallying call, your "Remember the Alamo." In one concise, punchy statement, you capture the essence of your message in a way that becomes memorable for your audience, both during the presentation and afterward.
—Tom Leech

Give the audience a slogan. We've run out of slogans. "Remember the Alamo!" "Remember the Maine!" "Remember Pearl Harbor!" What do we have to remember today? Our Zip Code.
—Al Lampkin

Secrets to Developing a Theme

Find out what's keeping them up nights and offer hope. Your theme must be an answer to their fears.
—Gerald C. Meyers

Find out what the audience worries about. Develop your theme out of that.
—Philip Crosby

In looking for a memorable theme you need only ask,

"What will touch their hearts?"

"What will stimulate their minds?"

"What will energize their very being?"

—Ralph Archbold

First determine if there is a theme for the overall meeting. Your theme should tie in the event's theme and what is in the current news.
—Somers White

I send a pre-program questionnaire (PPQ) to the meeting planner and with their help to several other attendees. Ask the audience what's needed and they will seldom lead you astray.
—Arden Bercovitz, Ph.D.

Is it time for you to rethink your mission statement? The above quotes may give you new insights.

Deciding on Your Presentation Theme

Your listeners are only going to remember 10 percent of what you tell them. The 10 percent that Churchill wanted Britain to remember was the mission which must have been something to the effect "Not only are we not down, we are never giving up, we shall take action until we die!"

He took that, made it into a short, pithy phrase, "we shall fight!" The British, as well as most of the English-speaking world, have remembered it for 50 years!

But there is so much information they must take home from my presentation.

Well, give them a handout with "all that stuff" you feel they need to have. They can study it later. But you need to make a decision on what you want them to *remember*.

First decide what your mission is—what you want your listeners to do differently after they hear you. What main thought *must* they remember to accomplish that? That is the core of your presentation. That is what you are going to develop your theme around.

Keep It Simple

They will remember your talk, if they can. So make sure they can. Try the "kiss" system: *keep it sweet and simple.* Simple does not mean insignificant, foolish, or childish. It means memorable, clear, and understandable.

> *When a man gives a speech, he takes a great chance at saying a damn fool thing. The longer the speech, the greater the thing.*
> —WILL ROGERS

Developing Your Presentation Theme

Speech classes teach that there are five kinds of presentations: persuasive, explanatory, instructional, oral report, and entertaining. I think there is only one kind of presentation. If you are doing an entertaining presentation, I think you are persuading the audience to laugh. If you are doing an instructional presentation, you are persuading them to learn. What is the one most important thing your audience must be persuaded to do differently?

> *Ask yourself, "If I had only 60 seconds on the stage, what would I absolutely have to say to get my message across?"*
> —JEFF DEWAR

Assignment: In one clear sentence, state what dominant idea your listeners must take home. This should be the essence of your mission statement. Now think of a short catch-phrase that supports that, i.e., "we shall fight," "I have a dream today."

Secrets on How Masters Have Used Themes

A well chosen theme creates interest on the part of the audience before they hear you speak as well as while you speak. Establish your theme as a result of knowing your "mission." If your mission is to show why changes are necessary, your theme might be "Change—Friend or Foe—the Choice is Yours."
—Christopher Hegarty

It is very important to develop a theme which can tie in all the important parts of your message. "The Olympic Fire" is my favorite theme and I can include my strongest belief of striving for Peace through Sports! From there I build my theories of Motivation and the Psychology of Winning and Teamwork—I can include all the stories of great athletes who've used these theories to achieve their goals and Win!
—Bob Richards

I developed my mission from the question people always ask me—"How do you handle it all?" The theme—"It's not what happens to you, it's what you do about it"—emerged from that after a year of actually giving the same speech. Now that theme is the trademark for my whole speaking career.
—W Mitchell

Go from something that is generally applicable to a recognizable problem the group has. Example: a few years ago we could have said America has a quality problem, then you could have brought that down to "we need to fix it here at our plant."
—Wess Roberts, Ph.D.

MORE SECRETS ABOUT STEP 5: THE KEY TO A MEMORABLE PRESENTATION—DEVELOP A THEME (A SOLID TRUNK)

Why will audiences remember your talk? First and foremost because you made it so simple they *can* remember. Decide what dominant thought they must take home. Develop your theme out of that. The theme is the vehicle that will support your mission.

A theme is a memory aid, it helps you through the presentation just as it also provides the thread of continuity for your audience.
—Capt. Dave Carey

A theme is the fuel of a presentation. Start with your objectives, add the fuel, then watch the creativity explode!
—HATTIE HILL-STORKS

...magic clarity is achieved by reducing our program to a statement of 25 words or less and repeating that statement over and over.
—JOHN PATRICK DOLAN

Aimless wandering over rough, unfamiliar terrain is sure to bring falls and scuffed knees. Aimless wandering through a theme-less presentation will surely bring falls and a scuffed reputation.
—HARVEY DIAMOND

The secret of successful speakers? Passion and compassion with a purpose.
—LILLY WALTERS

Step 6
Finding and Organizing Material in a Memorable Manner
_____Grow Strong, Sturdy Boughs_

You take a seed of interest in which you have found your passion, compassion, and definition. You find fertile soil for it—the right topic for the right audience. If the soil isn't fertile, and you have no choice but to present your material (in other words your boss says, "Look you teach this or you're out!"), you fertilize the soil by adapting the talk to your audience's wants, needs, attitudes, and capabilities. You force yourself to plant the seed in the ground, to get over your fear of the platform and making change. By being an expert you sink your roots down deep so no wind can blow you over. Now you grow strong, sturdy boughs and organize the material so it's not BAIR.

What?

Read on, it'll make sense by the end of this Step.

Designing and Organizing a
Memorable Speech

When you're designing your presentation, decide what three or four points you want to make. These are the main points of your outline—the boughs of the tree.

I have days and days of material, I can't get it down to three or four points!

I understand. But regardless of your agenda, the audience is only going to remember about 10 percent of what you *lecture*. If you were presenting to computers it wouldn't matter how much data you inputted, the disk clearly tells you when it's full—in no uncertain terms! When your listeners get "full," they just start to fade away. But since they are smiling sweetly at you as you lecture away, you are oblivious to the fact that you have lost them!

> *Speaking requires even more simplification than writing—a reader can "reread" a sentence, but listeners get easily distracted. Express yourself simply, then repeat the message.*
> —JACK ANDERSON

> *They can't go out and do 125 new things tomorrow. If they can just do one, two or three new things after they hear your talk, they will benefit mightily from your message. Narrow your talk down to those things, then use the many ways available to reinforce those things for your audience. Some will retain it visually, some auditorially, some kinesthetically. Try using all three methods to get your message home.*
> —W MITCHELL

How Audiences Process Your Material

Stephen C. Rafe makes a very interesting point in *How to Be Prepared to Think on Your Feet* that clarifies for me why we can't load your audience's mind down with too much information:

> *Let's consider what happens when you present two separate pieces of information:*
>
> *A-B   B-A*
>
> *So far, so good. Two ideas can only be presented in two different ways. However, as you read on, it will help you remember that the listener's mind can (and will) attend to, check, and cross information in as many ways as it can be presented—regardless of the sequence in which you may present each thought.*

Consequently, three pieces of information create a total of six different ways of presenting or processing:

A-BC   B-AC   C-AB
A-CB   B-CA   C-BA

Thus far, readers or listeners should be able to shift, resort, and recall— with reasonable accuracy—this number of topics. However, the complexity begins once you reach four major ideas. With four, the audience has to sort through 24 potential combinations and try to retain what it can.

A-BCD   B-ACD   C-ABD   D-ABC
A-BDC   B-ADC   C-ADB   D-ACB
A-CBD   B-CAD   C-BAD   D-BAC
A-CDB   B-CDA   C-BDA   D-BCA
A-DBC   B-DAC   C-DAB   D-CAB
A-DCB   B-DCA   C-DBA   D-CBA

At five major thoughts, the audience experiences serious overload—a possible 120 different ways to juggle your information.
—STEPHEN C. RAFE, HOW TO BE PREPARED TO
THINK ON YOUR FEET (© HARPER BUSINESS,
1990, REPRINTED WITH PERMISSION).

Now add to Stephen Rafe's observations. Each time you give your listeners even one piece of information, they immediately start applying it to some problem back home. This adds to the equation.

The listener thinks much faster than you talk. People generally speak at 150 words per minute, but think at 600 to 700. So your listeners are able to jump ahead and around the topic. They start adding in all kinds of factors from their own lives and experiences that have very little to do with what you're talking about. It makes the pieces of information they are juggling in their brains monumental to consider!

Now add to all that the problem of you saying a word that they interpret into something else entirely. Example: you say "fast." What does the word "fast," mean? "A fast horse" runs rapidly, a "fast dye" doesn't run at all. When you fast, you stop eating, but a fast person gets a lot done, or has a lot of dates!

Forget what you learned in school—more is not always better. Less is more.
—DIANNA BOOHER

Too many points spoil the soup. Keep them few and interesting and illustrate them with anecdotes. People remember points with stories attached to them.
—HOPE MIHALAP

Secrets on How Many Points
to Make in a Talk

In obtaining the following quotes I found it interesting that it was one of
the few issues that *almost* all the master speakers I interviewed agreed on.

No one can remember more than three points.
—PHILIP CROSBY

*I live by the magic of 3's—these can turn into many sub-points, but the 3's
ground me.*

—HATTIE HILL-STORKS

*Have three major points to make in your presentation and have three sup-
porting points for each of these.*
—ALLAN PEASE

*I like to get my talk down to three or four "big hit" things that people can
take home with them—like the way I write. I think people fall to sleep with
lists. Whenever a speaker starts off with, "Here are 10 points I'm going to
make..." I go into snoozeville.*
—DR. KEN BLANCHARD

*People won't remember more than four to six points— and they won't re-
member those unless you repeat them.*
—CAPT. DAVE CAREY

*I use a memory-peg picture to outline my key points to be made—never more
than 12—most usually six or less—and, yes, they do remember. Tell 'em
what 'cha gonna' tell 'em; tell 'em what; then, tell 'em what 'cha told 'em!*
—ED FOREMAN

*I generally make one point—my overriding message. I may support that
with illustrations, though. That's when I utilize the sacred "rule of three."*
—GENE PERRET

The Tried and True Triad

My personal favorite number for your main points is three. The human
mind has a real fondness for threes: Father, Son, and Holy Ghost; duty,
honor, country; faith, hope, charity; ready, set, go; morning, noon, and
night.

In *Sharing Ideas Newsmagazine for Professional Speakers*, Robert O.
Skovgard, editor of *The Executive Speaker Newsletter*, said,

*The most powerful and versatile speech writing devices or techniques in-
volve grouping of elements in units of three:*

"...of the people, by the people, for the people..."—Lincoln

"Liberty and union, now and forever, one and inseparable"—Webster
"...to dare, to dare again, ever to dare."—Danton

The "rule of three" can be applied anywhere that a dramatic heightened or intensifier is needed—to words, phrases, and sentences.
Douglas MacArthur's West Point farewell includes: "Duty, honor, country. Those three hallowed words reverently dictate what you ought to be, what you can be, what you will be. They are your rallying points: to build courage, when courage seems to fail; to regain faith when there seems to be little cause for faith; to create hope, when hope becomes forlorn."
The triad is difficult to misuse or overuse. It can break up large unwieldy blocks of information, knit together a paragraph and provide a touch of dramatic color.

THE RULE OF THREE
by Tom Ogden, master magician and entertainer

Series of three produce a rhythm that causes a positive and pleasing sense of completion and fulfillment. So many examples can be found in fact and fiction, in life and in storytelling, that it is valuable to relate the Rule of Three whenever possible to magic, both in individual effects and in routining.

Why does the Rule of Three work? The first item sets up the basic situation, the second item shows the pattern of expectation and the third item either completes the action or, more often, veers unexpectedly in an opposite direction to produce the surprise.

Needless to say, this Rule has immediate and obvious applications to comedy. Think how many jokes rely on a series of three. First "this" happens, then "this" happens, but then "*this*" happens instead. "There was a Jew, a Greek and an Italian..." "The farmer had three daughters..." The list is endless. Likewise, three jokes on a single topic seem to fulfill the Rule. The first joke sets up the topic. The second joke prolongs the laughter over the situation, and the third joke tops it off. How often have we heard Johnny Carson tell four jokes on a subject, only to die on the last joke, turn to Ed, and say, "I shouldn't have gone for the fourth.

"The Rule applies everywhere. To name some sets of three: the Trinity; the Three Bears; the Three Little Pigs; the Andrews Sisters; the Three Stooges; the Nina, the Pinta, and the Santa Maria; Eva Marie Saint. Are these all examples of the use of the Rule of Three? The Andrews Sisters and the boats, probably not. "Eva Marie Saint" does create a much better rhythm than just two names would, how-

(Continued)

ever—definitely a marketing plus. The number of Stooges changed over the years, and claiming "three" as the ultimate number for a comedy team would not explain Abbott and Costello, Burns and Allen, and so many more. But it is probably not coincidental that the Marx Brothers quickly honed their team down to three.

The Bears and The Pigs are perfect examples of the Rule of Three in storytelling. The Wolf was able to blow down the House of Wood and the House of Straw. But the switch came when he couldn't blow down the House of Bricks. The Three Bears is a more complicated use of the Rule of Three: it is actually three series of threes. "Someone's been eating my porridge, someone's been eating my porridge, someone's been eating my porridge, and they ate it all up. Someone's been sitting in my chair, and in my chair, and in my chair and they broke it all up. Someone's been sleeping in my bed, and in my bed, and in my bed and she's still there!" As for the Father, Son and Holy Ghost, well, I suppose it depends upon who's telling the story.

Deciding on Your Memorable Points

If you meet one of your audience members on the street a year from now, what three things would you hope they would remember? Look at your mission. What three or four things will help to accomplish that mission? Write those out on that handy scrap paper you have been using as a bookmark.

To make sure your tree isn't bare, we test each of those points against this 4-step BAIR test:

*B*enefit oriented

*A*dequately stated

*I*ndependent to the other points

*R*elevant to the mission and/or theme.[1]

Benefit-Oriented Points

The first point in our BAIR test is benefits. Look at each point and ask yourself if it is stated in terms of benefits to the listeners rather than just its features. Does it stress the results over the process?

If your topic was presentation skills and you wanted one of your sub-

---

[1]I got part of this concept from Tom Leech's excellent book, *How to Prepare, Stage, and Deliver Winning Presentations*, AMACOM, 1982.

points to be getting over stage fright, you might be tempted to make one of your points, "Deep breathing techniques." But this is a process, not a result. What is the result and/or the benefit of "Deep breathing techniques"? In this case, "getting over stage fright," "replacing fear with joy," "how not to throw up on the audience." Well, maybe that last one needs some work.

Adequately Stated Points

Now we test your mission against the second point in the BAIR test—is the point adequately stated? Does it say all you want it to say? We know what we mean. It is crystal clear in our heads. But thoughts are graphics, words are words. Is the graphic you are painting in their minds the one you intended?

By forcing yourself to write the words out on paper and clearly putting the whole concept down, you are forcing yourself to take the graphic out of your mind and put it in the mode used to transfer it over to their minds—words. As the words are just the vehicle, once it hits their minds, it becomes a picture. But by forcing yourself to clarify the words you send over, you have a better chance to control the graphic they are painting in their minds.

Independent of Other Points

Next, does the point stand all by itself? Very often one point will sort of slop over onto another one. All the points are related to the main mission, there will be some overlap. But divide them—as much as possible—into clearly separate points. When you do, your own perspective of the material will become clearer and more understandable. When that happens for you, it happens for your listeners.

> When editing, use the "stand alone filter." Take an idea, quote, or illustration and see if it is strong enough to stand alone without the support of the material that precedes or follows it in your presentation. If it needs further support or explanation to stand alone, either strengthen it or eliminate it.
> —MARK SANBORN

Relevant to the Mission and/or Theme

But that brings us to the last step in the test. Go back to the mission of the presentation. Are the points essential to help your listeners understand and accomplish the mission of your presentation? If they are not, rethink the points or rethink the mission.

Develop Your Own Original Material

There is nothing worse than hearing a presenter use the same tired old chestnuts you have heard a hundred times. No, that's not right, the worst is hearing them use the same tired old material you know they have flat-out stolen from someone else. But where does a presenter get new material from? *There is nothing new under the sun.* So how do you make it new?

If you start off with the premises we have so far— develop a mission (the seed), become an expert (sink your roots down deep), develop a theme to substantiate the mission (the trunk), then focus on the three or four points you feel they must take home—the rest will just start to fall into your lap from all kinds of places. Remember when you bought your car? All of a sudden you began to notice that same kind of car everywhere. That's because you heightened your awareness on the topic. By creating the focus on your presentation the way I have suggested, you will suddenly notice stories, statistics, and pictures in newspapers, magazines, books and even messages in the stories your friends and family tell you.

The kind of story to start with is the kind you are already comfortable telling. When you tell a story every day—you know, the kind your "significant other" starts rolling her or his eyes over—you have a story you are comfortable with and you have no doubt told over and over. These stories might make a great source for you to check for material.

But that's not original material.

Isn't it? Don't you retell that same story because it's new to your listeners? That's all that really counts. But that material you are comfortable with is just where you start. Now you will need to gather new material. Some of the really brilliant speakers I have heard who use a high percentage of original material say they are constantly on the prowl for it. Some carry a note pad. Whenever something interesting or humorous happens, they quickly write it down.

Don't be afraid to take old material and give it a new slant. I'll tell you this several times in this book because I feel it's important—Shakespeare said, "My best is dressing old words new." Take the old material, but make it new, make it yours. *However,* when you are using someone else's research and conclusions, make sure to give credit where it is due. Besides, crediting other authorities on a topic gives you more credibility.

> *New material comes thru alert living every day. Be aware of, experience life...then, share these experiences.*
> —ED FOREMAN

The specific ideas you wish to get across may not be original, but the way you get the audience to remember those ideas must be. I use a lot of humorous anecdotes and stories to illustrate key points. Many of these stories were developed from personal experiences I had and then embellished and expanded to be more effective.

—JEFF SLUTSKY, STREETFIGHTER MARKETING

TELL YOUR OWN STORY
by Stew Leonard, Jr.

I'm a believer in tellin' a lot of stories, that really happened to you. You don't need a script for them. Plus you can easily tell them with a lot of enthusiasm because they really happened to you, it made an impact on you. Chances are it's going to make an impact on the audience too.

I was speaking to a big association. Comedy Relief was held the night before. Next mornin' I read *USA Today*, they slide it under the door in everybody's hotel room. It quoted one of the comics. Said something to the effect that President Bush was asked to go out to the LA area to assess the damage done by the LA riots and the first place he stopped was Reagan's ranch. Sort of insinuating there was damage to Reagan's ranch too because he screwed the country up a little bit.

The first speaker gets up there and he tells that same little thing about Reagan's ranch I had read in *USA Today*. He made it sound like it was his thing. I sort of looked out over the audience and I could tell about half of the people laughed 'cause they hadn't read the paper in the morning, but the other half sort of looked at each other like, "hey who does this guy think he's fooling?"

I think the thing that hurt him as a speaker is that it completely shot his integrity for what he was then going to say about the association. Because you can't sort of re-package something and make it sound like it was your thing. The audience will find out, they're smart.

If he thought that line was really, really, really funny. If he was really excited about it and he laughed like crazy when he read it in the morning. He could have got up and said, "I want to share something with you that made me laugh like crazy this morning..." and he could then read that little thing out of the paper. I think that would have been great. But he had to love it.

Where to Find Material

Jim Cathcart of La Jolla, California, motivational speaker and seminar leader and coauthor of the audio album "Relationship Strategies," says, "If you give one hour extra per day of study to your chosen field, within five years you will be a national expert!"

Here's some ideas on how and where to find material.

- Go to local and county libraries. All the great minds of the world are there waiting to give you their information. Unfortunately, in this day and age you are likely to be the only one there. Well, you and one of the most overlooked resources in the United States today—the research librarian! If you have not tried talking to yours, you have missed a treasure right in your own backyard.

- Haunt bookstores. Especially used bookstores. You can find some wonderful books that are way out of print for pennies on the dollar. Everyone is quoting Tom Peters, and Peter Drucker, but what did the experts say on your topic 50, 60, or 100 years ago?

- Collect books of quotes and proverbs. What did all the great minds of the world say about your area of expertise?

- Subscribe to a computer search system. Libraries and colleges all have computer search services. You give them the topic, they obtain all the articles that have been written about the topic in the time frame you give them. You can also subscribe to the many systems available for your own computer at home.

- Join associations. Most of the real learning and exchange of business information in the world takes place at those industry associations. Members sit and discuss the real problems current in their work and come up with the modern day solutions.

- Go and hear other speakers on your subject. Don't ever assume that you know so much more than they, or that you can't learn from them. If they are really that bad, at least they'll teach you how *not* to do it.

- Assist other speakers and experts. Do your topic-area "gurus" come to town? Offer to help them. Pick them up at the airport. As you help them, they will give you all kinds of insights and ideas.

- Get a list of trade publications. Subscribe to the magazines, newsletters, and other publications in your area of expertise. Lists of these materials are available from the library.

- Write articles for all of the trade publications in your field. This encourages you to keep your research up to date and positions you as an expert to your potential audiences.

■ Constantly look for information. Keep your eyes open. When you are in an airplane, don't just sit there, read all the magazines and newspapers! Keep your scissors out and be ready to snip any goodies that have been printed on your topic.

A good many of the things I say as an after-dinner speaker occur to me during the hour or so before I get up to address the audience. I generally make notes throughout the evening, starting not just with the formal program but with my entry into the room. Almost invariably there is something that catches my attention or strikes me as odd or funny. It may be the wallpaper, a chandelier with three of its bulbs burned out, an orchestra playing disco music when the average age of the audience is sixty-five, or a tray of dishes spilled by a waiter.
—STEVE ALLEN, © 1986

I have gotten ideas for themes by reading anything I can get my hands on—fiction, plays, non-fiction, newspapers, stories, daily observation, my family. One time I got an idea for a speech on stress management from my seven-year-old daughter. She was dancing in a talent show with her sister and me. Right before we were due to go on stage she said, "Mom, please cut me out of the act." Haven't we all felt like that when the pressure is on?
—DANIELLE KENNEDY, M.A.

Is It Public Domain or Does Somebody Own It?

Cavett Robert's immortal rule:

First time the speaker says it: As Lilly Walters says, "quote."

Second time the speaker says it: As someone once said, "quote."

Third time the speaker says it: As I always say, "quote."

Notice I attributed that because I believe Cavett coined it and it's a specific quote. Otherwise, I wouldn't.

I try to do to others' quotes as I would want them to do unto mine. That's Longfellow's rule.
—DR. LAYNE LONGFELLOW

Jeff Dewar is an international speaker on Quality Enhancement. I helped him develop a set of funny but true statistics on, "What Does 99.9 Percent Quality Mean to You?" He offers what a 99.9 percent level of quality would mean in the following situations: "One hour of unsafe drinking water each month! Your heart would fail to beat 32,000 times per year. A total of 22,000 checks would be deducted from the wrong bank account each day." The list went on. This set of stats is so much fun it has been published in over 100 newspapers around the country.

Jeff was attending a seminar one day on Quality in his hometown in northern California. The presenter used the exact statistics, word for word, as if they were his own! At the break Jeff went up to him and very nicely said, "Thank you for quoting my statistics. They have certainly gotten around." The presenter said, "Oh, no, those can't be yours. I got those out of some paper in Atlanta. Here I've got the article right here in my briefcase. Look, here is the guy's picture who...why he does look just like you! But this guy's name is...." He glances at Jeff's name tag, "Hey, I'm sorry. If I'd have known you were going to be in my audience today, I would have given you credit."

Even if the author is not in your audience, someone who is a fan of the author may very well be sitting there and fuming. That same set of quotes showed up in a newsletter sent to me monthly by a speaker. She credited *Newsweek*, where she saw the quotes, but not the author, Jeff. His name was right there on the article. When I called her about it, she said, "Oh, I don't think the author's name was on that piece, hum...well, look, there's his name right there. Don't worry, I'll print a retraction." To this day I feel uncomfortable toward her, even though I fully understand it could have been an honest oversight.

I told Stew Leonard, Jr. what had happened to Jeff Dewar. He said the same thing has often happened to him.

> *Well, you know, my feeling is Jeff has to be a machine as far as turning out that kind of stuff, like those 99.9% Quality statistics. It's happened to me too. I get up to talk and people quote our rock, you might have heard it: "Rule #1—The Customer is always right. Rule #2—If they are ever wrong, re-read Rule #1". I'll be talking to the people at breakfast before I speak and they'll say, "Oh yeah, the speaker yesterday told us all about you, they said..." and they repeat our rock, or stories about me. I have to rush in and change my slides around.*
>
> *But, I figured I've just got to keep my talk fresh. I've got the luxury of being in business. So, everyday new stories happen to me. It's just a matter of weaving these new stories into the message of my talk. So when someone copies me, they're using stuff that's a year old. I'm sick of telling that old stuff anyway.*
>
> *If they're using your material you know you've got real talent. Just keep writing down those good ideas, put 'em in a book and sell 'em!*
> —STEW LEONARD, JR.

Secrets of When and How to Credit the Source

The best thing to do is use your own original material. But, when you use other people's material, credit the source. Originally, "credit the source" was the end of this section; I thought I was, well, good and done making my point. Then one of the speakers sending me quotes for this book sent me one dealing with giving credit, saying, "Give credit where credit is due." It occurred to me, "that's a good point in case, why don't we credit whoever said that?" I checked two quote books in my library, one of which was *Bartlett's Quotations*. No luck. So now I'm wondering, how far do you go to credit the source? On the other hand, if you credit every source on every point, you give a speech of footnotes with no continuity at all! I send out feelers to many of the Masters helping me with this book...

> *Some people say I ought to give a bibliography with my talks because I'm always referring to different people. I'm a "weaver." I weave ideas together. So I go out of my way to credit people. I don't think I need to fill myself up by taking credit for other people's stuff. I let my research assistants go as far as they can to find out who actually originated a bit of information so I can credit them.*
>
> *I often say in my talks, "As I talk to you I am really integrating and pulling together not only my thoughts but other people's. If there is anything I say that sounds familiar, that you feel somebody else has worked on, I would love for you to let me know."*
>
> —Dr. Ken Blanchard

> *Some quotes are so well identified with personalities that you almost have to credit them when quoting a line. The author doesn't need to be credited, but you have to credit them so as not to appear to be claiming the quote as your own. If you say, "I never met a man I didn't like," you better attribute it to Will Rogers because most people know he said it.*
>
> *I don't think good, memorable quotes ever become public domain. Shakespeare wrote in the 1600s, but he still owns "neither a borrower nor a lender be."*
>
> —Gene Perret

> *Just because you can't attribute it, doesn't mean you can acquire it. But even though you can't source it, you can still say it. Make a reasonable effort to find the source—check your quote books and ask your library—if that doesn't work, admit you don't know who said it."*
>
> —Mark Sanborn

> *...You might try—"as a wit once said"—"as the old saying goes"— "you've heard it before but it's still true."*
>
> *Something of that sort should settle the problem, in most cases.*
>
> —Steve Allen, ©1986

> *If you done it, it's yours!*
>
> —Ed Foreman

> *The best way to avoid infringement of other people's ideas is to develop your own.*
>
> —Michael H. Mescon

> *Credit the source as you received it, and then be ready to change it if you receive better information. I originally credited one to a talk show host— only*

to find it was first said by Thomas Aquinas. So I changed the slide. Since Thomas is dead, I doubt whether he cared.

I never use a full poem or substantial quote without permission from the author.

—TERRY L. PAULSON, PH.D.

Crediting is much easier to do when you write than when you speak. When I write, I make very sure to "footnote" where I first heard the information. In speaking, it is much more difficult to say, "as so and so said" for each reference. I find it more effective to hold up to the audience the actual newspaper, or magazine article where I found the information. On the back I have the actual quote written out so I can read it to the group. This validates my source in a physical way.

You should make a real effort to find the source of the information you are quoting. Go through a couple of quote books, like Bartlett's (they are even available on disks now), to try to find who said it first.

However, if you speak out of your own life and your own heart, you never have to worry about giving credit.

—FLORENCE LITTAUER, AUTHOR AND SPEAKER

HOW TO GENERATE IDEAS
by Steve Allen

One of my "secrets" for doing creative work of any sort is simply to do what I call "getting out of my own way." I discovered, quite early in life, that there is some strange creative center in my brain that, once stimulated, will give up a considerable volume of whatever I ask it to produce: jokes, stories, philosophical observations, or ideas for essays, newspaper or magazine features, television comedy sketches, plays, songs, and so on. Part of the process involves shutting "me" up, calming myself down, relaxing, and just listening to the ideas as an internal computer cranks them out.

I know it's all very easy for someone who has written a good many books, songs, plays, or whatever to suggest that you, too, can do likewise, and with equal ease. I'm saying no such thing. After all, I can't write a play as well as Neil Simon, a melody as well as Jerome Kern, a lyric as well as Stephen Sondheim, or a short story as well as John Cheever. But that's a point of no importance whatever. So don't worry if, when you first begin timidly listening to your own creative center, it doesn't immediately begin cranking out ideas that would dazzle Aristotle.

By simply agreeing to give a speech, or by self-generating a plan to do so, you will have stimulated your own mysterious idea center

What you must do next is listen to its responses. At this stage don't—whatever you do—serve as a censorious judge, telling yourself, "Oh, that's no good" or "That will never work." Stopping self-criticism at once is part of the process of getting out of your own way.Whatever thoughts occur to you, make an immediate note of them. It is assumed, of course, that you will have the common sense to keep yourself provided with pencil and paper or a small portable tape recorder. Then, by whatever means, grab any and every relevant idea that occurs to you. You may make your notations on separate slips of paper or on cards, or list them on one piece of paper. Some speakers prefer yellow lined legal pads for this purpose. On the left-hand side of the page enumerate the points as you make them. Then, over to the right, revise the order in any way that seems reasonable.

Now determine from your list or cards which points are the most important. Then either eliminate the least meaningful ones or include them only by way of a quick, passing reference, thus permitting yourself more time to develop the essential elements of your presentation.

Suppose that by this notation process you produce thirty separate ideas relating to the subject of your speech. As you review them you might decide that five or six points simply aren't suitable for your purposes. Who cares? You've still got all the others. And that's only from the first day's pickings. Assuming that you don't have to give your talk immediately, you'll probably have quite a few days—perhaps weeks—to listen to your internal creative center. If you're at all normal, you will almost certainly come up with not too few ideas, but too many.

From *How to Make a Speech* (McGraw-Hill), copyright © 1986, material reproduced with permission of Steve Allen.

Is It Fiction or a Flat-Out Lie?

My father has been watching the professional speaking industry for over 30 years now as he has kept Mom and me going. He has observed, in his jovial Irish witty fashion, "Speakers are like good Irishmen…neither lets reality get in the way of a good story!" Ninety percent of what most humorists tell you is fiction, "I saw these two guys walk into a bar…." We—the audience—know it didn't *really* happen. We accept it.

So, it's not a "lie," it's OK to dramatize and fictionalize stories for your talk. Right?

Sounds good to me, *I think.* I heard an excellent humorist say if it did not *really* happen, she would not use the story. At first I thought this extreme, especially for a humorist—we expect them to "pull our leg."

But when you are also a motivational humorist, you might want to take a serious look at this stance. You are in—as Ken Blanchard says—a privileged position. Whether you want it or not, there is a certain amount of hero worship going to come your way. If you are going to err one way or the other, it might be nice to be even more deserving of that worship and err on the side of honesty.

> *With an audience the most devastating thing a speaker can do is to say something that doesn't ring true.*
> —W MITCHELL

> *Tell them which are facts and which are opinions.*
> —PHILIP CROSBY

> *There is a difference between telling a story and reporting facts. An audience usually knows when you a trying to stir an emotion rather than report a fact. A little exaggeration to excite and inspire them is acceptable. But if you impart information you must be deadly accurate.*
> —JACK ANDERSON

What's a Chestnut?

We want a fruitful tree, not one with a bunch of old icky chestnuts on it. (A "chestnut" is a story or joke that has been told over, and over, and over.) There is a fine line between chestnuts and "golden oldies." A line defined by how many times your audience has heard the story. A chestnut in the United States can be wonderful in Zimbabwe and quite appropriate for a talk there—and vice versa.

It's not always wrong to use the same old material over and over. Although the story is old for you, for each audience it is new. However, if the audience members has heard the same story three or four times, you are going to get a very flat response.

Deciding if a story is a chestnut or golden oldie probably causes speakers more trauma than any other issue. Try going over some of the stories you are worried about with your event planner and a few of the audience members for their opinions. The ideal way to avoid chestnuts is to use only your own original material.

> *I always try to listen to as many of the speakers as possible that go on before me at an event. The audience may forgive me for using an old story they've heard. But not if they have heard it at the same meeting!*
> —TOM OGDEN

If your spouse and a friend in Los Angeles and New York all double-up...go for it!
—GERALD C. MEYERS

As soon as I hear another speaker share a story, that is my first warning it may fast be becoming a chestnut. The real danger of using an old story is not that the story doesn't illustrate the point, but that the audience will feel you are so naive as to believe they haven't heard it before...that you are simply not up to date.

But if you preface the story with, "you probably have heard this, but it's so appropriate to what I wanted to share with you...." You can always use old stories but make a new angle.

Like the famous old starfish story—thousands of star fish were beached with the low tide. A young boy stood on the beach and threw one at time out into the water so they wouldn't die. An old man came up and caustically said, "Kid, what do think you're doing? You can't possibly get even a fraction of these starfish in the water before they die! What possible difference is all your work going to make?" "Well sir," he replied as he leaned down, grabbed another and threw it in, "it makes all the difference in the world to that one."

That is one of the great old—if overused—stories. But you may think of a way to make a new point. Perhaps about what caused the old man's cynicism.
—MARK SANBORN

Some Biblical stories have been told hundreds of times with new insights mined by effective preachers. Some stories are so great we never tire of them. Some of my "used" audiences have been upset with me for not re-telling their favorite stories. Keep all stories relevant and alive. If you enjoy telling them, the audience will most likely enjoy hearing them.
—TERRY L. PAULSON, PH.D.

I always joke if I feel they have heard my story before and say, "I have my favorites that I love to hear over and over." Then sometimes I'll offer them the opportunity to tell me some new stories.
—TERRY COLE-WHITTAKER

The examples below are chestnuts I personally am tired of hearing. Hang on to this book, pull it out in 50 years, and they will seem like new stuff. But for today, please, they are overused.

Some opening chestnuts are:

"What a great introduction! That's the best introduction I've ever written!" (Or any variation of that.)

"Good morning!" Audience responds with a typical half-hearted "good morning" back. "Now that's not very good, come on now! GOOD MORNING!!"

Don't use this line, it makes your audience think that you feel they are
dumb: "You can always tell who the really energetic and excited people are, you always get here early and sit right up here in the front
rows."

Great, the majority—not the few in the front row—were just offended! If they were not motivated enough to sit in the front, then consider it your quest to motivate them. That may be why they brought you
in to make the speech. I don't like to be motivated by anyone who puts
me down.

Here are quick paraphrased versions of some of the stories I have
heard that have become chestnuts for me:

*A survey was just taken, it shows one out of every three people is
_____ (you fill in, ugly, crazy, whatever). Look at the person on
your left, now at the person on your right. If it's not them, it must be
you!*

---

*City slicker moved to country and bought himself a herd of pigs. Got real
excited 'bout startin a farm and wanted to breed 'em. Put 'em all in his
truck and brought 'em over to a neighbor who's got a stud.*

    City slicker asked his neighbor, "How'll I know if it took?"

    *Neighbor said, "Ain't no problem. You check on 'em tomorrow morning.
If they ain't grazing, they took. If they are grazing, bring 'em all back for
another go 'round."*

    *Next morning that city slicker is real excited. Jumps outta bed, looks out
his window. Damn! The whole herd is grazing.*

    *He puts all in the truck, goes to the neighbor's, and the pigs get another
go 'round.*

    *Next morning that city slicker is real excited. Jumps outta bed, looks out
his window again. Damn! The whole herd is grazing.*

    *One more time, he puts all in the truck, goes to the neighbors and the pigs
get another go 'round.*

    *Next morning he wakes up, "Honey, I just can't stand to see them pigs
grazing again, you go look."*

    She gets outta bed and has a look.

    "Well honey, are they grazing?"

    "No, but they're already in the truck and one is honking the horn!"

To date, I've heard that one done as pigs, cows, horses, and dogs. It's
cute, cute, cute, but it's done, done, done.

The football player with the blind father is a wonderful, beautiful,
touching classic story. In fact, I love it so much I asked who I thought
was the original source—Bob Richards—if he would transcribe it just
the way he would do it (see box). This story illustrates why stories become chestnuts—usually because they are *brilliant* to start with.

THE FOOTBALL STORY

Many people probably hear the "football story" from my original tape cassette of "Life's Higher Goals," copyrighted in 1957. It's a true story, told by Lou Little, football coach at Columbia University. The football player's name was Bill Sayles. I originally heard the story from Bill Alexander, a preacher out of Oklahoma City. Here is the story as it is heard in my tapes.—Rev. Bob Richards.

I close with this one last story—Lou Little tells it about his great football team. They were on their way to the Conference Championship. One last game! He had a boy on his squad who couldn't quite make the team for four straight years. Just before the game, three days before, Lou was given a telegram to give to this boy that his only living relative has just died. Well, the boy looked at the telegram and said, "Coach, I'll be back for Saturday's game."

The morning of the game he came up to his coach and said, "Lou, I want you to put me in this game. I know I haven't made the first team yet, but let me in for this kick-off. I'll prove to you I'm worthy of it!"

Well, Lou could see he was emotionally disturbed and he made all kind of excuses but finally thought, "Well, he can't do much harm in the kick-off!

The opposing quarterback took it on the goal line, moved up on the seven-yard line. A tremendous tackle, the boy had dropped him in his tracks! On the next tackle, you couldn't move him out of there. He made practically every tackle that day! Terrific downfield blocking. He was the reason why Columbia won the Championship!

Afterwards all the guys were pounding him on the back. When they were all done, Lou Little went up to him and said, "Son, I don't understand it. Today you were an All-American! I've never seen you play like this in four straight years. What happened?"

The boy looked up at his coach and said, "Well, Coach, you knew my Dad died, didn't you?" He said, "Yes, I handed you the telegram."

He said, "You knew he was blind, didn't you?" The Coach said, "Yes, I've seen you walking around the campus with him many times."

He said, "Coach, today's the first football game my Dad ever saw me play."

It makes a difference, friends, who those unseen eyes are watching.

By Reverend Bob Richards, Olympic Champion (Used with permission for *Secrets of Successful Speakers*, excerpted from "Life's Higher Goals" as told by Bob Richards.)

This wonderful story makes many beautiful points. The thousands of speakers who have all copied it from Bob Richards *all* think so. I have heard it told by "the brother" of the player, the player himself, the coach, the cheerleader, the wife of the dead father. I have heard that the coach was Notre Dame's Knute Rockne, Bear Bryant, and the local high school coach of all kinds of small town cities. It's just amazing how many people were in the football stadium that day. It's more amazing I have never heard one of them attribute the story to Reverend Richards.

Here are some audience participation chestnuts: You ask the audience to cross their arms. Then say, "OK, now cross them the other way." The entire audience moans, groans, and has difficulty figuring out how to cross their arms the other way.

This exercise beautifully illustrates how we get into a rut and how difficult it is for us to get out of the rut—to change old patterns (such as thinking up new audience participation exercises!). I think I have heard this exercise used in 90 percent of all training sessions I have ever attended. Another old audience participation exercise starts when you ask the audience, "Put your hand on your chin." But you put your hand on your cheek. Most of the audience will follow what you "show" them rather than what you "say."

> *Once I have heard the story or joke used twice by other speakers or entertainers, I avoid it.*
> —TOM OGDEN

> *You're always safe only when you use your own stories!*
> —DIANNA BOOHER

> *I can't prepare an entire new speech for each audience, so I just don't worry if a few old anecdotes get repeated.*
> —JACK ANDERSON

Before You Write the Speech

In this book and in my seminar on presentations, I use an analogy of a tree. I know a year from now you will only remember a few of the 11 steps we discuss, even though I have used a simple structural pattern. First, I have aimed at changing your actions in developing the presentations and your attitude toward writing them. Then I try to up your retention level in every step by using statistics, stories, and humor to try to emphasize those three essential points I want you to take home.

So, what are your three points?

My three points are:

1. Know exactly how you want to change the audience members' actions and attitudes when they leave your presentation—*develop a mission.*

2. Realize they won't remember more than a few points anyway, so decide *what three or four points they must remember* and design the speech around them.

3. Speak with *passion for your topic and compassion for your audience.*

In my seminars, keynotes, and in this book, I say over and over, "The secrets of successful speakers? Develop passion, and compassion with a purpose." If you have not clearly decided on your mission, your theme and the three or four main points the audience must remember, stop reading now and take time to think them through. You do not need to decide on the best way to deliver the information when you are unsure what the information will be.

Using Structural Patterns to Organize Your Speech

Now you are ready to decide on a pattern in which to place all your material. There are many. In this next section we will discuss a few structures—acronyms, analogies, problem-cause-solution series, story telling.

Organize Your Talk Like a Map

What may seem totally logical and organized to you can appear a jumbled mess in the ear of the listener. Take the time to be very clear of your sequence, your points, and your rationale. Make your thoughts an easy trail to follow.
—JEFF DEWAR

Organization consists of taking your two most important points and putting one at the beginning and one at the end of your talk. It's then a matter of building a bridge from one to the other.
—HARVEY DIAMOND

If you were telling yourself how to get from here to there, in the most enjoyable way, how many steps would it take? Write out the directions, file them in your mind, gild the path with laughter, and don't make the audience take any more steps than you would.
—HERMINE HILTON

Use experience stories. Explain what the problem was for you or your company and how you solved it. Give them three or four ideas they can use to solve similar problems of their own. Draw a little road map of how you are going to start and where you are going to your destination or end.
—IRA HAYES

Acronyms and Acrostics

Before we get into this, here's a word on acrostics and acronyms. Most Americans lump them together and call them both acronyms. Some day someone will walk up to you after a talk and say, "You know, that's not an acronym." You should know the difference between these two:

Acronym—a word formed from the first letter or syllables of the words, as UNESCO (from United Nations Educational, Scientific, and Cultural Organizations).

Acrostic—a composition in verse or an arrangement of words in which the first, last, or other particular letters in each line, taken in order, spell a word or phrase (as in NEWS, North, East, West, South[2]).

I am going to *incorrectly* call them both acronyms, knowing full well I'm *wrong*, but that you will *understand* me...which seems like a great trade-off to me! (The Europeans and Australians who commonly use and know the difference between an acronym and an acrostic are no doubt wondering what the fuss is about.)

Acronyms are fabulous memory aids to organize material when they're done right. A good acronym—in order of importance—does the following:

1. Is easily remembered

2. Has each letter represent the key thought in the concept you want them to remember

3. Substantiates your mission

One speaker I work with talks on "Change." He wrote a great speech full of super ideas to help his listeners deal with the tremendous changes going on in their industry. We both agreed the seven points he wanted them to remember were getting lost. Seven points, as we have already said, are way too many. But he and I thought they were all quite worthwhile and wanted to leave them in. He needed a good memory tool for them to use. Enter acronym stage left.

[2]*The World Book Encyclopedia*, 1964, Chicago.

He wrote out the word *"change"* and tried to make a point with each letter. I said, "Wait a minute, you already researched out the strategies that you feel they *must* remember if they are going to effectively cope with change. Why are you making up new ones? Were the old ones not right?" "No, they just don't fit the acronym I want to use." he replied.

Most speakers find themselves in this same trap. They get caught up in the process and forget the goal. I suggested, "Develop an acronym from the seven points you have already decided are imperative to your mission." First, we looked at each of his seven points and decided which key word represented the concept. Once we had those, we tried to find a word their initials spelled. By using synonyms for some of the words, we were able to come up with SMALLER. This nicely represented the mission of *reducing* the trauma of change, and it is easily remembered.

Another common mistake I see speakers make in using acronyms is to use the wrong word. Example, using the word "CHANGE," a speaker might try

C—Commitment to the project

H—Continuous hard work

A—A constant use of good listening skills

N—Negate negativity in your attitude

G—Generosity to your fellow workers

E—Enthusiasm for each day

Most of the above are fine. However, *A* will not help listeners remember the key point in this concept, which is "listening." The speaker needs to rethink the speech and decide on a new acronym or a new subpoint.

> We have four main principles we use at Stew Leonard's. One is "Satisfy the Customer," that is the focus of our whole company, making sure the customer is happy, that one is an "S." The second is "Team Work" which is a "T." That gets into how to motivate people and how to develop people. The third is "Excellence" which is creating an attitude where you want to do better, improve, get ideas. The fourth is a "WOW," which is make it fun. Create some fun or excitement in your office or business. That spells STEW. That is pretty much the talk I give professionally. But I'm constantly changing the content under each one of those four things. I bring in new stories and illustrations.
> —STEW LEONARD, JR.

Illustrations

It is easy to forget an idea, but stories, especially if they make your audiences laugh or cry, are very difficult to forget. Stories make the audience feel that these points and concepts you are teaching are universal because they are true experiences. The listeners feel, "Well, if 'it' happened to 'them' and 'they' are not only OK but doing very well, I guess I can cope too." An illustration is easy for the audience to follow and can fit into various time limits.

> *Stay with one subject and illustrate—illustrate—illustrate.*
> —GERALD C. MEYERS

> *Never underestimate the value of stories and humor in delivering and organizing your speech. People forget facts and graphs; they remember and retell memorable stories and anecdotes that can often illustrate the points and themes you want to advance. If stories were good enough for Jesus and Lincoln, they may be good enough for you.*
> —TERRY L. PAULSON, PH.D.

> *I like to use fairy tales with enduring values, like the "Secret Garden."*
> —WESS ROBERTS, PH.D.

Extended Comparison (Analogy)

Here we take the unfamiliar and hang it on the familiar—as I'm doing with this tree. When you use an illustration, make it one that is easily remembered. In helping to rewrite a speech on quality, I discovered many of the concepts the speaker was trying to make were C words— communication, commitment, clarity, etc. By using synonyms, I was able to make all six points into C words. I had him make one extra point that was also a C word. Then we made up slides with a map of the world and we had "The Seven Cs of Quality!" Great stuff, I was so proud of myself and my creativity. One problem, the Seven Cs don't hang nicely on the concept of the Seven Seas. I mean, what does *communication* have to do with the Pacific? Or *commitment* with the Indian Ocean?

For that matter, what are the *Seven Seas?* I remember the Pacific, Atlantic, Indian....But then I start to stumble—the Red Sea, the Mediterranean Sea? No, they're not part of the big seven. The Arctic Ocean? But that's an ocean not a sea. Does it still count as a sea? Oh dear.

Although I book this speaker often, and everyone loves what he has to say, they certainly don't remember it for very long. *I wrote it and I can't even remember it!* He does have a very high rehire rate with his past clients. (Maybe that's why they rehire him, they can't remember all seven points so they want him back to help them figure it out!) When you use an illustration, make sure it is easily remembered.

Problem-Cause-Solution

Here is an entire outline. Plug your information in and see if this structure works for you.

I. The problem is...
   A. It is important to you because...
   B. These people _____ (fill in the blank with right group) will get hurt by this problem.
II. The cause of the problem is...
   A. The main cause is...
   B. Another, lesser cause is...
   C. Another contributing cause is...
III. Some solutions to the problem are...
   A. Three possible solutions
     1. My first suggestion for a solution is...
     2. Second, we could try...
     3. Third we could do...(this is the one you really want them to do)
   B. My reasons for that solution are...
     1. It is better than the first solution I suggested because...
     2. It is better than the second alternative because...

What? So what? Now what?
      —Dr. Layne Longfellow

Here was the problem...
Here's how others helped us solve it...
We did it! It's GREAT to accomplish good goals.
      —Ira Hayes

Logic

To justify or support your position, try these four methods:

1. **Analogy.** Compare one idea or object with another. An analogy assumes that if things are the same in some respects, they are the same in others, and similar causes produce similar effects. For example, if a tree grows well by these principles, you should be able to use them to grow a great speech.

2. **Dilemma.** Provide logical proof that the other's opinion is incorrect. For example, to prove the world round—as the boats disappear over the horizon, they obviously are going over a rounded surface.

3. **Deductive logic.** The core of western thought is the syllogism by Aristotle. A *syllogism* is a form of argument or reasoning expressed

or claimed to be expressible in the form of two propositions—the major premise and the minor premise—containing a common term, and a third proposition—the conclusion—following necessarily from them. An example is: All trees have roots; an oak is a tree; therefore, an oak has roots.[3]

4. **Inductive logic.** Go from the specific to the general; An example is: Blue birds have wings, robins have wings, wrens have wings; therefore, all birds have wings.

Logical Reasoning
by Jeanine Walters Miranda*

Reasoning, or logic, is the way arguments and evidence are organized. The structure not only makes it easier for the audience to understand your point of view, it also makes the material believable. There are two kinds of structure found in reason: induction and deduction.

INDUCTION
An inductive argument is one whose conclusion is claimed to be probable but not certain. This kind of structure is most like reason by example.

Induction is what a detective uses to draw a conclusion about a suspect. We draw from evidence or experiences to come to a conclusion. As in what you use when you draw a simple conclusion such as, "I don't like spinach."

Inductive Process
If we are to draw our conclusion about spinach, the evidence might be...

When I was five, I ate spinach and became sick.

When I was seven, I was forced to eat spinach and became ill.

When I was nine, creamed spinach made me ill.

When I was thirteen spinach salad also made me ill.

At twenty I tried spinach again and became ill.

Conclusion by inductive process: spinach makes me ill.

---

[3]*The World Book Encyclopedia Dictionary*, 1964, Chicago.

The previous example is inductive thinking. It takes many instances and adds them up to a general conclusion. This procedure is the basis for our thinking and decision making. It allows us to make use of observation and reports. Our memories store away information and allow us to organize inductively.

Even though induction is basic to our thinking, there are limitations to using it. You must not assume that *your* inductive generalizations will match those of other people who have similar experiences. After all, just because you became ill when you ate spinach does not mean everyone else does. Individual definitions of *best* and *worst,* or experiences each person has had change conclusions.

Induction should be based on more than one example to best sway your audience. Actually, the more instances you supply, the more reliable your conclusion will be. The detective with only one piece of evidence, let's say motive, could not arrest a suspect and have it stick. He would also need opportunity, perhaps a body, and hopefully a smoking gun.

If I were speaking on communicating with troubled teens, an inductive argument I might use would be:

Johnny was truant from school 20 days.

His grades have gone from A's to F's.

He was suspended for drug paraphernalia.

Conclusion: Johnny is in trouble at school.

Writers and speakers make use of induction by presenting several instances and a particular subject, then invite their audience to share in drawing the conclusion.

DEDUCTION
The other major thinking structure is deduction. We use this method of thinking more in our daily lives than we do induction.

In the inductive process we make generalizations from separate but similar experiences. We are able to say spinach makes us ill because our experiences lead us to that generalization. When we need to make a decision about taking a chance in the present, we need to use deduction. It allows us to take our inductive generalization and apply it to a particular case in order to find an answer or conclusion. For example, we could take our inductive generalization that spinach makes me ill and apply it to the new solution.

(*Continued*)

Deductive Process

Spinach makes me sick.

Spinach souffle is tonight's main dish.

Conclusion: by deductive process I will get sick if I eat tonight's main dish.

The first statement is the result of our past experience, the inductive conclusion. The second statement is new, a specific case. The final statement is the conclusion of this reasoning process.

Deduction is the process of applying a generalization to a specific case and reaching a conclusion about that specific case. Almost every time we make a decision, we use deduction. It is also natural that our minds do it so quickly and automatically we use it without awareness.

A deductive argument for the talk on troubled teens would be:

Troubled teens get in trouble at school.

Johnny is in trouble at school.

Conclusion: Johnny is a troubled teen.

Using reasoning in your speaking helps the audience believe your conclusion because of the structure. When you give your audience only the conclusion of a reasoning process, you give them no way of understanding the bases for the final statement. If you ask your audience to agree with generalizations without a scrap of evidence, you are asking them to assume a responsibility that is not theirs. If you want your audience to believe what you say and understand your point of view, the structure of inductive and deductive reasoning helps you do this.

*This material was prepared specifically for this book and is reprinted with permission. The author is my sister, Jeanine, who teaches speech at the local college and high school.

Other Patterns to Structure Your Speech

Time: Evolve your topic from the beginning of the facts, through the present to the future speculation. We began here; we are now here; we are going here.

Geographic: North, south, east, west; left to right.

Change dry material by creating a "frame" of reference, i.e., "More change took place on earth during the 313 days the cosmonauts were circling the earth than during some entire centuries."
                                                —CHRISTOPHER HEGARTY

Now You Are Ready to Start Writing This Speech

Rudyard Kipling's Secret of Speech Writing

Sometimes, you stare at that blank piece of paper. You know where you want to go, but nothing comes out of your brain and onto the paper. Try Kipling's method, he had six "serving men" that helped him write:

> I had six honest serving men,
> they taught me all I knew.
> Their names were what and where and when,
> how and why and who.

Answer those six questions, what, where, when, how, why, and who, and you will find the information flowing.

> *You usually don't just sit down and write a speech. Gather ideas and thoughts and put in a file, then when you sit down to write the speech it comes together easier.*
> —PATRICIA FRIPP, AUTHOR AND SPEAKER

> *Once you have your objectives established, collect facts, research, quotes, theories, actual examples, humor, and memorable stories that will deliver your message. Mix them together to pace a presentation and organize your delivery. Memorize the progression of stories, then pair relevant content, quotes, and facts to each one. One story will lead to another sandwiched by the content you have prepared to add. They will not only love your style and message; they will remember and share it. You can forget your progression of facts, but you seldom will forget your progression of stories you love to tell.*
> —TERRY L. PAULSON, PH.D.

> *I never write out a presentation; I think it out. Then I make an outline, notes with real-life incidents to back-up the key points I'll present. Then I practice it, one on one, in daily situations until I'm comfortable with it.*
> —ED FOREMAN

> *Material written to be heard is different from material to be read. I never write a complete speech. I write short, well-prepared vignettes. Each of these "bite sized moments" has a life of its own. So when I get an assignment, I string together what I consider to be the appropriate vignettes to create a unique new life form.*
> —BILL GOVE

You have the three or four points you plan to make. You have firmly tested them. Now, you can organize the material. First you "tell 'em what you're gonna' tell 'em. Then tell 'em. Then tell 'em what you told 'em!" This is an old sales adage. It means start with the introduction—

"tell 'em what you're gonna' tell 'em"—go to the body—"tell 'em"—
and then present the conclusion—..."tell 'em what you told 'em!"
   Write the body first. Give all the points (the branches) you want and
the theme. The second thing to write is the conclusion. Restate your mission and the main points. Then call them to pick the fruit! (See Step 9,
"Motivating an Audience to Change Their Actions and Attitudes."
Lastly, write the introduction. Gain their attention and introduce the
subject. (Questions, stories, statistics, notable quotes, and illustrations
are all great grabbers in an introduction.)
   Studies indicate that the audience retains the majority of information
from the presentation in the first and the last 15 minutes. Certainly a big
chunk of the 10 percent they'll remember is in your introduction and
your conclusion. Make sure your mission and those three to four sub-
stantiating points are part of both of these.

This seems a bit much to keep straight.

It helps to have a worksheet to think it all through. At the end of the
book are two worksheets to help you organize your thoughts and get
started. However, you may prefer the mind map method, which we'll
discuss next.

*I organize a speech like a story. I open with something stimulating, then
give the background, then more stimulation, then more background, etc.*
   I use unfamiliar material first.
   *I have some of my standard exciting material that I know will work at the
end.*
                                                              —JACK ANDERSON

The most important part of a presentation:
   *Come out punching. Psychologists have proven that the first thirty sec-
onds and the last thirty seconds have the most impact. Do not start by
thanking the audience.*
                                                              —PATRICIA FRIPP

*Keep in mind the show-business adage on the advisability of getting off "too
soon," or always leaving them wanting more.*
                                                     —STEVE ALLEN, © 1986

Mind Maps

*If I'm concerned about having too much to say or what to cover in a speech,
I organize it by mind mapping the material. I put the topic or theme in the
middle of the page. Then brainstorm everything I can think of about that
topic. I write just a word or so that represents each of those thoughts. I put
little squiggles around each word, just for fun. I then look at the thoughts*

and number each one in the way I might use them. I don't draw pictures or get elaborate in terms of colors—my wife Marge does like to organize her talk that way.
                                                                    —Dr. Ken Blanchard

Yellow elephant.

As you read that phrase, did you think of letters Y-e-l-l-o-w-e-l-e-p-h-a-n-t. Or did you see an image? Of course, you saw the image. The mind thinks in images and pictures. Mind mapping was developed by Tony Buzan, author and brain researcher, as an alternative to outlining. He suggests you organize your material by drawing pictures. For example, you might draw a simple picture of a yellow elephant (assuming you were doing a talk that involved a yellow elephant), then a line with an arrow to the next thought you want to talk about.

When you try to force your mind to think in a traditional outline form—with words and sentences—you may wait around forever, staring at a blank paper, waiting for Roman numeral *I* to bounce into your head. But in mind mapping you draw each idea as it pops up, then connect the pictures later into a speech.

To explain mind mapping, I have started a small mind map of the thoughts I was just giving you (see Figure 6-1). First, I drew a brain. (When you draw a mind map, the picture must remind you of the material you want to talk about.) Then I drew lines out that represented the main points I wanted to cover.

As you draw your mind map, you can more easily see when you've got too much stuff in one place and not enough in another. If you can't easily connect one line to another, then you can see it may not belong in the presentation at all.

True mind map experts, which I am not, will tell you to use only one word per line along with the pictures.

Try using the mind map in Figure 6-2 to organize your speech. Draw simple pictures that represent what you want to say in the appropriate spots. Then start over with a blank sheet of paper.

Tips for Keeping Organized

Seems I have an awful lot of material to keep organized.

Here are some tips to help you keep it all straight:

- **3-×-5 cards.** My mother has used these for years. She kept them by categories: sales, customer service, etc. Before she prepared a speech she would pull out only the cards that applied to the speech she was devel-

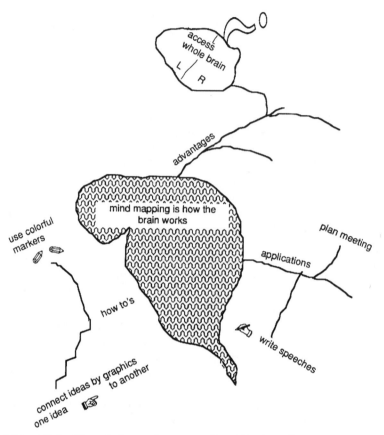

Figure 6-1. Use mind mapping as an alternative to outlining.

oping. She liked to put a simple picture on the card that reminded her of the story she would tell. Kind of an early version of mind mapping.

The good news about 3-×-5 cards is that they are easy to organize. The bad news is they are much too easy to drop when you're in the middle of your speech!

Cards have the advantage that their order can be changed as often as suits your purpose.

—STEVE ALLEN, © 1986

I have about 200 segments of talks put onto 5 × 7 cards. As I prepare a program, I think of the group, the theme, the intent, and pull out the number of cards that will fit the time allowed. Usually 12 per hour; however, I also use the same dramatic close.

—ROSITA PEREZ, PRESIDENT, CREATIVE LIVING
PROGRAMS, INC., MOTIVATIONAL SPEAKER

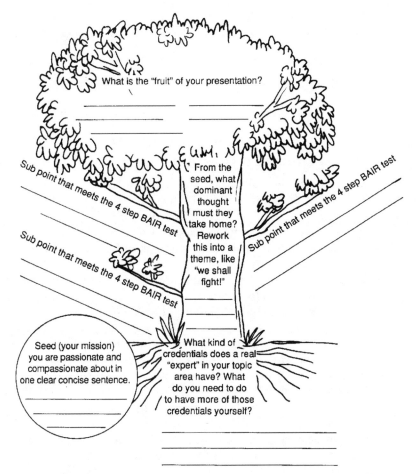

Figure 6-2. This basic mind map can be used to organize your speech.

- **Slides, workbooks, and overheads.** Once you have these organized, it's difficult to lose your place.

- **Outlines.** Most speakers find that a simple outline, one or two sheets, is the easiest. Perfect for the classic extemporaneous speech.

  Some speakers use color coding. The main "boughs" are one color - these are the points the presenter absolutely can't pass by. The next color would represent the humor story that helps to substantiate that main point. Another color is for the audience participation exercise. If you find yourself running out of time, you simply skip the colors you don't need.

- **Acronyms and acrostics.** By developing a simple memory tool for your audience, you will find yourself unable to forget it either!

- **Mind mapping.** Mental images used in mind mapping help you sort your material and identify easily remembered connections.
- **Props.**

   I use many props. The props act as cue cards reminding me of what to say next.
   —TOM OGDEN

Disaster Insurance—Be Flexible

Build the frames, but be flexible. Make the material so much a part of your life and thinking that you can adapt yourself to any circumstance. If Martians suddenly invade Washington, D.C., you are going to need to work it into your presentation. Some speakers are so entrenched in the exact words of their speech, they couldn't tell their audience to leave the room if the building caught fire.

Colonel Chuck Scott, one of the hostages in the Iran Embassy takeover in 1979–1981, tells a funny story about the week following his release from captivity. Before he and the rest of the hostages could be let out into public, they had to be certified as legally "sane" by no less an authority than the U.S. Army. Once, when he was telling this story to an audience, the lights all started to flash and the fire alarms went off. Without missing a beat, before the audience could panic, he calmly said, "…and unless you guys are all seeing flashing lights and hearing bells, they issued the wrong certificate." The audience members all started to giggle instead of panicking. Suddenly a panic-stricken voice came on the intercom, "Ladies and gentlemen, *don't panic!* There is a fire emergency on the the twenty-fifth floor. You will receive instructions if we need to evacuate!"

Speaking into the now dark room, Chuck said, "25th floor? No problem, fire burns up, we're 22 stories down from that. For a minute, I thought we were going to have a terrible catastrophe…I might have had to cut my speech short!" They all laughed at the silliness in his tone of voice. He did go on, in between the sirens and announcements. Finally the lights came back on and an announcement that stated the fire was— fortunately—a minor incident and now under control. But audiences have been known to panic and run for the door; deaths occur from people jamming into each other in a panic to get out of a crowded room. Chuck's flexibility saved the day—and his speech! In some cases, it might save a few lives.

MORE SECRETS ABOUT STEP 6: ORGANIZING THE MATERIAL IN A MEMORABLE MANNER (STRONG, STURDY BOUGHS)

Develop a theme that supports your mission. Then develop three or four points that are those "must-remember strategies" the listeners need to accomplish the mission. *You do not need to decide on the best way to deliver the information when you are unsure what the information will be.* Once you know your information, find a nice structure to hang it all on so it is even more easily remembered. Finally be flexible, in case the building is burning down; work something in to keep the situation well in hand!

Use a rifle, not a shotgun—target a few key points and hit them dead center.
—RALPH ARCHBOLD

Step 7

Editing the Material for Its Best Effect

——————*Prune the Deadwood*

You have developed a mission. You finally get stage fright under control. You slowly grow beautiful boughs that are very time- and energy-consuming to produce. You begin to feel like you're finally able to persuade and motivate an audience, lift your listeners out of their seats, and what do you do? You say this is it, I've made it, I'm not changing anything else for anybody!

But, your *continued* success as a presenter requires that you constantly look at your presentations and *cut away* what is weakest. Now you become a wordsmith.

> *The masterless man, afflicted with the magic of the necessary words, words that may become alive and walk up and down in the hearts of the hearers.*
> —RUDYARD KIPLING, SPEECH, ROYAL ACADEMY BANQUET, LONDON, 1906

> *As a smart person once said, "Good words are worth a thousand pictures."*
> —GERALD C. MEYERS

The question is," said Alice,
"whether you can make words mean so many different things."
"The question is," said Humpty Dumpty,
"which is to be master—that's all."
— LEWIS CARROLL, *THROUGH THE LOOKING-GLASS*,
CHAPTER 6

Why You Need to "Prune"

My rating sheets say I'm really pretty good right now! Why change?

You must change to grow. You're assuming when you did it last, it was perfect. That just can't be. "You are either green and growing, or ripe and rotten."

Besides, audiences change. Attitudes change. Last year it was apropos to use the "communist threat" as a drama getter; this year the Russians are good guys. You need to work into your speech what is current in the minds of your listeners.

Jeff Dewar, used to tell a story about one of Jeff's customers who was nervous about making a presentation. The man walks into the presentation room, he's terrified. Sweat drips from his nose, drip, drip, drip. Wonderfully dramatic! Someone had told him, "add some drama in there." So he did. When Jeff was a beginning presenter, it was a great story, for his ability at the time. Unfortunately, the story had very little to do with the mission of his presentation. As he grew into one of the leading experts on quality and related topics, this story became less relevant. But he had spent so much time developing the drama of the story, he found it incredibly painful to "prune it." However, once he did, he had room for new material. Now Jeff has international acclaim as a presenter.

You are either green and growing, or ripe and rotten!
— DANIELLE KENNEDY, M.A.

How Much to Change

Change about 5 percent each time you perform the same speech. This is a magic number for the speakers and presenters I've worked with. (Totally unscientific, it just feels right to me.)

Changes of a presentation are not limited to the material. One time you may work on lowering your voice. Would that mean a 5 percent change, in your mind? Maybe the way you stand, a new style of clothing, or hairstyle. Perhaps instead of overheads you try slides, or instead of slides you decide to try video.

I think change of more than 5 percent adds unfairly to your stress level and makes it too hard for you to concentrate on touching the audience. If you add too much, you're in effect starting over from scratch. If you don't add enough new things, the presentation becomes stale and you won't grow.

Deciding What to Cut

Tony Buzan, famous for his work on adult learning, brain research, and mind mapping, in one of his famous studies found that people will listen to you for 90 minutes, but they will only listen with retention for 20 minutes.

If a point takes more than 20 minutes to make in straight lecture, prune it. By that time you should have been able to state your mission and all three subpoints at least once. If you can't, reread this book. (Seriously, if you find you can't condense your talk that way, call in a coach to help you design the presentation.)

Over-prepare, under-deliver, stop speaking before they stop listening.
—Doug Malouf

When in doubt, cut. Add only to support or clarify a specific point.
—Col. Gene Harrison, Ret.

If you can't say it within 15 words, flush it.
—Doug Malouf

For psychological reasons it's not necessary to delve into here, it is notoriously difficult to edit your own material shortly after you've written it. Certainly you can start the process then, but the ego is generally plugged into the creation so firmly at that point that you'll find it painful to make deletions or other improvements. Set the material aside for a few days, therefore, so that you can consciously forget it. You'll be surprised by how many errors, typographical and otherwise, you can find when you look at it again.
—Steve Allen, © 1986

Audiences edit. That's why talks always get better. That's also why practicing a new talk with friends and colleagues before its premiere is essential.
—Dr. Layne Longfellow

Each story and some of the related content can be delivered to unexpected audiences. One comedian confided that he told every story he used seventy times before he ever used it in an act. Now, don't try it on the same person or you might be shot!

Try telling stories you want to use to every person you meet, saying, "I've got to tell you about...." Watch their eyes to look for premature glazing of the eyeballs.

Work and rework your story until you can say it quickly with the desired energetic effect you want. If it worked, they will want to know more about what you are saying and you can practice communicating some of your related facts and action statements. Try the three P's of speaking: practice, practice, practice.

—TERRY L. PAULSON, PH.D.

"I Can't Use That Material Again, It Bombed Once!"

Although speakers have reputations of having the biggest egos in the world, which is *mostly* true, we also have the most *fragile egos,* which is very true. As an industry, we are rather top-heavy when it comes to insecurity. As a result, when a new piece of material has less than spectacular results in a talk, we rip it out, crush it, and trash it. That is not one of the good "secrets" of the master speakers I hope you will take on for yourself. Instead, learn the techniques to overcome the failings of our fragile egos that seem inherent in our breed.

Before you decide to trash a bit of material, ask yourself, "did I give it enough time?" We get so panicky when a speech doesn't go well. We don't allow enough time for new material to grow into something usable. It may be that it just needed a little more practice.

A great presenter can carry an audience, even with bad material. Before you cut on those grounds, practice the material repeatedly with friends, family, and to yourself on tape.

*There are always **three** speeches, for every **one** you actually gave: The one you **practiced**...the one you **gave**...the one you **wish you gave!**"*

—DALE CARNEGIE, AMERICAN AUTHOR OF *HOW TO WIN FRIENDS AND INFLUENCE PEOPLE*

"I Don't Need to Edit; It Worked OK Last Time"

If you are going to edit your presentation, you need to *change* your presentation. Yes, the big 'C' word that immediately makes my palms start to sweat. Most presenters (myself at the top of the list) rationalize against making any change and just give into their fear of change with one of two thoughts, "I can't use that material again, it bombed once!" which we just dealt with, or "Why edit, it worked OK last time, I'm still alive." Both are just rationales we use to avoid change.

It's easy to be consumed by fear every time you make even a minor change in your presentations. But, as the old proverbs say, "if you always do…what you've always done, you'll always get, what you've always got" and "Every change is not an improvement, but every improvement is by change."

Remember "Fear is false evidence appearing real" (Zig Ziglar). Take a good look at your fear to change your presentation and style. Is the evidence supporting your fear "real"?

Jim Newman, speaker, president of the PACE organization, and author of *Release Your Brakes,* says, "Anything worth doing is worth doing badly."

What? Don't you mean…?

No, I don't. You have to do it wrong before you can do it right. If you make a mistake along the way, it's just one more step in the process of doing it right the next time.

To edit, you must change. Embrace the fear of change, fear is no bad thing for presenter. Fear is a power within yourself. Use the fear to lift your audience.

> *Far better it is to dare mighty things, to win glorious triumphs, even though checkered by failure, than to take rank with those poor spirits who neither enjoy much nor suffer much. Because they live in the gray twilight that knows not victory nor defeat.*
> —TEDDY ROOSEVELT, SPEECH BEFORE THE
> HAMILTON CLUB, CHICAGO, APRIL 10, 1899

Should You Edit Because You Are Bored?

Add for interest, comprehension and humor. Edit for boredom.
—HERMINE HILTON

When you have a piece of material or story that works well, do not add to it or edit it. Presenters who use the same material over and over normally start to edit because they're bored with hearing the same story over and over.
—ALLAN PEASE

I disagree with Allan. I think, when you get bored to death with a piece of material, it's time to retire it. If you're not excited about it, you will have a tough time getting your audiences excited.

The Most Eloquent Sound in the World

...silence! The less you say the better. Direct their minds in the right direction, then sit back and have a cup of coffee.

Once in awhile, when I'm delivering my humdinger, more wonderful than wonderful (according to my mother) keynote, my mind suddenly turns off and my voice goes into autopilot. As the panic starts to overtake my brain, "filler" words start to flow out. Afterwards I mumble something to my hosts about PMS, indigestion, or any other excuse I can think of why I had this frantic, searching, panicked look in the middle of the talk.

When this happens to me, I too often forget my own advice to other speakers: Use one of the best and most eloquent teaching techniques—silence—while you get your thoughts together.

When you feel yourself getting off track, don't fill up the void with words; pause. Give the listeners time to evaluate your prior words. It's one of the most eloquent things you can do.

It's not so much knowing when to speak, as when to pause.
—JACK BENNY

Pause. You are having a dialogue with the audience when you say something profound or ask them a question. Give them time to think before you continue.
—PATRICIA FRIPP

Persuasive speech, and more persuasive sighs, Silence that spoke and eloquence of eyes.
—HOMER, *ILIAD*

The notes I handle no better than many pianists.
*But the **pauses** between the notes—ah, that is where the art resides!*
—ARTHUR SCHNABLE

Cut Out the Unnecessary Words

Keep cutting out unimportant words or thoughts. What would you keep in the speech if you had to reduce it to two or three minutes? NO ONE EVER COMPLAINS ABOUT A SPEECH BEING TOO SHORT!
—IRA HAYES

Weasel words are words that suck all the life out of the words next to them, just as a weasel sucks an egg and leaves the shell.
—STEWART CHAPLAIN, THE STAINED-GLASS
POLITICAL PLATFORM, 1900

The most powerful presentations are short and simple. Winston Churchill's entire famous speech to Harrow School was

> *Never give in.*
> *Never give in.*
> *Never, never, never, never—*
> *in nothing great or small, large or petty,*
> *Never give in except to convictions of honor and good sense.*

and he left the podium! Churchill just cut out all the unnecessary words and wrote a speech that we still quote decades later.

> *Do not belabor any point by staying with it too long.*
> *Effectively present a point in a minimum amount of time.*
> —COACH JOHN WOODEN

> *Never use a long word, sentence, or story when a short one will do.*
> —JUDI MOREO

> *After I write a speech I do what my wife tells me to do every night; I take out the garbage.*
> —AL LAMPKIN

So, how do you cut all the wrong words out?

Tape yourself actually giving a speech, then make a transcript of the speech from the tape. Now go over it with a pen and scratch out all the words you *could* have left out! Now read it as it should have been said and tape it this way. When you get to those sections that you have cut out, leave in a pregnant pause.

Listen to this tape over and over. It's a method of learning what words to leave out. It will help you think in concise terms and help you memorize your speech.

One of the most humbling experiences I ever had was transcribing one of my two-day seminars onto paper. On paper English looked like my fourth language! I had no idea I was that verbose. As painful as it was for me, I strongly suggest this technique as a way for you to get rid of "weasel words" in your talk. Besides, I would love for others to share this fun (OK, miserably humbling) experience with me.

> *Tape record your talks, transcribe them, find the bad grammar, find the punch words even in regular speaking and edit out redundancy and practice it that way. I used to say "I set a new goal that day," then I realized the punchword, the point that needs to be remembered, is GOAL. I rephrase it, "That day I set a new GOAL."*
> —PATRICIA FRIPP

Each Speech Is a Workshop
for Your Next Speech

I find the best editing is done after the 1st and 2nd time I present the same material.
—ROGER BURGRAFF, PH.D., PROFESSIONAL
SPEAKER AND SEMINAR LEADER

I am still editing my oldest, best stories. A look, a gesture, a word is emphasized differently. It is a process that is honed by presenting and getting feedback and then re-working. Enhancing the presentation by editing cannot be done in a vacuum intellectually.
—ROSITA PEREZ

Audience interest, questions, and comments are my best editors.
—ARDEN BERCOVITZ, PH.D.

No humorist has ever had to hand out evaluation forms. You know when you do well and when you don't. I edit my material based on that audience's response. If pieces don't get the response I expect, I drop them or replace them. With honest self-evaluation and cold-blooded editing, the material becomes pretty powerful.
—GENE PERRET

MORE SECRETS ABOUT STEP 7:
EDITING THE MATERIAL
FOR ITS BEST EFFECT
(PRUNE DEAD WOOD)

Again, "you are either green and growing, or ripe and rotten." Change at least 5 percent each presentation. Keep moving toward "less is better." The most eloquent sound in the world? Silence.

Follow the advice of Ben Franklin. Ask yourself—Is it clear? Is it concise? Don't overload the audience—save something for the return engagement.
—RALPH ARCHBOLD

Editing goes hand-in-hand with organization. The IDEAL presentation will consist of only those things that make your audience think, cry, laugh and/or nod in agreement.
—HARVEY DIAMOND

Conversation and presentation are different. Presentation is carefully selected and edited.
—PATRICIA FRIPP

When in doubt, delete it.
—PHILIP CROSBY

Edit right up to the platform point—inspiration often strikes late.
—GERALD C. MEYERS

Step 8
Your Image from the Platform
_____ *Leaves of* *Brilliant Color*

In this Step we will work on the all good stuff that makes you attractive on the platform: your voice, clothes, mannerisms, and your image from the inside out.

*There is **no less** eloquence in the tone of the voice,*
in the eyes and in the air of the speaker,
than in his choice of words.
　　　　　　　　　　—FRANÇOIS LA ROCHEFOUCAULD, *MAXIMES*

You are your message.
　　　　　　　　　—COL. GENE HARRISON, RET.

Producing a Lovely Voice—Out of Your Throat

His words were simple words enough,
And yet he used them so,
That what in other mouths was rough
In his seemed musical and low."
　　　　　　　　—J. R. LOWELL, *THE SHEPHERD OF KING ADMETUS*

It's not so much what you say, it's how you say it.
                    —UNKNOWN

I studied voice and singing for 10 years.[1] My voice teacher in college would tell us that our vocal chords are tiny light tissues, lighter than butterfly wings. If you abuse them too often, you can develop real tissue damage such as vocal nodules, ulcerations, edema, etc., which can become serious medical problems. You know how people sound who have smoked all their lives or a football coach who has screamed for years on end. These people have abused those delicate tissues. They may never get their normal voices back again.

Rest your voice! Speakers who use the tool of golden silence often in their talks not only are more poignant, but they save wear and tear on their vocal cords.

You get the best vocal production when you stand up tall. This places your vocal chords, lungs, and diaphragm in a position that can send your voice more easily across the room. Practice with a tape recorder to hear how your voice sounds to others and which voice you like best.

Developing and maintaining good, strong vocal production is like developing and maintaining a good strong heart; it takes exercise. The following section discusses vocal exercises useful for improving your voice.

Voice Exercises

For a Lower, More Mellifluous Voice

When you think voice, think variation in pacing, volume, tone, and emotional feel. Variation provides interest and keeps attention as you orchestrate your message to the heart, to the head, and to the funnybone.
                    —TERRY L. PAULSON, PH.D.

1. Stand up tall but relaxed. Take your hands out of your pockets, let your arms hang normally at your sides.

2. Place your hands on your diaphragm. It is the muscle that is located where the rib cage divides above your waist. The diaphragm supports your tone as you talk.

3. Take a deep breath through your nose. Feel your diaphragm expand each time you take a breath. Then let the air out through your mouth. Sound is produced when the air goes over the vocal chords. So, breathe. Bring the breath in deep, then slowly let it out. Feel the muscle expand and retract.

[1]Dr. Roger Burgraff, a speech pathologist, edited the following section on voice production.

4. Now, let's do it again, and this time I would like you to have some sound come out. Try the alphabet—A, B, C, D. As that's coming out, have one hand on your diaphragm and one hand on your neck. Close your eyes and visualize your throat and vocal cords. Imagine everything inside there in *totally* relaxed, no strain, no forcing of sound. Feel totally relaxed, as if nothing is really moving, as if there's no strain anywhere.

For a Lower, More Authoritative Voice

5. Now say, "How low can I go?" as you allow your voice to go down the musical scale. Bring the note down lower each time. By bringing air in through the nose, the diaphragm will expand.

Totally relax your throat, and breathe in; then, as you let the breath out, say, "How low can I go?" and allow your voice to go down the musical scale.

Now you should be producing a new sound that is much deeper and lower. We don't recommend that you deliver your speech down there, this is just a vocal exercise. The best "low voice" placement is about one-quarter of the way up from the lowest pitch of your total vocal range.

6. Try it all again. This time, continue with the alphabet after the words, "How low can I go?" in that lovely lower level. Try allowing the voice to move up and down in pitch until you find that one-quarter of the way back up the scale spot.

Don't allow any strain or tightening to occur in your throat at any time. If it feels uncomfortable, see a voice coach. People with lower voices have more authority. Practice speaking in a low voice until it's comfortable for you. Kathleen Turner, of *Romancing the Stone* fame, says her normal voice is much higher than that lovely low voice she uses on the screen. She simply practiced until in time it became natural.

For More Resonance

7. Resonance is a sound quality, enriched by overtones, a quality that distinguishes Richard Burton's and Dame Judith Anderson's voices from untrained voices. It is that added sound which is made when the energy of the voice sets off vibration of air cavities and anatomical features, such as small bones and soft tissue. They vibrate in tune with the voice frequencies so you have oral and nasal resonance.

Hum. Put your hands on either side of your mouth and/or your nose to feel how it vibrates your teeth and bones in your face. If you don't feel it there, move your hands over your face until you feel where it makes your bones tingle. That is resonance.

Breathe in and hum. Feel it as it makes the back of your teeth tingle. Try to take that same tingle and make your forehead vibrate and hum.

After you've got the hum and the tickle making your frontal mask vibrate, open your mouth and say the vowels, with an *M* in the front of each one. Try it with hard vowels, then soft.

MMMMMayee

MMMMMeee

MMMMMiiiii

MMMMMooo

MMMMMuuuu

A hum is the essence of an *M* sound anyway, so these come out quite naturally.

8. Pick up a book or newspaper. Take a deep breath. Support the tone with your diaphragm. Think "how low can I go." Think about vibrating the frontal mask. Now start to read and play with variations in vocal variety, pitch, volume, and resonance.

> *Use a personally modified microphone that flatters your voice, if necessary. Breath deeply and speak from the belly, not the throat.*
> —CHRISTOPHER HEGARTY

Practice for 10 minutes a day. Tape yourself and listen to what voice sounds the best in your ears. Don't use a voice that causes any discomfort or strain! If it hurts, you are doing the exercise wrong and could do serious and permanent damage to your voice.

PROTECTION OF THE VOICE
by Dr. Roger Burgraff

The voice does carry meaning on its own apart from the words. You don't have to have a great voice to be a great presenter, but it helps. You do have to have a clear, durable, healthy voice to carry your message. There is no "right voice." There is a best voice for you.

Some are truly blessed with "great pipes." If you're not—don't worry—you can develop "good pipes." Here are some more tips and thoughts:

- Three Ms—more mouth movement—helps articulation and tends to promote "best voice."

- Prior to speaking: reduce or eliminate the use of coffee and tea, stay away from smokers, avoid dairy products.

- Pitch too high and pitch too low are both abusive to the voice and the listener's ear. Find the medium range that is comfortable for you.

- Slowing the pace helps your voice relax and lowers the pitch slightly.

- If speaking at an all-day seminar, try not to speak at lunch break. Instead, give your voice a break.

- When necessary, clear your throat gently. Begin clearing with a hum.

- Develop a sense of "openness" of voice to help relax it.

- For sore throat: Try salt water gargle. Lozenges are all right, but they may make you override the pain and fool you into overusing the voice when it requires rest.

- If your voice is raspy for 10 days or more and you don't have a cold or flu, see an ENT (ear, nose, throat) doctor. Ask for a direct laryngoscopy (a look at your vocal mechanism, with the use of a mirror).

- The voice likes wet and warm. I usually avoid heavily iced water and use instead cool to tepid water. Lemon water is all right if you enjoy it, but it's the water itself that is important.

- Best resource for working on pitch change: *Change Your Voice, Change Your Life* by Dr. Mort Cooper (Macmillan Publishing, New York, 1984).

- For help on voice evaluation, contact American Speech and Language Hearing Association, 10801 Rockville Pike, Rockville, MD, 20852; phone, 301-897-5700.

How to Decide on Your Personal Image

First, follow all the other strategies I discussed for growing your tree. Second, whenever you see pictures in magazines and newspapers, whose image makes you think, "I like that!" clip them out. I keep mine in a folder in my desk. Before I go out to buy an outfit, I review the pictures in my folder. Think about the mood you want to create with the presentation. Do you want this audience to feel interactive and warm? Do you have enough time to establish your expertise? Will your power image need to say it all? How much authority do you really want to exude? Look at the pictures you have collected and decide which images match the ambience you want to create.

What they don't teach you in image seminars is that everybody's idea of "power" is different. When I do my seminar, I show a series of slides, with two people in each slide. I use the slide to show what subtle differences in dressing and image do to the perspective of power.

The first time I used these slides in a seminar was a real *adventure*. I put the first slide up and asked the audience, who of the two people in this photograph has the greatest authority? To me, it was crystal clear. But my audience was split right in half! This was not the point I was trying to make at all. Luckily I had two more slides—I tried again. Same result. Half agreed with me, the other half thought the other person in the slide had more power. Same thing happened with the third slide! Every time I do the seminar I get the same result.

I have no doubts in *my* mind which of the people has a greater "power" image. It came as a shock to me that once you get past some rather basic rules of image—dark suit, solid colors, clean, ironed, etc.— the rest is up for grabs.

So what is a power image for speakers?

Your power image is whatever makes *you* feel like a presenter who can move and motivate an audience.

> *I want my appearance and demeanor on the platform to be first rate—whether it's something I buy or something I have to develop. It's not so important that the audience knows it; it's more important that I know and feel it."*
> —GENE PERRET

> *"I yam what I yam" (Popeye). I wear flowers in my hair and tell them why that's important to me. I like dramatic vibrant colors and sleeves that "move" to emphasize my gestures. I always consider my comfort up there as I use a guitar to make my points. I do what works for me!*
> —ROSITA PEREZ

> *The audience starts forming their opinions of you from the first moment they see you. If you make a mistake, make it on the conservative side.*
> —JUDI MOREO

Tips for Fabulous Fashion in the Footlights

> *I watched a famous woman golfer speak once. She carried a huge white handbag loaded with junk and plunked it on the lectern. We looked at it*

throughout her presentation. I don't remember a word she said, but I do re-
member the handbag.
                                        —JUDI MOREO

Fashion in the footlights is not governed by the same rules that tell us what is appropriate fashion when we are one on one. As a presenter, you need to dress for success—*from across the room.*

When you try on the clothes you are considering using on the platform, do you stand about 5 feet from your mirror as you review your image? I always did. Until it hit me one day. The audience will be 10 to several hundred feet away! Lines, colors, and images change drastically when seen from a distance—as your audience sees you.

Walk *way* across the room from your mirror. Walk as far as the majority of your listeners are from you on the platform, and then decide if you like what you see. Men, that patterned tie looks great up close. But it confuses your audience's eyes from a distance and distracts from your listeners' concentration on your topic.

How Much Authority Do You Want Your Image to Generate?

Before we go on with tips on how to create an authority or power image from the platform, ask yourself, "How much power and authority do I want my appearance to generate?" If you project too much authority, your listeners will never know how much you care because they'll assume you're not the caring type. Authoritative people seem to create that kind of environment. So, you may want to dress with less than the look of the Absolute Authority.

Still, you need to know what the rules are of creating an authority power image before you decide if you want to break them. If you're presenting for only an hour, you don't have as long to build credibility with people. You need to rely on your image more heavily to help you establish credibility. If you have several hours, it won't matter how good your image is. If you don't follow the other steps in growing this tree, your listeners will see right through the temporary effect you create with your image.

Tips on Image for Men

John T. Molloy, author of the world famous book, *Dress for Success,* said in a keynote I heard, "There are only three appropriate colors for men in a business setting—dull, dark and drab." I think a step or so beyond Mr. Molloy's "drab" category is acceptable. A good quality suit, perhaps just a shade or so lighter than the traditional dark grey, black, or dark blue, but still within that realm of "dull and dark" can be very nice and at the same time help the speaker stand out on the platform. If you have any doubts as to what the standard traditional "success" look is, see Molloy's *Dress for Success*.

Tips on Image for Women

Women have a tougher time than men figuring out what to wear in a business setting. Since the turn of the century, men have been wearing "dull, dark, drab" trousers, vest, and jacket. Sure, the lapels and tails changed slightly, but a man's suit has hardly changed at all compared with women's fashions.

At the turn of the century, women wore Victorian bustles, huge hats with feathers, ribbons, and stuffed birds draped in odd places—over their shoulders and on their heads. Not what you see walking into the board room today!

Although men have only worn "dull, dark, drab" this century, women have been appropriate in the entire color spectrum. So as we have entered the business world, deciding what is acceptable to wear can be hard. Here are a few quick guidelines:

- Subdued, solid colors will make you appear more authoritative.
- The higher the neckline, the less frivolous you appear.
- A tailored look gives you more power and authority. "Tailored" means form fitting, not baggy. If you want a more powerful look, and you're wearing something that's meant to button, button it. It's natural and stylish for women to have a blouse left unbuttoned at the top. Or a jacket that should button, worn open. It's a "pretty" look, but it immediately takes away from your authority.
- If you want more authority, put your hair up and pull it away from your face in a tighter, tailored look.
- A high heel gives you more sophistication.

Power Image Tips
for the First Impression

Image is based on people's first impression assumptions (which, by the way, are often wrong). Your performance on stage will change the audience's first impression of you anyway, but it won't hurt to try and create a good first impression that might help get your message home. Here are a few ideas on image assumptions you may not have thought of:

- For more authority, a dark suit rather than a sports jacket and slacks.

- Graying hair and wrinkles that put you into the 45-to-65 category have more authority than dark shiny hair and a youthful complexion.

- Someone with a sun-tanned look always seems *too* casual. People assume a serious professional would not have time to sit in the sun.

- Wearing glasses makes people think you read more, are more intelligent, and older, so therefore they *assume* you are more intelligent. (If you wear them on the platform, get the nonglare kind so people in the audiences are not looking at two little mirrors reflecting lights into their eyes.)

- "Taller" gives your appearance more authority. "Taller" has very little, if anything, to do with real authority and power. We are only talking about the first impressions. Someone who *stands* tall can give much the same power image effect.

Using Color to Enhance Your Image

A Munich Psychological Institute study showed that children improved their I.Q. scores if they were tested in rooms painted with "happy" colors: light blue, yellow, and orange. But those who were tested in rooms painted in "ugly" colors—black, brown, and white—got lower scores.

You can use color psychology to help create moods within your audiences too. First, decide how much authority and power you want to create, then use color as a tool to help you achieve it. You can use color in the room and in your materials as well as in your clothes.

Color Meanings

The following are some meanings associated with various colors. Also remember that dark colors have more authority, power, and control. Bright colors get more attention and can help keep people attentive. Pastels can make you appear soft, perhaps even weak.

Blue. Blue is most likely the most popular color. When you wear dark blue, people think you are intelligent, knowledgeable, credible, powerful, and you have a solid strength. Soft blues, e.g., sky blue, are calming.

Red. Red is energetic and dynamic. A strength color that implies movement, danger, fast things happening.

Yellow. Yellow is bright, cheerful, an action color. It's also a high-anxiety color.

Brown. Brown can be very calming. Unfortunately, it can be so calming it's boring. In theater, they often put the person who is not supposed be "smart" in a brown suit.

Black. Black is very authoritative. But it can be too authoritative and overwhelming such that some will want to keep their distance.

White. White is clear and crisp and contributes to an appearance of purity and youthfulness. But under spotlights white can be glaring, because the lights will bounce right back off the white you wear and into the audience's eyes. The audience won't see your face, just a white suit.

When you are on television, don't wear white. Men too, wear a blue shirt, off-white, ivory, anything but white, which makes you look pale and creates technical problems for the camera people as the lights jump off the white and create spots.

Choosing the Type and Color of Material for Your Clothes

Patterns make your eyes blink. Every time your eye blinks, it takes away from the brain's concentration on the topic. When we look at you from across the room, we should see *you*, not your necklace, tie, or jewelry.

Don't buy fabrics that have a shine or glimmer under bright lights. (Beware—lights in department stores, are not the same type that hit you on stage.) Be careful or you will be shining a light into your audience's eyes, almost like a mirror. Instead, buy material with subdued colors and mild patterns. A *very subtle* pattern or a very light pin stripe is acceptable.

Coordinate your colors with more than just your hair and skin colors. You decide on a dark blue suit, light blue shirt, solid steel blue tie. Now you walk out in front of the audience in front of that dark blue backdrop. Lights! Camera! Action! You disappear! Great for a magic show. Not so good for a business presentation. To avoid this, wear a color that makes you stand out from the background. Try to coordinate your colors so you don't clash with the room color.

How do you know what the room color will be?

Before you get dressed—preferably the night before—check out your entire room setup, including room color. If this is impossible, bring two suits, a dark and a light.

It's Hard to Persuade Anyone When Your Feet Hurt

Wear "wearable" clothes. Try your outfit on for a nice long period, at least as long as the presentation. If it's a several day presentation, one day is enough. If you're pulling at your drawers or cringing every time you take a step because your shoes are too tight, you won't have the concentration to be able to persuade your audience to do anything. Your focus turns from them to yourself.

Women have a more difficult time than men when it comes to shoes. Men wear shoes that are meant to be walked in. Women have been taught that high heels are "the thing" for the well-dressed businesswoman. If you can stand in high heels from sunrise 'til sundown and not feel excruciating pain, your feet just can't have nerve endings.

Ladies, let's be honest, there is only one reason to wear high heels—they make our calves look thinner. However, no presenter has ever told me, "I had them in the palm of my hand! Persuaded and motivated! Suddenly, someone looked at my legs and said, 'Oh heavens! She has heavy calves! How can she possibly know what she's talking about?'"

I, on the other hand, have taken a stand for women's rights. I just don't care how heavy my calves look when I'm on the platform (when I'm on a date it's a different story!). When I'm giving a full-day session, I wear shoes I can walk, move, and be energetic in all day long. True, adrenaline will often carry me through the first day, regardless of how uncomfortable I am. But at the end of that day I have sat in my hotel room in tears because of my silly, vain choice of shoes. Day two was not a pretty picture.

Mona Moon, professional speaker and seminar leader on, among other things, presentation skills, has a clever trick. She has a set of high heels which she wears until lunch. She buys flats in the same material which she slips on for the afternoon. No one but me seemed to notice. Nice compromise, smart idea.

Never wear white shoes—unless you want your audience to look at your feet the entire presentation.
—BOBBIE GEE

Match the Meeting's Ambience

If they're having a western hoedown, or a Hawaiian luau, dress to match the mood. You look pretty silly if you come out in a tux and they have jeans and cowboy boots on. It's important for the speaker to help the meeting planner create the mood and environment for the event.

Find out what the majority of your audience will be wearing and dress just a tad nicer. Don't give all your authority away by dressing "too casually," but don't spoil their fun either. Just because it's at the beach and they will be wearing bathing suits does not mean you should! You should be in a casual outfit, perhaps a muslin-type Caribbean-looking suit. (Men, this might be a great time to pull those white suits out of storage!)

> *I come dressed up, but I'm ready to dress down to make a human connec-*
> *tion to the audience. The first impression should match your introduction*
> *and the credibility you want to build. Even when I'm told to dress casual, I*
> *start off in a suit and take off my coat after they know I have one! Once you*
> *have connected with an audience, they won't care what you look like. But*
> *30 percent of an audience can be so image-oriented that inappropriate attire*
> *can turn them off in a way you will never be able to recover. Never be afraid*
> *to ask what is appropriate and then, as a rule of thumb go one step up from*
> *what they ask for.*
> —TERRY L. PAULSON, PH.D.

> *...my choice of clothing comes from a heart decision. What can I wear today*
> *to make my audience feel good about me and about themselves? I want my*
> *clothes to merely be a frame around the love that permeates from my heart.*
> —DANIELLE KENNEDY, M.A.

Makeup

Gentlemen, don't skip this section! Yes, I mean you too. The tiniest bit of oil in your skin looks very shiny to the audience and in photographs. A bit of face powder every hour or so does wonders.

If you have never purchased face power, go to any department store that has a makeup counter. Men, just look helpless and explain to the nice attendant you are a presenter—you need something to cut the glare under the lights. They'll be very understanding and helpful.

> *I often use a light amount of face makeup on my nose and temples, especially*
> *if there is a spotlight; I never use a lip gloss, it looks like lipstick. If I'm play-*
> *ing to a crowd of 2,000 or more, eye liner. Wives or girl friends will love to*
> *give you lessons.*
> —TOM OGDEN

How to Hide Nervous Shaking

Even tried-and-true masters of the platform can lose their control and start to shake. Not a good image enhancement technique! Here are a few tricks to help you appear normal in an abnormal situation:

- Don't hold your notes or workbooks in your hands. Find something to set your notes on. When you shake, so does whatever you are holding.

- Put your hands behind your back. Notice how the royal families always stand. Maybe they get a bit nervous too.

- Grasp your lectern if the shakes hit you. It's not a power stance, you should be naturally gesturing. But watching you shake uncontrollably is much worse than watching you hang on to the lectern.

- Try giving a simple group exercise, such as "Discuss with your neighbor three ways you can apply what you've learned so far today." This gives you a few minutes to get hold of yourself, go back over your notes, and visualize the audience being uplifted. It will soothe, calm you, and get you back in control.

Avoiding an Ugly Image

You can never buy back your reputation.
—BOBBIE GEE

When Jimmy Swaggart had an extramarital affair, he was met with more than mere disapproval. He was just about crucified by the public. Why? How would you have felt if Hugh Hefner, of *Playboy*, was caught doing the same thing? We were outraged with Swaggart because his "roots" were based in being "moral." When he did something in opposition to his roots, the world condemned him. He wasn't "walking the talk."

When you're presenting, an audience does not see you as just a person. The audience seems to put speakers into a superhuman category. After all, we are the ones who think we're so much "better than the rest" that we can get up on stage and give advice. No one knows better than a presenter how unfair that assessment is, but if you decide to take the platform, you will meet with it constantly.

Right or wrong, the moment you show up to give a speech, all eyes are on you. You're always on stage.

Colonel Gene Harrison, retired from the Marine Corps, speaks on ethics and integrity. He never ever drinks alcohol in front of any of his clients or audience members, before or after the speech. He feels it doesn't fit the image he wants to project. (He's never had a drink in front of me either.)

At the social hour before a dinner speech, Gene would always have a glass of Perrier as he mingled. Until one day, when one of his attendees came up to him before the speech, gave Gene a knowing grin, and said, "Guess you need that gin to calm you down for our group!" It had never occurred to Gene that people might think he was drinking anything other than water! Now he drinks it out of the bottle or holds the can. It looks tacky and makes shaking hands with the guests difficult, but he feels it's important to his image.

Chuck Reaves, a sales motivational speaker, often has a light Christian message weaved in his business speech. He told me he has given up going to the "social hour" before an event. He says it's not worth the negative moral image he may get entangled in. He put it this way, if he talks to a woman too long, they think he's "hitting" on her. If he drinks, then laughs loudly and from the heart—as he always does—they think he might be a drunk. If he dances with the boss's wife, he's too frivolous. Now he just stays in his meeting room or sits at the head table waiting and lets people come to him.

Once, when I asked a meeting planner how the speaker of the evening before had done, she replied, "Oh fine," I heard the hesitation in her voice. I immediately inquired, "You sound hesitant. You don't sound as if we really met your needs. Please tell me." "Well," she responded, "He was a terrific speaker, but he sure didn't waste any time getting *friendly* with some of our ladies." Oh boy, I thought. "Thank you for letting me know," I told her.

I called the speaker and said, "Look, what you do on your time is your business. But when you represent Walters International, they are trusting me to send them someone who speaks well and presents—at least— a mildly *wholesome* image!"

The speaker responded, "Lilly, I sat in the lobby and one of the attendees came over and sat next to me to talk for about 10 minutes. Whoever saw us did not see what they thought they saw."

This seems like it's none of your business. Can you really afford to be throwing stones here?

I'm not telling you how to live your life. And no, I certainly can't afford to throw stones. But I want you to realize as you decide on your own rules of conduct that you are being judged by rules far different from the ones the average person is judged by. Even if you decide to protect your reputation and not sit in the lobby for even 10 minutes with an audience member, you are still going to get raised eyebrows and false assumptions over other innocent actions.

I'm not suggesting you give up drinking or socializing with your audiences. I am suggesting that you consider that you are constantly being scrutinized when you are given the opportunity of wearing the title "Speaker."

About five years ago I was in Washington, D.C., speaking to the National Council of Parents for Drug-Free Youth. Mrs. Reagan spoke and Brooke

Shields, who had done a couple of commercials for the group, was also there. I was the wind-up speaker that evening. The audience was enormously responsive, they laughed at all of my jokes (which, incidentally, is a sign of intelligence!). They said nice things about me, so I went to bed excited and pleased that I had participated.

The next morning I was down in the restaurant, awaiting my turn to be seated. There were about a dozen people behind me. The host had gone out to seat the couple in front of me and I was patiently waiting my turn to be seated.

Now I don't know how you stand when you stand, but when I stand, I just stand. For example, I do not know how to stand "motivated," so I was just "standing." Three ladies walked in from the other side of the restaurant to get in the line, and when they spotted me they started talking about me in whispers that you could only hear about a hundred and fifty yards away. The first one commented, "There's our speaker from last night." The second one added, "Yes, and he's obviously a 'night' person." The third one concluded by saying, "He must be, he sure doesn't look motivated to me!"

To repeat myself, I don't know how you stand when you stand, but when I stand, I just stand. I don't know how to stand motivated. I don't know whether the ladies thought I should have been standing there looooooking out at everybody in the audience, you know, griiiiinnnning at 'em, waaaaaving at 'em and jumping up and down while I was doing it. That's motivation? That's insanity!

—ZIG ZIGLAR

Perception is reality in the minds of your clients. I avoid risky situations— I don't "chat" alone with people in dark corners for more than a few minutes. I don't go into the bar.

—TOM OGDEN

I allow a man to walk me to the elevator door—but no farther. They all see him go into the elevator with me—they don't see him come right back down.

—PATRICIA FRIPP

The problem is, there are a few people who abuse the privilege of being a speaker. Some people in your audience, who have problems, come to you for help. Because you are up there as the expert, people think you have answers to everything. I've seen a few speakers consult vulnerable audience members right into bed. When you are up in front of a group, sharing yourself and your knowledge, you are in a very privileged position. People look up to you. You need to watch it. We are also in a vulnerable position. I heard Billy Graham will not eat a meal or have a meeting with a woman without someone else there. It's not a bad rule for speakers.

—DR. KEN BLANCHARD

Ethics in today's world must needs be unbending; you're a role model up there on the platform.

—DR. LAYNE LONGFELLOW

As regards alcoholic beverages, you'll have to make up your own mind. I wouldn't dream of taking a drink before I entertain or lecture, although there are some people who prefer to have a little beer, wine, or perhaps some-thing stronger before they go to the platform. However, a good rule would be "If in doubt, don't do it." The danger of having several drinks before you go on stage is that you can end up being a true horse's ass and simply never know it.

—Steve Allen, © 1986

Red Motley on Smoking, Image, and Focus

A few years ago, I heard a tape of Red Motley that was recorded almost four decades earlier, in the 1950s. He talked about the importance of im-age. For many years president of *Parade Magazine*, Red was one of the greatest speakers of his day.

His message made a great impression on me about the image we pro-ject. See the box for a transcription of that original recording. It's re-markable when you listen to his thoughts on smoking, then think of how long ago this recording was made. At the time every star was puff-ing away up on the silver screen, but Red took a stand on professional-ism and excellence that sounds like something Tom Peters (author of the "Excellence" series) might say today; well, Tom Peters would say it to-day with a few changes in delivery style!

WHAT FOR?
by Red Motley

I won't permit a salesman that works for me to smoke while he sells, if I catch him, I'll fire him. They know that. And why? Well, I learned the hard way, the way most pros did.

Years ago I was invited by the head of one of the divisions of a great motor car corporation to sit in while the advertising agent of a New York agency made the presentation. He must have had $25,000 worth of hardware, and comprehensives and charts, and market analysis studies and everything else.

When he got all through, my friend, the head of this division, left the room first because he was the big wheel, and as he shook hands with this president of this New York agency while leaving, he said, "This wasn't very important to you, was it?"

The agent's face turned as white as my shirt. Of course it was im-portant to him, with 7 or 8 million dollars involved.

And then my friend gave me the tip off, he said, "It wasn't as important as 4 cigarettes."

Then I remembered. That man hadn't been going more than 5 minutes before he made that old familiar search for that pack. He got the cigarette out, he tapped it, he lit it, he puffed, somebody had to find him an ash tray, he broke the continuity, he lost his audience, 4 times!

And what for? Four lousy cigarettes! I don't smoke cigarettes, but I smoke cigars. But I don't smoke 'em anymore when I sell. Because I began to wonder how many times I'd been selling a dirty, second hand, chewed up cigar butt, as I pointed at a price list or some of the things on those signs or what not. What for? Not common sense!

Oh yes, I know, I have ash trays on my desk. I have salesmen come to see me, and they say, "May I smoke?" very politely, and I always say, "Of course." Then under my breath, "You damn fool." And why? Because I find myself looking at this chump, dragging that stuff down into his navel, and then for 5 minutes as he talks it comes out of his eyes, ears, nose, and every place else, and I'm fascinated by it!

What for? What for? What did he go there to do? To do an imitation of a smokestack on wheels? You went there to sell 'em something, didn't you? Not blow smoke in his face. It's just common sense that you gotta know how you look to the prospect.

But I'll give you six, two and even, that 95 percent of the people in this room have no idea how they look to the man across the desk, they've never taken the trouble to find out.

I didn't either, until one night, another salesman said to me, "Motley, you went to college didn't you?" and I said, "Yes," and he said, "You gotta Phi Beta Kappa key didn't you?" and I said, "Sure. Why?" "Well," he said, "I don't understand why you insist on making people believe you're a tough guy, that you have no education." I said, "what do you mean?"

"Well," he said, "talking out of the corner of your mouth."

I said, "I do not!"

He said, "You do too!"

The argument went on far into the night. It was a draw. I didn't believe it.

I went out to see a friend of mine, the advertising man at the Chrysler Corporation, R. M. Roland. I said, "Roland, you're a friend of mine, tell me the truth, do I talk out of the corner of my mouth?"

(Continued)

He said, "You certainly do, and I've often wondered why."

Well, Mrs. Motley and the kids were in hysterics for months while the old man practiced his pitch in front of the mirror. But I don't talk out of the corner of my mouth anymore.

How do you know how you look to the guy? I remember the last fascinating specimen that sat across from me. I found myself marveling at the durability of the human ear, that could stand that sort of thing. That gouging, that digging in the ear with that forefinger. Then I found myself speculating, what would happen if I ever succeed in diggin' through and getting inside that damn ear! It's unfortunate, the tragic part is that he didn't know he was doing it. He didn't have sense enough to go and find out how he looked to the guy on the other side of the desk.

I instruct my salesmen not to take their hat and coat in the office, when they make the call. I've had a lot of fellows say to me, "Well, there isn't any place to put it."

I've said, "Throw it on the floor and put the dry cleaning on the expense account." They say well, lot of times you leave it out there, might be stolen. I say, "All right then, take out an insurance policy and put that on the expense account too."

Why? You spend a lot of time getting the body in front of a prospect, then what do you do? Why you lug your hat and coat in to advertise to the guy that you're a bird of passage, you don't have to pay much attention to me, I'm not going to stay very long, Mister.

You spend a lot of time trying to meet 'em on a equal footing, don't you? And there's that picture of that dynamic salesman sittin' across from you, with an overcoat, a brief case and a hat piled up on his lap, stripped for action.

Doesn't make sense.

Edited from a transcript of the actual famous speech given in the 1950s. Reproduced with permission of the Lacy Institute. Audiotapes of the live presentation available from the Lacy Institute, South Yarmouth, MA.

Image from the Inside Out

It's good to get rid of the obvious habits that might distract listeners. However, all image problems are just symptoms of how you feel about yourself. The presenters who have the greatest impact on their audiences follow very few of the traditional "rules" of image. Tom Peters paces back and forth across the stage and often looks like he slept in his clothes. Ken Blanchard often wears a sports coat. Hermine Hilton, a memory expert, wears pants instead of a skirt, and her hair often looks like she forgot to brush it when she got up that morning. Yet all three leave their audiences wanting more and raving about their fantastic impact.

If you have an obvious "flaw" in your image, e.g., "too fat," "annoying voice," "too short," "handicapped," "not educated enough," please understand, the audience is not very concerned about you. They are concerned about what you are going to do to make them feel better. Consider your impression of the following list of presenters—did their "flaws" affect the brilliance of their presentations?

Too fat: Winston Churchill

Annoying voice: Helen Keller

Handicapped: Franklin D. Roosevelt

Not educated enough: Will Rogers

> *You know what happens, people get too worried with this looking like a professional speaker deal. Everybody tells you, "Here's how to give an executive presentation..." and "You're suppose to wear a blue suit and red tie." And you know what happens? Here's a lively, colorful, dynamite person that is stuffed into this square box. All the enthusiasm and excitement is just drained right out of them. You should try to look nice up there, but more important, look like you.*
> —STEW LEONARD, JR.

> *Clothes should match the audience. You can choose your clothes and you can train your voice, but your personality is best the opposite—unchosen, untrained, natural.*
> —DR. LAYNE LONGFELLOW

> *People tell me again and again my wheelchair and my unique physical appearance pretty much disappears. My movement back and forth across the stage are just one more sign that helps convey that although I am disabled I am not unable.*
> —W MITCHELL

MORE SECRETS ABOUT STEP 8: YOUR IMAGE FROM THE PLATFORM (LEAVES OF BRILLIANT COLOR)

Although they judge you the minute they see you, they will *rejudge* you by what you say and do as your speech goes on. Your power image is going to finish with how you project "a passion for your topic, and a compassion for your audience."

They expect a professional presentation, so they expect to see a "professional." Dress appropriately for the occasion, but don't be one of the crowd. Be just a step above.
—WESS ROBERTS, PH.D.

I suppose it's nice to have a good speaking voice—but I know many stars who don't.
—BILL GOVE

More often than not a speaker's image will remain in a person's mind long after the words have been forgotten. You can never be overdressed or too polite. It sends a message of the respect you hold for your audience.
—HARVEY DIAMOND

Look like today, speak like today, use today's stories and you will be thought of as a today's speaker.
—DOUG MALOUF

Step 9
Motivating an Audience
_____Call Them to Pick the Fruit_

All personal breakthroughs begin with a change in beliefs.
—ANTHONY ROBBINS

You take a seed; find the right place for it to take root; actually plant the seed in the ground; you sink your roots down deep; you have one solid trunk that comes up; you have strong, simply organized boughs that come out of the trunk; then you decorate it all with leaves of brilliant color. A tree is known by its fruit. But what is the point of a fruit tree? You need to **call the audience to pick the fruit.**

Great Titles Entice the Audience

It is by no means necessary to have an actual title before you begin to write. We may be sure that at the top of the envelope on which he wrote his now-famous speech, Abraham Lincoln did not write the words "The Gettysburg Address."
—STEVE ALLEN, © 1986

Titles should get their attention. "Leadership Secrets of Attila the Hun" got people's attention. They wondered if anyone could be serious about "Attila" being a great leader. It stimulated the curious, the genuinely interested.
—WESS ROBERTS, PH.D.

People judge a book by its cover, and they'll judge your presentation by its title. "Sizzlin" Elmer Wheeler, a famous sales speaker of decades gone by advises us to sell the "sizzle," not the steak. Let's suppose your topic may be communication skills. Well, what's alluring, what's the sizzle, what's the benefit of communication skills? Add that into your title to help entice audiences into your meeting room.

La Rue Frye, director of Conventions and Expositions for ASAE (The American Society of Association Executives), came up with a great theme test[1] for meeting planners. I have adapted it as a method to help make presentation titles more enticing.

Take your mission and/or your potential title, and ask yourself the series of questions below. Even better, get some friends together and have a brain-storming session using the test on your title. They will be more objective than you are. The first time I run presenters through this test in my seminar they always reply to each question, "Yes, my title *certainly* meets that point!" The rest of the group looks at each other uncomfortably, not knowing what to say. Because the rest of us certainly did not see what was such a certainty for the presenter. If your answer to one of the following questions is, "Of course my title does that, just as it is!" ask your friends for advice, then hush up and listen to them—never an easy task for us speakers!

Presentation Title Test

- Does the title stress benefits not features?

- Does the title stress results over process?

- Does the title stress the WIIFM factor, which means "What's In It For Me?"

- Does the title instantly reflect major objectives that you wish to accomplish with your presentation?

- Does the title suggest a personal tangible goal?

- Does the title reflect the concerns or problems facing the industry?

- Does the title serve as a subject matter umbrella under which the majority of your speech material can be encompassed?

- Does the title suggest action?

- Does the title lend itself to dramatization?

- Does the title contain an element of mystery?

- Does the title stimulate the imagination?

---

[1]*The Meeting Manager*, association publication of Meeting Planners International, Dallas, December 1987.

- Does the title embody more than one element? Does the title have a double meaning?
- Is the title easily remembered, orally and mentally?
- Does the title have a familiar ring to it?
- Is the title a catchy phrase that will permeate conversation after the presentation?

This is discouraging. I can't think of good creative ideas off the top of my head.

Perfect! If the above was easy for you, you were doing it wrong. Great titles rarely come easily. Titles that always attract an audience well are ones that say blatantly or imply "How to _____, so you can _____."

Consider the *One Minute Manager* by Ken Blanchard and Spencer Johnson. A great title. It doesn't say "how to," but it implies "How to become an effective manager in just one minute!"

The name of my last book is *Speak and Grow Rich* (Prentice Hall). The implied how to? How to become rich by speaking.

Give your presentation a title that's going to motivate people to attend in the first place. Get them to the orchard before you worry about how to get them to pick the fruit!

> *When I put a talk together I spend every waking hour thinking about and researching each of the points. I usually pick the title out of one of my points. For example, in my speech, "The Power of Positive Doing," I might use, "IT IS EASIER TO ACT YOURSELF INTO GOOD THINKING, THAN IT IS TO THINK YOURSELF INTO GOOD ACTION!"*
> —Bill Gove

Five Levels to Motivate an Audience

In his excellent book, *How to Prepare, Stage, and Deliver Winning Presentations* (AMACOM, 1982, p. 71), Tom Leech says you need to bring your listeners through 5 levels to motivate them.

1. **Listen.**   Make sure they're listening. Once you have them listening, you can bring them to the next level.
2. **Understand.**   Present in such a way that they will understand.
3. **Believe.**   Get them to believe you.
4. **Retain.**   Make sure that you deliver your presentation in such a format that they can retain what they've learned.
5. **Act or Do.**   Make sure your presentation helps your audience to do and to act.

Let's take each level one at a time to see how you can more easily bring your listeners successfully through each level.

Level One: Get Them to Listen

Why People Don't Listen

How do you ensure your audience is going to listen? First, let's look at why they *don't* listen. In the textbook *Looking Out, Looking In*, (Harcourt Brace Jovanovich, 1993, p. 253) authored by Ronald Alder and Neil Towne, there are nine reasons people don't listen:

1. **Message overload.** When you spend most of the day listening, listening, listening, you simply input too much information into your brain to retain all of it.

2. **Preoccupation.** Perhaps they had a fight with their spouse, they are hungry, or have pressing business at work they wish they were getting accomplished.

3. **Rapid thinking.** We think at about 600 words per minute. On an average, people talk at about 140. So, you say a few words, your listeners' minds have just raced ahead of you to something else.

   My sister Jeanine, a college speech coach, says you need to find ways to keep pulling their thoughts back to you every 15 seconds. Zig Ziglar uses unusual body movement to bring his listeners' attention back to his topic every 30 seconds or so. He squats down low, then stands up, he moves around the stage. It's an interesting method. As one of the highest-paid sales speakers in the world, he is unquestionably effective.

4. **Effort.** Active listening is just hard work. When you're actively listening, your respiration rate goes up. Your heart starts to beat faster. People can't keep it up for a long time.

5. **External noise.** Noise is anything that distracts. You could even classify "noise" in this sense as a distracting appearance which is created if the presenter wears a glaring hot color, such as hot pink or orange.

6. **Hearing problems.** Fifty percent of people have hearing problems—that's right, 50 percent!

7. **Faulty assumptions.** They assume you said something that you didn't.

8. **Lack of apparent advantage.** The listener does not recognize the benefits.

9. **Lack of training.** Did you ever take a course in school called "Listening 101," or "Beginning Listening"? No, most of us didn't.

Yet, statistics show we spend 32 percent of our time doing mass listening, and 21 percent of it in face-to-face listening. So 53 percent of our time is spent in listening, yet we've never had any training in it.

Bright eyed college students in a lecture hall, aren't necessarily listening to the professor, the American Psychological Association was told yesterday. If you shot off a gun at sporadic intervals and asked the student to encode their thoughts and moods at that moment, you would discover that about 20% of the students, men and women, are pursuing erotic thoughts.

Another 20% are reminiscing about something. Only 20% are actually paying attention to the lecture, 12% are actually listening, the others are worrying, daydreaming, thinking about lunch or, surprise, religion. This confirmation of the lecturer's worst fears were recorded by Paul Cameron, 28, an assistant professor.*

*San Francisco Chronicle, 1982.

Now to Grab Their Attention

Be Enthusiastic. A Stanford University study on sales success showed that only 15 percent of success in sales was due to knowledge, whereas 85 percent was from *enthusiasm*.

Charisma is the transference of enthusiasm.
Be excited about your message and your audience will be also.
    —RALPH ARCHBOLD

Use spirited, exciting delivery to convey how wonderful the results were...and they can do it too.
ENTHUSIASM LETS YOU DO THINGS BETTER THAN YOU REALLY KNOW HOW.
    —IRA HAYES

Speak on a Subject of Importance to Them. Stress the benefits.
1) Give them a reason to change by stating benefits.
2) Show the negative results of not changing.
3) Try to give simple, immediate "how to's."
    —ROGER BURGRAFF, PH.D.

Create a vision of change they perceive to be in their best self-interest.
    —COL. GENE HARRISON, RET.

To motivate people, present your message so that it addresses their pressing needs and interests. People listen to what affects them and respond to what promises to enrich them in those areas.
—TOM LEECH

Don't waste your pearls of wisdom until you've opened their eyes to their value. Make part of your introduction a timely exposé on why they need what you are about to offer. Borrow on timely articles from magazines or newspapers that capitalize on other companies or organizations like the one you are speaking to that failed to listen or learn. You want that person to say, "That could be me (us)...." I let them know my objective up front, "I don't just want positive evaluations and bizarre behavior for four days, I want you to be different three months from now. Don't just think of other people who ought to be here; spend most of your time looking in a mirror. After all, the only person you really control is yourself, and even that is in question on Mondays. At the end of this program, I want you to share one thing you plan on doing differently as a result of my presentation. That will be our summary. After all, what you receive to make a difference is more important than what I say." They don't have to buy the whole load; you want a few targeted changes not just "happy face" evaluations.
—TERRY L. PAULSON, PH.D.

Speaking a Language They Understand.   I don't mean English compared with Swahili. I mean stay away from "techno-babble." Don't try to impress with your amazing grasp of the English language, chances are they will just smile and look at you intelligently rather than let you know they don't have a clue as to what you're talking about. You're far safer if you use the KISS method—keep it sweet and simple.

Make Them Think or Act in the First Few Minutes.   Find ways to surprise them. Perhaps, ask them to take out a pen, stand up, or move over a seat—anything to create a surprise that reinforces the mission. Use the age-old techniques of: sound, vision, fragrance, and anticipation.

Humorous Openings

The opening of your presentation plays a big part in how well people will listen to you. *Executive Speaker,* a newsletter which studies speeches done by top executives, also publishes *Openings,* which studies the best openings of great speeches. It says that in the more than 130 examples of the most frequently used attention-getting devices, the most frequent is humor.

A few of my favorite openings are

■ I loved it when Groucho Marx opened with, "Before I speak, I have something important to say."

- In the book *How to Hold Your Audience with Humor,* Gene Perret tells about a brilliant opening by Phyllis Diller.[2] She was addressing an audience in Las Vegas, and, due to a minor injury, her arm was in a cast. "I'd like to begin with a public service announcement: If there is anyone here who has just bought the new book *The Joy of Sex,* there is a misprint on page 206."

- Westinghouse vice chairman and chief operating officer, Douglas D. Danforth, commented on the business climate of the 1980s, "It is widely prophesied that the business climate of the '80s will display the classic symptoms of a New Year's Day hangover—not healthy enough to go jogging, but not sick enough to bury."

Other classic openers include the following:

- Ask a question ("Were you there when...")
- Historical reference ("Fourscore and seven years ago...")
- Poem or rhyme or quote
- Music or other unusual sound audience would not be expecting
- Show the benefits by stating a promise ("When you leave today, you will have the solution to...")

> *Shock them with a contrarian view—then retreat to an acceptable idea.*
> —GERALD C. MEYERS

Assignment: Look at the previous section on listening. What will you do to ensure that your audiences "listen"?

Level Two: Understand

What happens if listeners don't understand? They go right back to level one. They're not listening, and you need to start over. Let's work on some techniques to ensure that your audiences will *understand* what you are saying.

The listeners are more likely to understand you if the material is clearly organized, which includes the following:

You have clearly defined your mission.

You have a simple and easily remembered theme.

---

[2]Gene Perret's excellent book is now out of print, but he has others, equally as good, available at your bookstore.

You only use three to four main points.

You hang the whole picture on a simple clear structure.

The material must be delivered in digestible amounts. Dr. Albert Mehrabian's research also found that audience members listen to you for 90 minutes, but they'll only listen with retention for 20.

> *So simplify the information as much as possible, and use audio visual aids to speed up the process.*
> —DR. ALBERT MEHRABIAN

Your material must encourage and respond to feedback. At least every 20 minutes, break for an audience interaction of some type: Q&A, a discussion session, and so forth.

Your illustrations should be simple and easy to understand. Melvin Belli, the famous trial attorney, said one of the secrets of his success was using simple illustrations.[3] When he was a child, he read the *Book of Knowledge* series. He loved the way the books explained things. Instead of saying the Empire State building is "so many" feet high, it would say, it's as big as putting 30 (or however many) railroad cars end to end up to the sky! This method made the concept so clear to him as a child, that he used that technique in all his trials to make the juries understand the concepts he was attempting to convey.

Get the audience to experience the concepts themselves through audience participation. Audience participation is—in my humble opinion—the best learning tool. Listeners explicitly remember the things you have them do themselves. That's the good news. The bad news is it would take a book twice as long as this one to do audience participation justice. Luckily, there are many excellent books on the topic. Jeff Dewar and I also produced a two-hour video called "Games Presenters Play—How to Design Audience Participation Experiences." The book by the same title is in progress.

Assignment: What will you do to ensure that your audiences "understand"?

Level Three: Accept or Believe

Once you get your listeners to listen and to understand, you need to bring them to the third level—to accept and believe you. Of course the

---

[3]*Sharing Ideas among Professional Speakers Newsmagazine*, Royal Publishing, April/May 1990, p. 15.

audience may understand you but simply disagree. You probably didn't offer the right arguments in the right amounts, to the right audience, at the right time—it happens!

The listener is more receptive to accepting and believing what you have to say when you add the "three proofs," an old Greek philosophy from Aristotle:

1. **Ethos** means your ethics, likability, and credibility, courage. This is where you, your honor, and your personality are judged.
2. **Pathos** is the passion, the touching of the heart strings. Tell the stories that make them laugh and cry.
3. **Logos** is the logic behind it all. You need to answer concerns and objections and give facts and details to prove and substantiate your position.

You always need all three ingredients if you intend to bring the audience to accept or believe you. However, the personality type you present for will determine the "mix" you use of these three ingredients. If you're presenting mainly to analyticals (see the personality analysis in Step 2), you want more of the *logos,* and less of the *pathos* and *ethos.* If you've got relationship-oriented types in your audience, such as teachers and counselors, you'll want to add more *pathos.*

What famous story used all three attributes in their purest form to make up each of its main characters as caricatures? Give up? I'll give you a hint...

> If the Wizard is a Wizard who will serve...
> Then we're sure to get
> a brain, a heart, the Nerve.

That's it. They went *Over the Rainbow* to the Emerald City to meet the *Wizard of Oz.* The *logos* character was the Scarecrow, the *Pathos* was the Tin Woodsman, the *Ethos* was the Cowardly Lion. Combine all the ingredients as successfully as L. Frank Baum did and your presentations may be remembered for as long as his classic tale.

> *The Secret of Successful Speakers?*
> *Passion (ethos) and compassion (pathos)*
> *with a purpose (logos).*
> —Lilly Walters

In my presentation "The Secrets of Motivation," I give three little simple truths about life: You are what you think. You are what you go for. You are

*what you do. It doesn't sound very profound, but millions of people today
don't know these simple little thoughts that can change your life!*
                              —BOB RICHARDS

Assignment: What will you do to ensure that your audiences "believe
or accept" you?

Level Four: Retention

If your listeners accept and believe you, you can bring them on to the
next level—get them to retain the information. Retention is only par-
tially applicable during the presentation, because most of it happens afterward. Listeners are more likely to retain information when you use
visuals to play a great part. See Figure 9-1.

*Back up your points with visual aids (oversize props...charts...blown up
letter, etc. People watch television...they only listen to a radio. [Using
props, etc.] lets you become a video...ALIVE...and you will be refreshing
and unique.*
                              —IRA HAYES

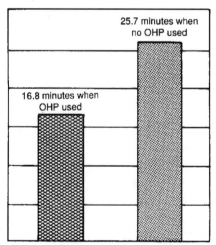

Results: Use of overhead projector reduced
average meeting length by 28 percent.

Figure 9-1. The influence of overhead projector usage on average meeting length. (*From
the Wharton Study, Wharton Center for Applied
Research*)

Retention is aided when you repeat the information. Another study quoted the following statistics regarding repeats and retention:

Number of Repeats	Amount of Retention
1	<10%
6	>90%

I organize my material using what I call the PIP Technique. The first "P" stands for your premise: what point are you trying to get across? The "I" stands for illustration. That's what makes the point understood and memorable. Stories are among the best illustrations, but quotes, humor, group exercises and poetry also qualify. The final "P" is for the point that you'll verbalize to summarize and emphasize just exactly what it is that you want them to remember from the illustration.
—**MARK SANBORN**

Tell 'em what you're gonna tell 'em. Tell 'em. Tell 'em what you told 'em.
—**UNKNOWN**

Also use workbooks, quizzes, and/or group discussions as methods to repeat the information.

Another retention improver is to give the audience time to absorb what you say. It's much more powerful to make the point and then just be silent and let your listeners think about it. Let them reach the conclusion by themselves. Just point them in the right direction and let them go. According to Bob Pike, creator of "Creative Training Techniques Seminars," "People don't argue with their own data, but they can and do argue with yours." Joseph Joubert, a French moralist, said, "We can convince others by our own arguments, but we can only persuade them by their own." Or as Ben Franklin said, "A man convinced against his will, is of the same opinion still."

Audience participation exercises are an excellent method to allow your audience to experience the learning. Edgar Dale, a researcher, developed what is now known as "Dale's Cone of Experience." He says people will remember

20 percent of what they hear

30 percent of what they see

50 percent of what they see and hear

80 percent of what they hear, see, and do.

Teach with the use of humor and heart stories. You may not remember the exact information, but chances are you'll remember the joke or the story. These are largely graphic images, and images are more easily remembered than abstract information.

Learning takes place when you kick them into a higher attention level. Touch their hearts, their minds will follow.

Assignment: What will you do to ensure that your audiences "retain" the information you deliver?

Level Five: Get Them to Act or Do

Listeners are more likely to take action from a presentation if it's not too much trouble. If you're asking them to solve all the famine problems in the world tomorrow, chances are they're not going to do it. But if you give them one little action they **can** do, like "Please donate $20 at the door as you go out," or "Join the association—you have forms at your seat!" you've got a good chance of success.

If you have incorporated their ideas, people will often talk themselves into your point of view. Create audience participation experiences that allow them to come to the conclusion on their own. They can argue with your data. It's hard to argue with their own.

When you conclude a session, reword your remarks using the terms they have come up with in discussions.

> *How the heart listened while he pleading spoke!*
> *While on the enlightened mind, with winning art,*
> *His gentle reason so persuasive stole,*
> *That the charmed hearer thought it was his own.*
> —THOMSON, *THE SEASONS*

> *Don't tell them what they should do.*
> *Tell them what you did…let them have the idea themselves.*
> —SUZIE HUMPHREYS

Finally, the audience is more likely to take action if the presenter gives an altar call. Reverend Bob Richards is an Olympic gold medalist in the pole vault and a national decathlon champion. He often speaks to high school kids on motivation and the Olympic games. He told me he would often conclude a presentation by saying, "Who knows, but there is an Olympic Champion right here in this auditorium! One of you may be willing to pay the price—you can if you'll work, if you'll dream! You know who you are. Thank you." Then he'd walk off the stage.

> *After many speeches, some little, least-likely to succeed, fat, short or skinny, underdeveloped kid would come up and say to me, "Mr. Richards, I'm go-ing to be an Olympic Champion!" Or, "I'm going to win a Gold Medal in four years. I'm the one!" And many of those unlikely kids were "the ones."*

They believed they could do it. They answered the call and went on to become Olympic Champions.
—REVEREND BOB RICHARDS

At the end of your presentation, what are you calling them to do? Are you asking for the sale? Are you calling them to pick the fruit on your tree? *Assignment:* What will you do to ensure that your audiences "act"?

You stir audiences because they respond to an earnest message.
—JACK ANDERSON

When Does Change Happen?

Every change is not an improvement,
but every improvement is by change.
—UNKNOWN

Change happens in the boiler room of our emotions—so find out how to light their fires.
—JEFF DEWAR

Change only really happens when people are dissatisfied with the present situation, and have been shown an alternative course of action. Create an urgency of dissatisfaction and lead them to the first step of action.
—RALPH ARCHBOLD

You can impact several areas: (1) A message strong enough to light an "internal" spark, a desire to change; (2) reenforcement of individual ability to change; (3) and an initial thought on how to start the change.
—CAPT. DAVE CAREY

Give examples of other's success stories. Inspire them to taste the results and to realize that the value of the change is greater than the way things have been.
—TERRY COLE-WHITTAKER

I don't motivate. That has to be done at three in the morning when they are alone. I open doors. Invite them to come in. It's their decision whether they do or not.
—ROSITA PEREZ

MORE SECRETS ABOUT STEP 9: MOTIVATING AN AUDIENCE TO CHANGE THEIR ACTIONS AND ATTITUDES (CALL THEM TO PICK)

Before you can motivate an audience to change, you need to get them in your meeting room! Develop an exciting title to draw them in. Once they are there, bring them through the five levels: (1) listen, (2) understand, (3) believe, (4) retain, and (5) do.

> *Presenters are salespeople. If you want your audience to buy your idea you must SELL IT, and SELL IT WELL. "Use Dougie's 4-A Rule: You must get their Attention. You must Arouse their interest. You must Appeal to their emotions, and you will get some Action!"*
> —DOUG MALOUF

> *Give each audience something they need but don't think they already know [which means]: Never try to sell selling to a salesman, just give him an idea that's new—so he can outsell you.*
> —HERMINE HILTON

Step 10
Tools to Deliver the Speech and Build Rapport with Your Audience

_____*Till the Soil*

Relate to them and let them relate to you.
—PHILIP CROSBY

I used to think the audience was something to "work over"—dazzle 'em with my verbal skills. Now I know the audience is part of my support system. A painter can paint alone—a writer can write alone—but a speaker is only a speaker when he has an audience to address.
—BILL GOVE

Material cannot do it alone. The personality and delivery make it come alive.
—PATRICIA FRIPP

Making Contact with Your Audience

You don't want to just talk to the person in the front row, because they are easy to connect with. I try to think about connecting with the people in the very back. One thing I like to do before the speech is go to the very back of the room, the furthest away from where I'll be on the platform, and sit. I feel it helps me identify with the person who will be sitting there when I talk. I get a sense of what it feels like to be back there. I try to sit there awhile in the session before mine when the room is full. When I give my talk I can make a better connection with the entire room.

—W MITCHELL

Every person who steps on the platform, whether they want to admit it or not, is a performer. And for performers, showmanship is paramount. I've seen Bob Hope revitalize weary soldiers with some snappy jokes, I've seen him bring surges of pride and patriotism to them with a few words of praise, and I've seen him bring tears to the eyes of battle worn warriors with a tender song.

You motivate an audience with a worthwhile, truthful message. Then you just deliver the hell out of it.

—GENE PERRET

To Use or Not to Use Notes

I don't think it makes a bit a difference if you use notes or not. The difference comes when you hide behind the notes and avoid the audience. Originally Winston Churchill believed in the "I don't need notes! I rely on my extemporaneous skills" philosophy. Then he bombed doing a trade union speech—he forgot the whole thing. Thereafter, he came armed with everything written down, including pauses, *pretended* fumbling, anticipated "cheers," "hear, hears," "prolonged cheering," and even "standing ovations!"

As he didn't have the wonderful advantage of a computer, he would dictate his presentation to a secretary. Then he would edit it with scissors and paste. Finally, the secretary would rewrite it with a special typewriter with extra large print. He always had it put into "psalm form." He read his speeches, word for word. They looked like this...

We shall fight on the beaches.
We shall fight on the landing grounds.

We shall fight in the fields
and in the streets.

We shall fight in the hills.
We shall never surrender.

Do what you need to do to get the message into your listeners' minds and hearts. The magic is in the way you mix your flexibility and spontaneity with the memorability of a good structure.

Too many nervous speakers scatter their eye contact, drone on with memorized lines or read prepared texts, and wonder why most of their audience seems to be engaged in silent prayer. If you've done your preparation, you can risk putting away the prepared notes and coming from experience.
—TERRY L. PAULSON, PH.D.

I never use notes, they interfere with me.
—DR. KEN BLANCHARD

Sometimes I'll write down the name of the CEO or others I want to mention in my talk or the theme of their meeting. Other than that, I don't use notes.
—W MITCHELL

Don't read your speech. With a felt pen write key words that you can see easily that will remind you of your next points.
—PATRICIA FRIPP

Eye Contact

Try to reach the entire audience. My mother performed to a group of 15,000 one time. She said you have to pretend to see their eyes even when you can't. Envision them.

Make sure your eye contact is spread throughout the entire audience.
—PATRICIA FRIPP

I imagine that I'm talking to the person in the back row. The people in the front stay with you anyway. You lose the ones in the back—then that discomfort spreads forward. I try to look at each person in the room for at least an instant. It makes each member feel you are talking just to them.
—TOM OGDEN

A good speech is a one on one conversation with each audience member.
—RALPH ARCHBOLD

Toastmasters International says to try to hold each person's eye for about 4 to 5 seconds. Mom says, "Look at each person for as long as it creates a *mind touch* with them." From the time I was very little she would say, "You look at them long enough until you feel 'em start to lift. Then you leave them up there, and go on to the next person."

I used to just scan the audience, never really looking at any one person. Now I'm confident enough up there to have actual conversations with members in the audience. I will talk to them for 20 seconds, then have a conver-

sation with somebody else. It has made a big difference in establishing a rapport with them.
                                        —W MITCHELL

Don't just focus on anyone, find the "energy boosting" people in different sections of your audience that nod their heads and smile. Never stay focused on the "energy sappers" with their faces in park, or your butterflies will quickly turn to energy sapping eagles.
                              —TERRY L. PAULSON, PH.D.

Once you make a good eye contact with a person in the audience, they will feel you are talking to them for the rest of the speech.
                                  —DR. KEN BLANCHARD

The Magic V

Let's say there are 500 people in your audience. It's very difficult to make actual eye contact with 500 people. However, there's a trick to help called the Magic V (see Figure 10-1). When you look at someone, everyone in a *V* behind that person thinks you are looking at them.

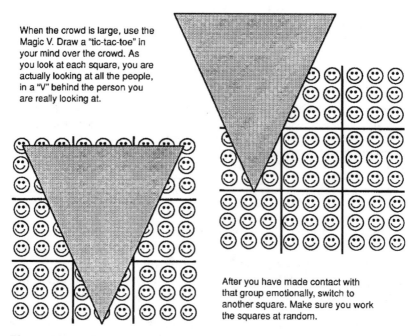

When the crowd is large, use the Magic V. Draw a "tic-tac-toe" in your mind over the crowd. As you look at each square, you are actually looking at all the people, in a "V" behind the person you are really looking at.

After you have made contact with that group emotionally, switch to another square. Make sure you work the squares at random.

Figure 10-1. The Magic V.

Divide the room up into a tic-tac-toe board. Look at one of the "squares" and use the *V* and the mind touch to lift that section. Once you have them, move to another square.

Mingling before the Speech

Get to know the audience before the speech. Then even if you can't see them in an audience of 4,000 people—the auditorium is dark and the stage brightly lit—you can still say things like, "Joe out there I know is struggling with…" or "Mary is having problems with her kids Jack and Jane, but you know what she did about it? She…." When I take the time to know the people in the audience it helps enormously. Even if you can only get to know a few, the rest realize you are involved and you care—you didn't just fall off the shelf and pop out the speech and then run off to the next event.
—W MITCHELL

In situations where I am going to entertain, I usually arrange not to be seen before the moment of my introduction. Such modest glamour as a television performer can project is best concentrated on the moment of appearance. If you're sitting in full view for two hours before you walk on stage, a bit of that mystique wears off. On the other hand, if I'm going to lecture—in either a serious or a humorous vein—I generally prefer to be part of the group before being introduced, since the raw material of the situation—whatever actually happens during the earlier portions of the program, the serving of the lunch or dinner—will usually provide material for jokes or philosophical observations.
—STEVE ALLEN, © 1986

Using Lecterns

My brother, R. Michael Walters, an attorney, speaks on "Dealing With Difficult People." (Who better than an attorney? Does the phrase, "it takes one…" come to mind?) Anyway, his perspective is unusual for an attorney. He says you need to revert to the oldest laws of all to deal with people—the laws of human nature. The first thing to do when you are confronted with an angry customer or irritable client is to get on the same side of the counter or table as they are. The ancient laws of human nature say that that is where a friend is. Only the enemy hides behind the barriers.

If you are comfortable enough, get out from the barriers like lecterns.[1]

---

[1]A lectern is the tall thing, usually with a microphone attached, that you put your notes on. A podium is the thing you stand on, sometimes called a "riser." Most people you deal with won't know the difference. If it's important for you to have either a lectern or a podium, send them a sketch, so there is no confusion, or write out a brief description: "please provide a 12" h by 10' w by 10' l podium (riser). No, I'm not kidding.

Get out from behind that lectern if at all possible! You may look and sound terrific, but any obstruction between you and the audience will decrease your effectiveness.
—ANITA CHEEK MILNER

The whole idea is to shorten, even eliminate, the distance between you and your audience. You want them to identify with you.
—CAPT. DAVE CAREY

Your Words Say One Thing, Your Body Another

When you are communicating about important emotional topics, or while you attempt to persuade your audience of something, your voice, gestures, postures and movements take on extreme importance.
—DR. ALBERT MEHRABIAN

Every speech class will tell you to "use gestures." Then they quote the famous Albert Mehrabian study on communication of feelings and attitudes:[2]

Modes of Communication	Percent of Message
Verbal (words)	7
Vocal use (tone, pitch, etc.)	38
Visual (body language)	55

There is no doubt Dr. Mehrabian's findings from his extensive studies are correct. Often your mouth says one thing while your body says another. People see you adjusting your clothes, picking, fiddling, and scratching, and they get distracted from your message. Then they lose confidence in you.

So, why do I feel you don't agree with this?

I agree—with qualifications. Speech coaches, like me, come up with these gems, "Everyone should use gestures." But only your own natural gestures—the kind of gestures you use when you communicate in a loving, friendly manner with people you are comfortable with and care about.

Usually, the body constricts when you are consumed with stage fright. So as coaches, we try to force you to use gestures. But when coaches do that, we're dealing with the symptom, not the problem. Your

[2]Albert Mehrabian, *Silent Messages,* Wadsworths Publishing, 1981, p. 76.

lack of natural gestures means you are thinking too much about how you look to the audience.

The audience only wants you to make them feel, know, and do things differently—better—than they did before they sat down in your audience. The only audience members counting your gestures are the ones who are not paying the slightest bit of attention to what you're talking about anyway. Using unnatural gestures is your solution to a problem that is symptomatic of your not focusing on their needs.

If your child, or someone you loved more than anyone else, came to you and said with tears and suffering in their eyes, "Please, *help me*. I'm going to be fired at work. My boss said if I could only understand that thing you teach about, I could keep my job. Please help me." I promise you would give a speech that used natural gestures, enthusiasm, passion, and compassion. Because it would come from your heart.

When you are able to let go of your worries about how great you are going to look to them and start worrying about how to help, lift, motivate, and change their actions and attitudes, the gestures will fall into place naturally.

You must make them feel you care more about them than they could ever care about themselves.
—MARY MARTIN, FAMOUS STAGE ACTRESS

Words represent your intellect. The sound, gesture and movement represent your feeling.
—PATRICIA FRIPP

Be a real person. A "persona" is often seen for what it is: a "phony" veneer.
—CHRISTOPHER HEGARTY

SPEAK RIGHT FROM THE HEART
by Stew Leonard, Jr.

One day while having lunch with a modern acting king
I asked Paul Newman his advice to my speech opening.

He said "don't listen to the 'pros' just speak right from your heart
The people in your audience will sense your humble start."

So below I wrote this poem and I hope you like its ring.
I read it to myself before my speech's opening.

You see I've heard lots of speeches to many big groups
And I've heard motivators who stir up the troops.

(Continued)

I've also heard funny speakers with hilarious jokes
And I've heard storytellers with great anecdotes.

But the one I like the best in a class so far apart
Is the one that I know, speaks right from the heart.

Some speakers are polished but seem cold as ice
Some others say nothing they're just plain and nice.

Some speakers will call you "an intelligent crew"
But don't really mean to and talk down to you.

I've seen every style, I've studied the art
And the kind I like best speaks right from the heart.

So if you're asked to speak, leave your script on the chair
Hop up onto the stage and show them you care.

Be humble and happy and speak one on one
And show them you're having a whole lot of fun.

Don't try to be clever, don't try to be smart
Instead just be natural...speak right from the heart.

(Reproduced with permission of Stew Leonard, Jr.)

But I have to do something with my hands.

Simply do with your hands what you would if talking to a member of your family. Put one hand in your jacket pocket and gesture with the other. Or—if the occasion is very informal—put them both in your pockets. Scratch your nose if it itches, make a gesture if it illustrates a story or point, or clasp both hands behind your back. It's not a big deal unless you make it one. If you're one of those rare individuals who, despite the best advice, is still faced with the what-to-do-with-my-hands problem, you might resort to the use of props. This is a trick that professional actors and actresses learn early in the game. The next time you see a play, film, or television drama, note the objects the performers touch or handle. They may employ guns, tennis rackets, pocket combs, books, eyeglasses, cigars, crocheting paraphernalia, a beer glass, a football, a coffee cup—any of the thousands of objects with which people normally come into contact. I'm naturally not suggesting that you stand on the speaker's platform with a pistol or tennis racket in your hand. But there are items you can naturally employ in the context of your assignment: typed pages, index cards, a pointer, a pen, an object you might be talking about. Some talk-show hosts hold 5 × 7 cards in their hands while conducting interviews. William F. Buckley holds a clipboard, with notes attached. It will be better if you don't have to depend on such props, but—if you feel the need, feel free."[3]
—STEVE ALLEN

[3]From *How to Make a Speech,* © 1986 by Steve Allen, McGraw-Hill, p. 67.

How Do You Handle the Audience When...

You *Don't* Know the Answers to Their Questions

Whatever you do, don't say, "Look, I don't want to cover that today." or "Sorry, we just don't have time." Inside they're thinking, "Why else are you here, if not to answer our questions?" Even if you can only do it superficially and quickly, answer their questions.

Heaven forbid it should happen that you don't know the answers to their questions, but just in case try opening the question up to the audience. You can say, "What an excellent question!" Look at the rest of the group and say, "What is your experience on that?" With luck, someone will know.

If you opened it up to the audience and still didn't get a good answer, you then need to say, "That's a very insightful question that I hadn't thought of before. Give me your business card. I'm going to research the answer, and send it to you," and do it!

> It's extremely important to respond to questions from the audience with an "I don't know but I'll check into it for you" when asked a question you can't answer.
>
> —CANDY LIGHTNER, FOUNDER MADD

They Won't Ask Any Questions

A presenter's nightmare. I gave a keynote to a group of meeting planners. The client was very specific, 20 minutes of talk, 40 minutes of Q & A. *No problem,* I thought! Famous last words. I finished with the lecture, looked out at the audience and said, "Any questions?" It was like talking to a painting. Not a query. I'm looking at 40 minutes of program with nothing prepared.

This never, ever happens to me now. To help save yourself from making the same incredibly stupid mistake I made, break up the audience into small subgroups to come up with questions. When you look at an audience and say, "Now who has any questions?," it translates into their minds as, "Who is the dumbest person in the room? The one who didn't understand what I've said perfectly—as did the majority of people sitting here." Which is, of course, the farthest thing from what you really meant, "What didn't I cover clearly? What have I left out?" So why not say that?

It is less threatening to break into small groups. Ask the group to discuss, "What questions came to mind while I was talking?[4] Please come up with three or four questions that you wish I would have covered

[4]I first heard this terrific idea from Bob Pike of Creative Training Techniques.

more clearly." After they talk among themselves, ask them to share a few of these questions with the entire audience. An added attraction of this method is that they often answer each other's questions. So by the time questions get to you, they really are very insightful.

I think you're asking for it when you ask for questions—then just stand there and stare at them. They would like an opportunity to talk anyway. So I like to break them into groups of three to four and say, "Take five minutes and talk to your neighbors about what I have said, see if you can come up with one question that, if answered, would help the audience."
                                        —Dr. Ken Blanchard

Another strategy is to plant questions. There are almost always people who come in early while you are preparing your presentation. Often they have a comment or a question they ask at that point. Ask them to help you. "That is a very interesting observation. To help me get the questions rolling during the Q&A session, would you ask that again? Most people feel uncomfortable asking questions in front of a group. It helps if someone with confidence—like you—gets them started."

OK, you're stroking their egos. They know it, you know it, but you're sincere. You really do need a leader to get the ball rolling. They'll be honored to help you.

Sometimes Rosita Perez talks to people before the presentation and asks them to help her. She gives them little cards. At the appropriate moment she'll say, "Now who had #1? Will you read it please?" Number 1 will stand up and read, "Tell us about the...." She says, "Ah yes," and she goes into it. An interesting memory technique to keep her speech in order. It also makes the audience feel very involved.

Right up front...I often will state a thought and leave it incomplete, and indicate with my hands I want them to finish it by filling in the word. They do so immediately. That sets the tone for a give and take that is automatic—and exhilarating!
                                        —Rosita Perez

*What do I do when they won't ask any questions? It happens often (I **hope** because they are spell bound). I usually make a few jokes until the first one asks a question, then the dam opens and they all start asking questions. I usually have at least a full hour of questions from my audiences.*
                                        —Jack Anderson

You Ask Them to Read Something, Then Realize They Can't Read!

One of my speakers asked someone in an audience of executives to read a rather long paragraph. After only a few seconds the speaker realized with horror, the man was almost illiterate! The entire group was trapped in the terrible feeling of "how do we get out of this?" The speaker froze, the audience froze. The only one moving was the poor man struggling desperately to slowly—and inadequately—sound out each syllable.

David Ruzek, a real estate sales trainer, says he accidentally came up with a solution. When the same scenario happened to him, he said in all honesty, "I'm sorry, I can be so rude! I should have asked if you had your reading glasses on." He looked at the others and asked, "could someone else read that please?" A volunteer picked it up, the man who couldn't read was able to save face, and they went right on with the seminar. David said he didn't realize the truth until later, when one of the others who knew the man couldn't read, came up and complimented David on his delicate handling of the situation.

If you do ask people to read something, ask for volunteers. You can never tell when you will have dyslexics, vision disabled, those with English as their second or third language, or even illiterates.

English Is Their Second or
Third Language

Even in English-speaking countries, this has become a serious issue for presenters. See the accompanying box by Marcy Huber for some tips.

---

10 TIPS FOR PRESENTING TO CROSS-CULTURAL AUDIENCES
by Marcy Huber, President of The Center of Language Training

1. **Speak slowly, simplify your language, and enunciate well, but never, never talk down to them.** Most of the people are well educated in their own language, but it may take time for them to process what they hear.

2. **Pause while speaking.** Don't be afraid of silence; Americans think they have to talk all the time, but people from other cultures are used to silence. Japanese businessmen can't understand how Americans can talk and think at the same time! (Guess what? They can't!)

3. **Idioms can be confusing.** We use so many idioms, and people whose first language is not English tend to take them literally. A woman in a seminar came up to me and said her boss asked her to "touch base" at 11:30. It was then 11:20, and she asked me if I knew where the base was. Was it inside or outside?

(Continued)

The American idiom for doing something exactly right is, "He hit the nail on the head!" The Japanese idiom is, "The nail that sticks out gets hit." (The group is more important than the individual.) The two cultures have totally opposite approaches to the same nail!

4. **Avoid idiomatic verbs.** Are you aware of how many idiomatic verbs we use in everyday communication? One workshop participant flipped open his notebook and said his boss asked him, "Will you go ahead with this project if I go over once more how to go about it?" He gave me a blank look and said, "Please translate. I know what 'go' means, but this doesn't make sense."

5. **Be aware of humor.** Humor doesn't translate well. Check with the meeting planner to find out who will be in your audience, and then try out your humor with some people from that culture first. Plays-on-words are not understood, because they are usually taken literally.

6. **Sarcasm is rarely understood.** One computer programmer told me he would *never* understand Americans. His computer had gone down the day before, and he lost half of the program he was writing. When he told his boss, she said, "Wonderful! You just made my day."

7. **Many Asian cultures are very uncomfortable with direct eye contact.** Try to pick the Americans in the audience and look at them, or look at the walls, or hold your handouts and stare at them.

8. **Often people from other cultures will show little reaction as we speak.** We feel as if we are talking to a stone wall. We have no way of knowing if we are "getting through," and may never know! Whatever happens, never, never get angry or talk down to the audience. Statements such as, "Yoohoo, is anyone out there?" are totally inappropriate, and you can be sure the audience will now "tune you out" if they were listening before.

9. **Questions to the presenter are almost impossible for people from some cultures.** They have been taught to respect authority, and you are the authority. They won't ask questions for two reasons. One, they don't want to look stupid in front of their colleagues, and two, it is conceivable that you might not know the answer, and then *you* would "lose face" or be embarrassed in front of the audience.

> If you are unsure if your message is being understood, ask people to form small groups and discuss specific points or write the information you have just presented in order of importance for them. Then, as you circulate among the groups, you will invariably find they do have questions and you can answer them in a "safe" way. Another possibility is to have cards available so they can write their questions.
>
> 10. **Be yourself. Be natural and sincere.** Your sincerity will be very evident to the audience, and will persuade them to your point of view even though they may *understand* every word you said.

You Are Speaking to an "Empty House"

I hate it when a small group is spread throughout a big house, yet you will always see six rows of empty seats in the front and people standing in the back. People just have an affliction about sitting in the front. I always try to pull them forward. I tease them with lines like, "The Lottery tickets for the Mercedes are taped under the seats on the first four rows." I cajole them when they come in late with, "these seats up front are the best in the house." Other than that, you can't let it bother.
—W Mitchell

You can actually make use of it to get sympathy for your predicament and even as raw material for a humorous approach. On one occasion, at a dinner attended by fewer than had been anticipated, I said, "I don't feel bad about the size of this audience, ladies and gentlemen, so there's no reason you should, either. Jesus Christ addressed a very small gathering at the Last Supper. And he didn't get many laughs, either, come to think of it."
—Steve Allen, © 1986

I first try to get them to move forward. Then I remind myself that the ones who did show up deserve the best that I've got and I try to give it to them.
—Jeff Slutsky, *Streetfighter Marketing*

You Want a Standing Ovation

My mother says a standing ovation always starts on the left, toward the front, then works into the rest of the audience. She looks right at that first person who stands, gestures toward them to draw the rest of the audience's notice that way and says, "Oh, thank you!" That usually gets more of them on their feet. Question number one is, do you want a standing ovation?

What? Of course you want to get a standing ovation!

I've spoken when I got them and when I didn't. (I like it a lot better when I get them!) But when it comes right down to it, ovations are not why we're there.

Mark Sanborn says that after he spoke to a management meeting in Brainerd, Minnesota, he didn't get a standing ovation, but it was one of the most rewarding experiences of his life. Flying home he wrote a poem, "I Didn't Get a Standing Ovation Today."

I DIDN'T GET A STANDING OVATION TODAY
by Mark Sanborn

I didn't get a standing ovation today
But I learned afterwards a woman in the front row with cancer
Nodded in agreement as I spoke of overcoming circumstance.

I didn't get a standing ovation a week ago
But a small group stayed late after the program.
They bought the beer and we shared great stories.

I didn't get a standing ovation a month ago,
But a manager from that program sent me a note.
He said my presentation encouraged him to keep trying.

I did get a standing ovation recently,
I gave a pretty good speech, but after the applause,
I don't remember much else that was remarkable that day.

I didn't get a standing ovation today
Instead, somehow I connected with the human spirit

You want a standing ovation?
Speak in a room with no chairs.
Otherwise remember the main reason why you're there.
        —JEFF SLUTSKY, *STREETFIGHTER MARKETING*

I don't ask for it, I don't encourage it, I don't expect it—but it happens a lot.
        —W MITCHELL

I always go for the standing ovation. A great speaker and poet showed me the greatest tip to get one. She says to the audience, "I want to do one last thing before we close. Why don't you all stand up. Put your right hand on your left shoulder, and your left hand on your right shoulder. Give yourself a hug, you are very special people. Now, go out into the world and make a difference!" They are already on their feet, you have your Standing O!
        —DR. KEN BLANCHARD

Your Standing Ovation Turns into a Dud Closing

You deliver a great presentation. You go into your big dramatic close. A thunderous standing ovation follows! Everyone is shouting and the adrenaline is pumping! You launch into the Q&A. Everyone is excited, the questions are coming along strong. Then it begins to slow down...further...further...the last question is milked out of the audience. You look at a silent crowd and say, "Is there anything else? Nothing? OK, well, nobody? Uh, OK, then let's go..." and off you shuffle.

That's what you leave them with? No, no, no! Instead, have *two* great endings. One *before* the questions and answers, then the Q&A, then you cut the Q&A off, preferably after a particularly brilliant response on your part and go into a really big humdinger close! Now you walk off the stage and back to your autograph table while they are on their feet and applauding wildly!

You Need Higher Ratings on Your Rating Sheet

On the rating sheets of all speakers, the lowest marks from the audience always seem to be on "practicality of topic," or a comparable category, like "Do you feel the topic was applicable to you?"

Audiences often have a hard time deciding how they are going to apply what you talked about to themselves. One way to help them is to first get them to decide why they are there at all. Even if they were sent by someone else, they usually have a few hopeful expectations and objectives.

Often, you ask your audience outright at the beginning of a presentation, "What are your objectives for being here?" Their minds freeze up. You need to help warm up their brains.

To start off my full-day sessions, I have them write a quick list, "If you could gain only three or four useful ideas from this seminar today, what would they be?" After they write their own ideas down, I assign a group leader and have a small group of four to six come up with an overall list that combines everyone in their small group into one master list. Now I assign each person a "report" topic from that master list. At the end of the day, they will report what they learned on that topic to the rest of us.

If you have 200 people and they came up with 20 things they want to accomplish, you assign 10 people per topic. If you have 10 people and they come up 20 topics, then each person gets two topics.

Since I started doing this, my ratings under the categories of "practical and applicable to you" have changed dramatically. You see, it makes attendees extra-sensitive to the fact that *they* must pick up as many practical tips as possible on the objective they selected.

(Have them fill in their boss's name here:)

_____

_____

_____

Dear M_____ ,

 Thank you for sending me to Lilly Walters' seminar on "Secrets of Successful Speakers." I know this was not a low-cost "economical" seminar. I appreciated the investment you have made in me.
 The things I learned that I feel I can apply to our company's needs are

_____

_____

_____

_____

_____

Thank you for sending me.

Sincerely,

Figure 10-2. A sample of the letter seminar participants can complete to get them to focus on the presentation's benefits.

 A sneaky way to force their awareness into looking for good ideas and ways to apply those ideas, is to have them write a letter to their bosses, _which you will mail!_ (See Figure 10-2.)

Isn't this risky? Won't they feel offended?

Whether they are offended depends on your attitude as you give them the instructions. If you are condescending, you bet you're going to have problems.
 This is most effective for the people who get "sent" to your presentation but don't really want to be there. If you let them know at the beginning that they will be doing this, it makes them pay much closer at-

tention. If you get stuck with this sort of group, let them know at the beginning that they have been "chosen" to go. They are the sort of person the company is willing to invest money in. It vastly changes their outlook on the presentation.

Hecklers Invade Your Presentation

I thought hecklers were only at nightclubs?

I wish. You are most likely to find hecklers in your audience if you're presenting at functions that

- Are in the evening
- Start after the audience has had a long day
- Have an "attitude adjustment hour" (translation: four martinis and pretzels)
- Serve wine or other alcohol at the dinner, and
- Serve a dinner consisting of a heavy meat, e.g., roast beef or steak, a starchy something with gravy, and a heavy dessert

Which means most presenters have a war story or two about hecklers. Luckily only one or two.

While he was with us, Dr. Kenneth McFarland was called the "Dean of Public Speaking." Once, while doing a presentation, one person in the front row was just being obnoxious. Finally Dr. McFarland said, "I can't continue. I'm sorry, but that man must be removed."

Someone came down, they took the individual out. Dr. McFarland started to go on with his speech; within 10 minutes, the entire auditorium was empty! Everybody had walked out.

The rest of the story—which Dr. McFarland didn't know—was that this man was this association's president from the year before. His wife had just died from a very long, painful, and lingering cancer. They'd been a much beloved couple within the association, and that day everybody had bought him a sympathy drink. When he was publicly embarrassed, they all individually felt "It's my fault. I did this to poor ol' _____." So they all left with him.

Father Michael Mulvaney, a speaker and counselor on self-esteem, traveled a great distance at his own expense to do a talk for a high school group. (A nightmare in itself. High school students are either the most fabulous audiences in the world, or they are hell!) That day the group seemed antsy and inattentive. One small clique in the back had a girl who was so rude that she had her back turned to Father Mulvaney as she blithely went on with her own conversation! Finally, this kind and good—but very tired and frustrated man—singled out the girl with her back to him, and in an exasperated tone said, "Look, I've traveled a long way just to be with you today. I deserve to be treated with *some* respect. You can at least give me the courtesy to turn around and look at me! You have no right to be so rude." The girl was very embarrassed and distressed to be singled out. With tears of humiliation and shame in her eyes she said, "Father, I'm so sorry! But these are our deaf students, and I was translating your talk for them." As you can imagine, he wanted to drop through a hole in the ground and never reappear.

If you single out a heckler and try to nail them to a cross—as they justly deserve for interrupting the presentation—you will be the bad guy. No matter how much the audience agrees with you that the heckler is wrong and you are right, the heckler is still a member of their peer group; you are the outsider.

What can you do when it happens to you?

Walk into the audience. Bill Wolff (a speaker on self-esteem and executive at KNX radio, a CBS station) was not being heckled, but during Bill's talk, a loud, obviously drunk person was talking to the other people around him. Not missing a beat in his talk, Bill simply walked over to the loud guy, put his hand on the man's shoulder and kept right on with his presentation. The drunk pulled out of his haze enough to realize someone else had the floor. The drunk turned to looked at Bill and listened. Then Bill casually walked back up onto the stage, never stopping his dialog. Bill said the audience all smiled. They knew what had happened and appreciated the "soft" way Bill handled it. I thought it was a stroke of genius!

Unfortunately, one minute later, the drunk was telling another loud story to his table-mates. Usually, others in your audience will lean over to obnoxious people and tell them to knock it off. In Bill's case nobody was saying a word! So Bill tried the same process again. The drunk shut up, Bill went back onto the stage. The drunk went into another story! Bill tried a third time—same result! Bill couldn't understand why the audience wasn't helping him out. He finally gave it up and just talked louder. After the talk several people came up and apologized. One said quietly in Bill's ear, "I wanted that idiot to shut up...but he's our CEO."

I turn to the people with him and say, "Is he with you?" or "Did you all come on the same bus?" That will usually get the others with the heckler to quiet him down. If that does not work, I walk off the stage, walk up to him

and say, "that's a great line, incoherent, but a great line." Over the audi-
ence's laughter, I turn off the mic and say in his ear, "you must be quiet,
you are disrupting the group." Then I smile at him and walk away. 99% of
the time it works and the audience thinks I have just been gracious.
—Tom Ogden

Have some gentle jokes ready. Gentle and clean jokes *sometimes* help. Like "Sir? Excuse me, I work alone!" "Let's play a little game. Only the person with the microphone gets to speak." "Now, now, your part doesn't have any lines."

Do not use off-color, nightclub humor to "stab" hecklers, unless you're in a nightclub. We may laugh at off-color humor in a nightclub, but if you use it in a training session or a business presentation, you are going to get criticized.

Although a gentle joke or two in your pocket is a good idea, it's not your *best* strategy.

No matter how many witty lines you have for hecklers, they can always
come back with just one more..."Oh yeah!"
—Joey Bishop

Teach the meeting planner how to help you. This is my favorite strategy. But be very careful in the way you request help. They don't want to think that you have a negative picture of them. Always tell the planners it is very unlikely to happen in *their* group. Explain to the planner, "In the very unlikely event that someone might be a tiny bit silly at your banquet tonight, I need you to be prepared to help me. Just be ready to go to the heckler and say, 'you have a message' or 'you have a phone call.' Please get them out of the room and deal with it outside."

Usually I let them rant until the crowd boos them down. I always try to an-
swer the heckler seriously-when I can. But, if they are too abusive, I answer
lightly with a joke like, "you have the right to remain silent."
—Jack Anderson

Don't mistake a legitimate skeptic for a heckler. The way you handle your-
self is more important than how you handle the heckler. Be fair. Be firm, and
end the heckling quickly. For example, "It's obvious you and I see things
very differently. I can live with that! And I hope you can too!"
—Christopher Hegarty

Polite and respectful with everyone—no matter what—that's the order of
the day.
—Capt. Dave Carey

Ask the heckler to identify himself and his company. They usually prefer to
be anonymous.
—Judi Moreo

Don't argue with hecklers. (1) Ignore them, (2) laugh with 'em, (3) laugh at 'em, (4) let the audience handle them.
—ED FOREMAN

Don't ever talk back to a heckler…look away and talk to some other part of the audience…and Keep Going.
—IRA HAYES

You can only be heckled if you believe more in the heckler than you do in yourself.
—HERMINE HILTON

Humor heals the heckler.
—GERALD C. MEYERS

If the heckler is a two year old, break the group into pairs to discuss some aspect of your talk. Go up to the caretaker of the child and ask him or her to assist you with something—where others won't be able to hear your discussion. Then ask the person to take the child out. But show them how much you are concerned that they will miss the talk. Offer to call them to personally discuss their issues. Or offer a gift of a tape of the talk, a copy of your notes from the day, whatever.

It is very touchy dealing with babies. You can come across as cold and un-caring. If it becomes annoying ask a committee or staff person to offer as-sistance to the lady by taking the baby out of the room. The mother wants to listen to your presentation also.
—FLORENCE LITTAUER

The "Stars" in Your Audience Think They Know More Than You Do!

These "stars" seem to sneak into many audiences. Whatever you say, they have a *witty* thought to add…a *small* correction…an *interesting* anecdote…at least in their eyes. If you ask them to "knock it off," it will lessen your authority and your *pathos* with the group. If you allow them to keep on, you may need to rent the room for an extra day.

It's not just the disruption of my agenda, it's what happens in my mind…es-pecially if they are making some pretty good points!

I understand! You think, "Oh, Great! The whole audience thinks this person knows more than I do!" All right, stay in control. Focus on the audience. If the information is good, rejoice. After all, you are there to help them get this sort of information.

But if it is pulling the presentation to far out of the pattern you need for your message, try some of Terry Paulson's ideas. Terry once had a whole week with a star in his seminar. He said it was enough to drive anyone crazy.

Terry says it is important that you don't embarrass these stars. When you realize you've got a problem with one, he suggests you move the whole group into a quick five-minute exercise and take that person aside. First, thank him or her for participating. Explain, "It is a delight to get people who participate as wholeheartedly as you do. However, when there is an obvious leader, *like you*, the others just sit back and are content to let you lead. I need to find ways to bring them out of their shells, and get involved. So, when I notice that they are retreating again, I'm going to give you a secret hand signal, which will be your cue to hold in any comment. Eventually they will get involved. I appreciate your help. Between the two of us, we will be able to get them learning." Terry is able to bring the person onto his team, a win-win.

Terry has another suggestion. These types are blurters. When you ask the group for feedback, they always beat the rest to the punch and blurt out their comments, which tends to shut the rest of the group down. Instead, Terry combats this by asking the entire group to write down two ideas. Then he calls on specific people he noticed writing but who had not yet participated as much as the others. He always goes up to the "stars" at the breaks and gives them the chance to talk and tell *their* stories. It's how they learn, and Terry is there for everyone.

> *You always get a few who think they know more than you do. I ask them, in a fun way, if they would like to do the session for me. Another way to handle them is to walk out right where they are sitting and do the rest of your talk right there, or with your back to them.*
> —Dr. Ken Blanchard

Your Joke or Story Bombs!

Now, this may never have happened to you. You may want to just pass over this section! No? Have a few bombs under your belt? Don't feel bad. Speakers who say they have never had a story or joke fail are telling you a whopper—or they've had a frontal lobotomy and wouldn't know if the joke fell flat or not.

You're looking out at an audience, waiting for a laugh. You get the old familiar feeling of I could just leave now, they'll never notice I'm gone. Don't despair, I think it's a fantastic opportunity for one of the best laughs of your presentation.

You see, you are looking at them thinking, "I'd rather be dead than standing here looking at an audience who isn't laughing when they are supposed to." They are looking at you thinking, "we were supposed to laugh there, weren't we? Oh dear, it was funny. I was just about to laugh, but nobody else did and I'd feel silly laughing by myself. But look at that guy, he is dying up there, I'm so glad I'm not him!" Their emotional discomfort level is rising at just about the same dramatic speed as yours.

Emotion is a power, use it! You will get a fantastic laugh if you follow it up with a good old-fashioned, time-tested comeback, "saver" line. I know several speakers who purposely set up these situations to ensure that second great laugh. Some of my humorists and entertainers use these savers:

- Jerry Winnick, motivational comedian and writer for Johnny Carson and other TV comedy, says he waits for a laugh, and if it doesn't come he looks at the audience with a quizzical expression and says, "You know, you people have marvelous self-control!"

- Al Lampkin, entertainer and speaker, tries, "I've got 12 more rotten lines like that. I can wait...."

- If no one is laughing, Dale Irvin, a comedian, actor, and writer, will say, "Excuse me, but some of these I do just for me." If only one person seems to be laughing at the joke, Dale uses, "Excuse me, would you mind running around the room, so it sounds like everyone is enjoying this?"

- Ken Blanchard sometimes will look at the audience and say, "Well...my mother really, really enjoyed that one."

I have heard others over the years use, "I've got a book for sale out in the lobby, explaining all these. You may want to pick up a copy on your way out." You can look at someone in the audience that everybody else knows and say, "John, that is the very last time I use your material!"

Humor is very personal. You may have read some of the lines above and thought, "This is dumb, I could never say that!" and you'd be absolutely right. If it feels good, use it. Listen to good humorists and nightclub entertainers, write down the great lines they have, then use what feels funny for you.

On the other hand, many top presenters say they would never use a save line. So, there you have it! If it feels right to you, use it.

When my joke or story "bombs"? I just pretend I was perfectly serious, go right on to the next point, and let them wonder.
—JACK ANDERSON

No matter what happens with hecklers, bad lights, poor mikes, small attendance, the Golden Rule of Professional Speakers is: You are not responsible ***for*** *the behavior of your audience. You are only responsible* ***to*** *them!*
—BILL GOVE

*There are all kinds of tricks to learn to help prevent problems. But the right strategy will come to you at the right time if you try to have "A passion for your topic and a **compassion** for your audience."*
—LILLY WALTERS

Working with Hostile or Irritable Audiences

Don't worry if your audience walks out on you during your talk, start worrying when they start walking toward you.
—AL LAMPKIN

Hostility isn't all bad.

Excuse me?

Figure 10-3.

Hostility is a power. It is much easier to redirect power than to create it. You are actually better off with a hostile, angry crowd than you are with an apathetic one.

But redirect you must. Anger is a low brain function. People don't think or reason well at that level. It's your job as a presenter—an ethical presenter—to pull listeners into a higher brain function so they can clearly think about the issue and make a rational decision about your proposed solution.

Many great orators have used the "angry mob" mentality to push their audiences into action. God willing, no one like that has picked up this book. For the rest of you who want to *redirect* their negativity, here are a few tips.

> *A good speaker is a good listener who hears what lesser speakers fail to.*
> —SOMERS WHITE

Psychologists and psychiatrists tell us about a common problem. Their patients fall in love with them. You thought that was a joke? Nope. It is called the *transference syndrome*. In very simple terms it means when you give someone the opportunity to talk from the heart, and you just listen to them, they fall in love with you. Simple as that. We are so hungry for someone to just listen to us with understanding and without criticism of us, that we transfer our love to them when we finally get it.

When you are faced with an audience that is hostile, try to find ways to give your listeners the opportunity to talk about themselves. Group sessions where they come up with solutions to whatever made them angry can be very effective.

> *Great ideas, it has been said, come into the world as gently as doves. Perhaps, then, if we listen attentively, we shall hear amid the uproar of empires and nations a faint flutter of wings, the gentle stirring of life and hope.*
> —ALBERT CAMUS

It is easiest to feel anyone's mood by listening. It is hard to use your listening skills while you are speaking, but there are ways you can listen and talk.

Watch the audience, feel their presence while you talk. When I'm giving sessions of over 30 minutes, I have them do a group exercise within the first five minutes. It's my time to watch and listen. There will always be some people who just sit there. They won't open the workbook, they don't follow the exercise instructions. Their body language screams at you, "I don't need this. These other people might, but I'm *much* too superior for this silly stuff." Invariably you will get several of these who sit close together. You will also see the ones who eagerly open the workbooks and smile at each other.

At the break, try to move the people around. Break up the groups of grumps, try to seat them next to the eager ones. Hopefully they will spread some of their enthusiasm and the negativity will be distilled.

You can dissipate some of that "I don't need to be here" anger if you let audience members know at the beginning that they have been "chosen" to attend. They are the sort of "superior" person the company is willing to invest money in.

I was talking to a group once, I was getting no energy back from them. So I stopped the talk and said, "Let me give you a little feedback, who cut off your nerve endings? I feel like I'm doing all the work. Something is going on here. Is there anybody willing to share what is going on here?" They told me they were forced to go to these seminars every year and nothing ever happened to them, they were just a waste of time as far as they were concerned, they would rather be back at work. So I told them to go back to work. "There is no point in being here if you can't focus in." A few went back. But the rest who stayed were ready to learn, or at least shocked into giving me a chance.

Warren Earhart had a great saying—"Life which you resist, persists." If something is bothering you and you don't deal with it, it does not go away, you just gunney sack it. But it prevents you from taking in new stuff. The same is true for your audience members.

When I work with government groups I say, "Look, before we get started I want to take about 10 minutes and break you into groups. Let's play 'Ain't It Awful!' I want you to tell me all the things that are awful about being in the government that I ought to know." You see, they are all sitting there bitching about me, "he doesn't know about us," "he doesn't understand our problems."

John Jones—a wonderful trainer—has a wonderful statement, "When in doubt, confront. When all else fails, try honesty." So first try perhaps, "what's going on here?" to confront the issue. If that doesn't work try honestly telling them how you feel, "I'm feeling very uncomfortable."
—DR. KEN BLANCHARD

Start Your Persuasion from Their Side of the Argument

Find out what troubles them and sympathize, show them some sincere compassion. No matter what the topic, you can usually find *something* you can agree with. Start there. If they think you are on their side, they start to relax, which puts them in a higher brain function. Now they can be rational in their assessments of your position.

Shakespeare uses this technique in *Julius Caesar*. In that famous speech, when Mark Antony gives the eulogy over Caesar's body, the crowd is very hostile. They are glad Caesar is dead. They are hostile because they think Mark Antony is going to tell them they should be ashamed to be happy over Caesar's death, which, of course, is what Mark Antony wants them to feel.

First, he feels out the crowd. "Gentle Romans!" he exclaims. He gets booed down. The seed is not taking root because the ground is not yet fertile. He tries some fertilizer. He assesses the situation, he realizes the crowd is angry.

He tries again. This time starting with a point they can accept: *"Friends, Romans, country men, lend me your ears. I come to bury Caesar, not to praise him!"*

This takes root. Now they are listening. He tells them that Caesar was an ambitious man, and it must be so, because Brutus said so, and Brutus is an honorable man. They agree with him. They start to relax, which makes them go into a higher brain function.

Antony now seems to be agreeing with them when he explains that because Caesar put money into the treasury and brought all that wonderful wealth back for the citizens of Rome, it must prove he was rotten and ambitious. After all, Brutus said so, and Brutus is an honorable man.

Mark Antony started off agreeing with the angry, hostile audience, then slowly he fed in his own concepts. Finally, the crowd realizes the truth of the situation and turns on Brutus.

Once you sincerely and believably agree with the people in a hostile crowd, they have no reason to fight. Their anger begins to diffuse and they start to listen to your message. Anger is a place of very low level brain function. You need to move them to a higher brain level if they are to make decisions that are lasting.

> *Probe until you find their stumbling blocks—then use these to build a bridge to bring them to your side.*
> —HATTIE HILL-STORKS

Try not to disagree with them on anything unless they are so far away from your personal belief system that you can't find even the tiniest bit of truth to agree on. I was giving a "Front Line Customer Service" seminar in South Africa. One of the steps in dealing with any conflict is to agree with, in this case, the unhappy customer. One Indian man in the front row seemed very upset and uncomfortable. I stopped the seminar, looked at him, smiled and said, "Tell me what I need to explain better."

He responded with a heavy accent, "I cannot find agreement with your statement, 'always agree with your angry customer.' Sometimes when they are returning things to our auto parts store they try to say it is my fault, that I ordered the wrong part. But I have not ordered the wrong thing, I have their order form in their handwriting."

I replied. "I understand. But if you want to avoid the conflict, you need to try and find *something* in all their ranting you can agree on. That makes them relax. Then you can go on and solve the problem."

He shook his head and looked down, even more uncomfortable, "You do not understand my situation." Remembering my own advice about not disagreeing with my audience, I said, "OK, you be the customer, I'll be you. Show me what happens."

I thought he would just role play from his seat where he could feel "safe." But he stood up. He looked down so long I thought I had really made a mistake in starting this. Suddenly he looked right at me and said in a loud angry voice, "You stupid _____! You have ordered the wrong part! Your people never get anything right. Only a store as bad as this one would hire a stupid _____."

This was one of those times that time stood still for me. Here I was, an upper middle-class California girl. The worse prejudice I ever had to cope with was whether my car was as nice as my neighbor's. I'm doing a seminar far away from my home and understanding, giving Pollyanna advice to a man who is facing a problem I can't even comprehend. I thought, what amazing gall I have to even attempt to teach someone with this kind of problem.

I remember feeling tears come to my eyes. I just told him what feelings came into my heart, "People who say these things to you are in terrible pain. The hate they have for themselves must be unbearable. Can you imagine saying something like that—even to someone you don't like? The only way words like that can come out of anyone's mouth is when they are so miserable and unhappy they can't think well.

"Think what you would do if a physically or mentally handicapped person fell down on the street, and you helped him up. You wouldn't think twice about hostile, angry words he might use as you helped him up. You would know his mind is just hurt. That would communicate more loudly than his words to you.

"Think of these hostile people that come into your store like that. Then you can hear those same painful words and find that tiny bit of truth you can agree with.

"How about saying, 'Sir you are right. Our company does feel stupid anytime we have allowed a valued customer like you to be unhappy.'"

He came up to me after the seminar and hugged me with tears in *his* eyes. I guess it was the right thing to say. I had never given that advice before to anyone or said any of those words. As Mom says, "sometimes you are just a conduit."

Again, try not to disagree. Instead find some bit of truth you can agree on.

When should you disagree?

Try to win others to your point of view by finding common ground for agreement. As the old maxim goes, "You catch more flies with sugar than you do with vinegar." But there will come a time when you need to take a stand. As soon as you say, "No, I do not, will not, and cannot agree," you have drawn the battle line—which you may win. But if the *war* was about winning this person over to your side, you win the battle and lose the war.

This breaking point is usually much further down the line than we are ready to admit. We usually let our pride jump in our way too early, rather than waiting until a true ethics and integrity issue is at stake.

Before you get ready to draw the line and flat-out disagree, ask yourself, "have I really gotten to the point where my integrity is an issue here? Or is my pride at issue because someone does not agree with my point of view?" If the answer is your pride, try to give in and just agree to disagree with them.

But, when the time comes that you are being asked to bend your honor, ethics, or integrity, go ahead and draw the line. If you are giving a talk, you are voicing your opinion. Opinions, by their nature, are arguable. Sometime, somewhere, you are just going to have to offend somebody. It's fate.

> *If you find they have a differing point of view from yours—and they let you know it during the speech, you can still be gracious. Once, when the host was apologizing afterwards over a few of the audience members loud disagreements, I said, "Don't give the matter another thought. I appreciate your invitation because I get a little tired of talking to people who already agree with me. It's more interesting to address people with other points of view."*
>
> *You might also, for example, say something like "Now, I know a number of you here this evening differ with me on this particular point, but I very much appreciate your having invited me to speak to you about the matter, because it gives me the opportunity to explain why I feel as I do."*
>
> *If you say something of that sort, in a cordial tone, the majority of your audience will show you the courtesy of at least listening. Don't expect that everyone present will be converted to your position on the spot, but at least you have the opportunity to engage in reasonable dialogue, one of the distinguishing marks of a civilized society.*
> —Steve Allen, © 1986

Life is about different perceptions. Because you disagree, it does not mean they, or you, are wrong.
—Dr. Ken Blanchard

If the Audience Just Doesn't Care

If they're apathetic, quickly state the benefits in the first few sentences of your talk. It may take some creative digging on your part to find benefits in a seemingly hostile situation.

If you are asked to present on "Executive Parking Lot Maintenance" to the nonexecutives of a company, you can bet they won't care much

about your topic. Their attitude is going to be low. Find out what benefits there are in "Executive Parking Lot Maintenance" for the nonexecutives. State them quickly in the first few minutes. Now you have them
listening.

*All people care about something. A speaker's job is to connect what they
care about to your topic.*
—HATTIE HILL-STORKS

Save the Audience and You from
Getting Dragged Down
by the Hostiles

Don't play to the grumps, play to those who are having a good time.
Emotions are contagious. Play to the emotion you want to encourage.

Now correct me if I'm wrong. Do you normally look at the person
that's sitting in the back of the room, sighing in boredom and looking at
his watch? Do you think, "If I can just get to that one person...."

As you look into the faces in your audience, you will get replenished
or depleted. Just like dropping your bucket into a well. But 2 percent of
every audience is looking for a reason to get ticked off at somebody and
are going to snatch your bucket and keep it down there in those dismal
depths!

Find the person in the audience who is obviously having a good time.
There is always going to be 2 percent of the audience who thinks you are
horrid, but there is also 2 percent who thinks you're fantastic[5]—and it
won't really matter what you say. (These statistics hold *fairly* firm as
long as you are *fairly* competent.)

Don't play to the 2 percent of the people who think you are horrid.
Play to the people who just think you're great. As you're playing to
those excited people, their emotions start to circulate. Pretty soon the
hostile people are looking at everybody else who is having a good time
and they start to think, "That must be funny. Didn't make any sense to
me, but must be good stuff!"

*Try to play to the people in the crowd who are sober, the drunks will think
you were great no matter what you did. (Actually the drunks won't really
remember your talk at all, but they don't want anyone else to know they
don't.)*
—TOM OGDEN

---

[5]I have paraphrased this a great deal from a statement made by one of the executives of
CareerTrack, one of the largest seminar companies in the world. They survey the literally
thousands of attendees who go through their seminars to find out what they liked and dis-
liked the best. They found that about 2 percent of any audience didn't like the presenter,
regardless. Two percent liked the presenter, regardless.

Get Trouble Makers on Your Side before Your Presentation

If you suspect from your preprogram analysis that you may have trouble, find those people in the audience who are the "leaders" of the hostility and interview them ahead of your presentation. The ones who are hostile are either the ones in the back of the room muttering under their breath to their neighbors, "this is garbage, I can't believe this idiot" or they sit in the front row like a hungry panther, tail twitching. You're just sure the minute you take a deep breath they are going to spring for your jugular!

If you interview them ahead of the event, you will get great ideas on compromises and strategies to help them. Then you can start off the presentation by quickly saying "You know, Ron (the trouble maker you interviewed) came up with some great ideas...." Since Ron is one of their leaders they immediately relax and listen. Ron is sitting, not in the very front ready to pounce, not in the back, but right in the middle. He turns to his neighbor and says, "About time they got somebody in here who knows what they're talking about!"

> *Look for people in the back of the room who don't look like they even want to be there. Go up to them before your talk, introduce yourself with a smile, and ask for their input. Use some of their input in the first ten minutes, and watch those potential enemies beam with pride and growing support for your program. You will seldom win people over from a distance; you will do better by getting them involved.*
> —TERRY L. PAULSON, PH.D.

Transfer the Angry Crowd's Hostility

Humankind loves to rise up and fight, if we have a bad guy to fight against, a scapegoat. Unfortunately, we are all too easily swayed by this technique, not always for the good: throughout history, for example, demagogues have used this technique to serve their cause. But it doesn't make the *strategy* bad because it was used by bad people. If you use it, do better. For example, in the battle against smallpox, doctors used their skills to motivate an entire world to rise up and conquer smallpox. The only smallpox left in the world is in two vials in a laboratory.

> *While it would no doubt be better for the world if you could always truly instruct and enlighten your audiences, the fact is that you will often get more applause and cheers by appealing to their passions and prejudices— sometimes, sadly, even their hatreds.*
> —STEVE ALLEN, © 1986

Use Humor to Turn Their Minds from Anger

Try to get an angry crowd to laugh at whatever has gotten them upset. If the entire audience is all on the same side of an issue, you are in luck. Get out your ethnic joke books (the ones with the jokes you should normally never ever use!). Redo the joke so that the "ethnic" issue in the joke gets changed to the issue the audience is "upset" about. Instead of, "Two Jews walked into a bar," you try, "Two corporate analysts walked into the lunch room at _____." They're very willing to laugh at that. Once you get them laughing, they are no longer in the low brain function area.

During the presidential debates between Reagan and Mondale, Reagan came up with a classic line. One of his speech coaches, Roger Ailes (author of *You Are the Message—Secrets of the Master Communicator,* Dow-Jones Irwin, 1988) knew the other side was bound to bring up the age issue. He helped Reagan with a terrific comeback. Sure enough, the inevitable question came up. Did Reagan feel "the age issue was going to be a problem"?

He confidently replied, "I want you to know that I will not make age an issue of this campaign. I am not going to exploit—for political purposes—my opponent's youth and inexperience."

Many agree the campaign was won from that comment on.

> *Humor at the beginning is a good tool to stay likeable with a hostile group. I had one classic example: I spoke for the American Trial Lawyers. I had just written a column blasting lawyers, as you can guess, the group was hostile. One lawyer had circulated a flyer that quoted my column with their conclusion that I was trying to put them out of business. I started right off by holding up the flyer and saying, "I see my appearance here has already been advertised," which got a nervous but genuine laugh. Then I said, "Someone says in this that I'm trying to put trial lawyers out of business. Not true, my son is a trial lawyer...so there's at least one I'm not trying to put out of business." This got a little more laughter. Now we were able to go on with the talk and they listened reasonably and luckily liked what I had to say.*
> —JACK ANDERSON

> *Always review the material for negative references.*
> —RALPH ARCHBOLD

> *Never pick on ethnic groups or individuals.*
> —PHILIP CROSBY

Answer Questions

Too often, when I see a speaker face a hostile audience, someone will interrupt and say, "I have a question!" The speaker replies with, "You

know, I'm not sure we will have time for questions, but if we do, I'll
make sure to get back to you."

Bad call. The whole audience just said to themselves, "Liar! The
speaker is avoiding the issue." You may have every intention of getting
back to that question, but they won't believe you.

You are there to serve their needs. If you find yourself in the undesir-
able position of facing a hostile group, try to allow time for them to vent
their questions. If you don't, they will brood on their unvoiced questions rather than your comments. When they ask a question you do not
want to answer try the following.

> *Just give an answer that actually answers another question. Answer about*
> *something on a closely related topic you are comfortable talking about.*
> —JACK ANDERSON

Keep the Angry Audience Members
Talking Whenever You Can

You can turn a dull person into an interesting one by finding their area
of interest. My best friend Melodie and I took her four-year-old niece,
Miranda, to Marineland. Miranda is a beautiful, doll-like child. But she
was so quiet I secretly thought she must have some kind of learning dis-
order. At one point we were watching the big killer whale show with
Orkey and Corkey. I wasn't sure if she had enjoyed anything up to that
point. Whenever we questioned her, "Are you having a good time
honey?" she just nodded.

Well, Orkey and Corkey came flying up out of the water to do the famous "get the crowd wet" scene. Unfortunately, we were among the
lucky members to be baptized. We and lovely little Miranda in her
pretty lace dress—which she had been so careful of all day—got soaked.

Melodie and I looked at each other and grimaced. "We're in big trouble now," we communicated by face language. But as I might have expected, not a word from Miranda.

A few hours later, after a fun—but quiet—adventure at Marineland,
we were settled in the car on our way home. "Well sweetie," I asked, not
expecting an answer by now, "did you have a good time? You got a little wet today, didn't you?"

"The bad boy whale got my dress wet!" came a loud little voice!
Melodie and I looked at each other in shock, a full sentence!

Hoping to draw her out, I asked "Are you sure it was the boy?"

"Yes. Boys are messy. The nice lady whale didn't get me wet. My
brother Jason is never good 'bout keeping his room clean, like me. He
gets dirty in the yard when we play and once he got all wet in the sprin-
klers. So it must have been the boy. The walrus wasn't as big as the

whale, but he waved at me, he didn't get my dress wet...." She never stopped the whole way home. We just hadn't asked the *right* question.

When you develop interactive sessions for a group that is potentially hostile, design it with lots of opportunity for them to talk. It gives them a chance to diffuse some of that anger and hopefully get some constructive ideas to handle the "problem."

Arrange interviews ahead of your presentation to determine what questions will keep them talking. Think of the right questions that will get them talking about the problem and, more important, the solution.

MORE "SECRETS" ABOUT STEP 10: TOOLS TO DELIVER THE SPEECH AND BUILD RAPPORT WITH YOUR AUDIENCE (TILL THE SOIL)

Speak to every person in the audience, even when you can't see them. Take the time to bring the hostile element over to your side.

When I'm losing them I sometimes try, "You're such a great audience, I'm going to do something special—entirely different than I normally do." They wake up and pay attention. I go right on and do what I always do. However, they don't know that.
—Tom Ogden

Ask the audience for some help in regard to something you appear to have forgotten.
—Coach John Wooden

Do things that challenge and "shake up" the audience so they "feel the need" to change. For example, walk into the audience and ask, "How many of you are above average in intelligence?" Many hands will go up. Then ask, "How many of you are above average in how to think, how to be truly ingenious?" Almost no hands will go up. Ask those people who did raise their hands to the second question to stand up for a test and most often no one stands up. Now they "feel the need" to learn how to think.
—Christopher Hegarty

Don't pontificate, lecture or speak! Do discuss—intrigue—excite—arouse—challenge.
—Gerald C. Meyers

The most important thing to remember in any program is first to flatter your audience. If you do that at the beginning, you're home free.
—Letitia Baldrige, international corporate
etiquette expert

How do I customize? By doing my homework about the audience. Reading their newsletters, memorizing names. A client wrote about a talk I did for them: "Calling people by name and recognizing them from photos in our magazine awed everyone!"
—ROSITA PEREZ

Don't talk down to them. Direct stupid things to yourself, not them.
—IRA HAYES

Step 11

Avoiding the Problems and Pitfalls of the Platform

_____*Protect It All from Wilt*

Remember the Boy Scout motto: Be prepared.
—COL. GENE HARRISON, RET.

In growing your tree, you **start with a seed**—a mission you are passionate, compassionate, and purposeful about; **find fertile soil**—the right place to plant it; you get over your own fears—**plant it in the ground; you sink your roots down deep**—you become a credible expert; **you grow a single trunk**—an easily remembered theme; you form **no more than three or four strong boughs**—the points you want them to remember; you **decorate the tree with leaves of brilliant colors**—your image and voice; you **call listeners to pick**—get them to walk up the five levels of listen, understand, believe, retain, and do; and you **till the soil**—enhance your delivery and build rapport with the audience.

Now let's talk about some tips, ideas and strategies to keep the whole thing from wilting. Prevent those nasty little problems when Murphy

comes in to plague us—like when you forget your talk, the building
burns down, or the critics attack you.

*Take care of the arrangements or they'll take care of you—in ways you wish
they hadn't. Being ready is the mark of a professional—that means yourself,
your presentation and the arrangements. It's entertaining to watch
Murphy zap a careless presenter, but it's embarrassing and frequently
costly if the zapee is ourselves.*
—Tom Leech

*My case is perhaps unique in that I use such mistakes and accidents to get
laughs. Even a serious speaker, however, can do the same. If, let's say, you
happen to trip walking across the stage or coming up the steps to the platform, you might quip, "I had an interesting trip coming here tonight, but
not as interesting as the one I had just now." If your notes blow off the
lectern, the microphone falls off the stage, or something of the sort, you
might say, "A few years ago there was reference to one prominent public
speaker who—it was said—couldn't chew gum and talk at the same time.
Well, I've just discovered I can't give a speech and handle my notes at the
same time."*

*In such circumstances you don't have to be as witty as Voltaire or Mark
Twain to get a sympathetic response from your audience.*
—Steve Allen, © 1986

It's Show Time! Staging Your Presentation

Wouldn't it be wonderful if everyone who built hotels would actually
come to a few presentations and see the problems presenters face? To be
fair, the new hotels are trying to get it right. Trying, not always suc-
ceeding.

It always seems that if you put your screen over there, where they
have designed the room for it to sit, some big column will be in the way.
Or, if you use that great expensive screen that comes down out of the
ceiling with a flick of a button, the audience will be looking at the
screen, but also at a mirrored wall right behind and to both sides of the
screen. Which of course reflects the lights from the projector right back
into their eyes. And if you put the lectern where they had it in mind to
go from the layout of the room, the audience will be looking into cur-
tainless windows behind the lectern and right into the setting sun.

Think of your presentation as a production, a play. In a play the audience never gets the feeling that anything is going on except the fantasy being created in front of them. They are transported into the
"drama," nothing else is noticed.

But there is a crew back stage, a director, and a production manager creating a beehive of activity. The mood off stage is in vast contrast to the lazy scene occurring on stage. When actors calmly walk off stage, in formal dinner attire, they might have only 10 seconds to reappear in bathing suits for the next scene. Costume people are standing in the wings as the actors casually exit stage left. One rips the clothing off an actor as another is putting the new costume on. Within seconds the change is made and the actor calmly reappears on stage.

The magic of the theater, and of a master presenter, comes because the audience never knows about the staging you do to create a magic experience for them. As a presenter, you are the actor, the director, and usually the crew. The audience must always have the feeling—from you—that it's effortless. It's as if by magic the lights go on and off, screens come down. Your planning and preparation should be so extensive that all their concentration will focus on your message, just as it does in good theater.

Be the first person in the meeting room. Check out everything before the audience starts to arrive.
—IRA HAYES

Bruce Springsteen always did his own microphone checks and arrived hours early at the venue. Don't be a prima-donna. Roll up your sleeves and check things out ahead of time.
—DANIELLE KENNEDY, M.A.

I've worked with and for many of the legendary entertainers. Each one of them prepares religiously for each performance. They check the lighting, the sound, the stage, the theater...anything that will have to do with their performance.
—GENE PERRET

Ideal Room Setup

Every book on presenting and meeting planning will spend time on classic room setups. I promised you a different prospective in this book, so I'm only going to give you a few points the others tend to miss. If you need more, try Tom Leech's excellent book, *How to Prepare, Stage, and Deliver Winning Presentations* (AMACOM, 1982).

When you are trying to decide on the ideal room setup, stand in the back of the room and imagine yourself talking to your audience. Decide what room setup will allow you to have the most direct contact with your listeners.

When you're looking at the audience, you've got no problem. But what are they looking at? Are you in front of a screen that is active? This has the same great effect as if you stood up in the movie theater and faced the audiences while the picture was still going.

The night before, test the entire room setup. If you don't like it, check with the host of the event, then change it. Don't wait until 5 minutes before the event to inform the meeting planner you don't think it will work.

Always send your preferred seating chart to meeting planners before the event. That way they can call you with problems (like it messes up the schedule for the rest of the day for the other presenters). Then you can work out an alternative. Always bring an extra copy of the room setup to the venue. Murphy loves to help the meeting planner forget it back at the office.

If you're comfortable enough, don't hide behind a lectern. If you need a lectern to rest your notes on, put it slightly off to the side so you can actually move up closer to the people. Go to whatever part of the room you have decided will be the front. Walk around, pretending to give your talk. Put your notes where it takes the least amount of effort for you to glance at them. If that means moving the lectern to a weird location, or adding something extra in the room, do it! (Before the presentation!)

If you are using an overhead, try to get a projector with a switch on your side. One that allows you to turn it off without leaning across the machine.

There are many ways to set up a room. I like the setups in Figure 11-1 for interactive sessions that are 2 hours or longer. It allows the audience to talk to each other, without having their backs to me. It is also just different enough from the "normal" setups that it helps to get them interested quicker. (At least that's my theory!) Round tables can also be used for these setups, but leave the side of the table closest to the presenter open. However, you may find that the people on each side of this "blank spot" toward the presenter are so far away from each other they have a difficult time speaking to each other across the table.

> *The wrong room setup will sabotage my best efforts. Only I know just how the room must be set up to work for me. I am in the room the night before to check. If it's not right, and all else fails, I do it myself.*
> —ROSITA PEREZ

Lighting

Where do the lights in the room shine? Will the lighting illuminate you, but leave any screens you use dark enough to see?

> *I'm amazed at how many ballrooms have no stage lighting, and no one planning the event has thought to change the available lights around to shine on their own stage instead of on the plants in the corner. I think the planner really loses by not planning the lighting.*
> —W MITCHELL

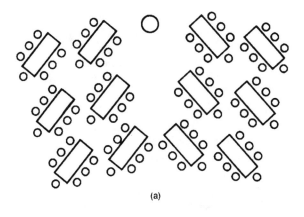

(a)

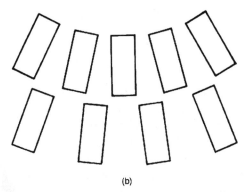

(b)

Figure 11-1. Two types of room arrangements for interactive sessions of two hours or longer.

If you are doing a presentation for a large group, you will need to get a spotlight. A necessary evil. I find them terribly uncomfortable and they don't allow me to see into the eyes of my audience. I try to get them to lift the house lights whenever possible so we can all see each other.

If the spotlights shine in your eyes, you are in the right place.
                                                        —ALAN J. PARISSE

What to Do When the Building Burns Down Around You and the Audience Members Have Heart Attacks

What foolishness! What are the chances of anything like that happening?

Actually not very high. However, the fire that devastated the MGM Grand in Las Vegas burned faster than a person could run. I have stayed at hotels that report up to eight medical emergencies per day. One of those emergencies could easily be in your audience. You are in a privileged position. The audience will look to you for leadership. Have an emergency procedure in mind.

Always find out where all the closest fire exits are to your room. Actually walk down them to the street. When I was presenting in Africa, we had a fire exit right in my meeting room. When I went through it, I could only go about 20 feet before I was stopped by a door with a huge chain and padlocks. I asked the manager how we were supposed to get out in case of a fire. "Oh, we don't have fires here. We are more worried about terrorists bringing bombs in, so we padlock these exits." (Not terribly reassuring.) At my insistence, he showed me an alternate route out for us, just in case.

Ask someone at the hotel or venue how they want you to handle medical emergencies. "Just call us, we'll get the paramedics." Great. Where is the closest phone to your meeting room? Assign someone in your group to help you, someone whom you have also informed where the nearest phone is and the procedures to follow in an emergency. That leaves you free to handle the audience while someone else gets help.

When an emergency is over, you must acknowledge it to defuse it. Humor is a nice way to relax them again, if you can find a way to use it. In the story I told you earlier about Colonel Chuck Scott and the fire alarms going off in his speech in Boston, he concluded that emergency by saying, "I know a humorist who was giving a speech in Cincinnati. He had a guy *die* of a heart attack right in the middle of his talk. Being a humorist he was almost glad about it, 'cause now he can go around the country saying, 'I really killed 'em in Cincinnati!' I'm very glad I can't say 'I burned 'em up in Boston.'"

Emergencies are spontaneous...so am I!
—Jack Anderson

One night, I think it was in Chattanooga, a pigeon disturbed me and the audience by flying around the meeting room. Finally a big husky guy opened the window. I said, "Let's all concentrate on that pigeon. He is subject to positive thinking, and he will go out that window." He sure did! I then made a few light remarks. This big husky guy I knew to be the Chief of Police. I said, "If the Chief of Police can't get that pigeon under control, I'll miss my guess! He handles crooks and criminals, he should be able to handle this little pigeon! But maybe we should let this bird stay. He just wants to get in here because of the speech I'm delivering tonight. Seems everybody wants to improve their mind with Positive Thinking these days!"
—Dr. Norman Vincent Peale

Staging Your Entrance

Being in a wheelchair, sometimes my greatest staging problem is just getting up on the stage!
—W MITCHELL

When you come up to the lectern, enter boldly. Give the feeling of excitement and enthusiasm for this audience.

Stop, look, and listen, before you start to speak. Take a moment and read the audience, and what they need. This pause also gains their attention.

I was sitting at the head table, there were a thousand people in the audience of an association. Someone gets up to give his little annual update. He's had the whole thing written out, like three pages worth. He goes up there and the first thing he does is rearrange the podium for about ten seconds, get his notes neat and all that type of stuff, which I think is damn rude. Personally, I don't think you should keep people waiting for you. You should be sort of waving almost saying, "Thank you for inviting me" before you get to the microphone.
—STEW LEONARD, JR.

You will ordinarily receive a smattering of polite applause when you are introduced. You are fortunate if it lasts as long as it takes to walk from your chair to the microphone or lectern. Whether you are totally unknown or a figure of world prominence, you always feel a bit disconcerted if the applause stops before you reach your target area. Walking those last few seconds in silence does little to inflate your confidence, so don't dawdle.
—STEVE ALLEN, © 1986

When you walk to the podium, remember to take yourself along. That's the natural, energetic, forceful you that got you there, not a wooden imitation.
—TOM LEECH

Working with Introducers

You are waiting just off stage. The announcer says, more or less, "Our presenter today has done this and that and that other thing. Please help me welcome...." The announcer smiles at you, you walk in.

So far, so good. Now what? The introducer is wondering, *where do I go now?* He takes a half step toward you. You stop to let him pass. He stops, confused. You move slightly to the left, uh no, the right, oops, you bump into each other. The introducer quickly reaches back to pick up the introduction he left on the lectern, then pulls quickly away as he sees you reach for the lectern at the same time.

Sound familiar? Lesson: Rehearse with the introducer ahead of the event. For some introducers, reading your introduction in public is the scariest thing they have ever done. Send your prewritten introduction to the introducer ahead of the event. Then carry an extra copy with you (Murphy's

Law). Add instructions at the bottom of the introduction. Consider using the "Psalm" form that Winston Churchill used when he read his speeches (Figure 11-2). It makes it simple for introducers.

"I give the introducer a written introduction and ask them not to vary from it. Before the talk I ask the introducer to go over the introduction with me. (I want to see the introduction they have in their hands and make sure it's mine!) I always carry an extra copy with me if they don't have one. Even, if they made up their own, I encourage them to use mine. This can be delicate. First, I praise the one they have written themselves, and tell them how much I appreciate the effort they have put into it. I explain that this introduction (giving them mine) has been tested over several hundred speeches and makes my talk more effective and impactful as it doesn't give anything away I'm going to say in my talk. It also gives them information I won't be talking about. Although I would never push it to the limit and insist—it's their show after all is said and done and I'm their employee—they always use mine.
—W MITCHELL

Let your introducer build your credentials by listing educational and professional accomplishments, but avoid the oversell. The content and style of your message should be the ultimate test of your expertise. In fact, once you let others build you up, learn how to take some air out of your own balloon by making fun of yourself. Only confident people are capable of taking their jobs and accomplishments seriously, but themselves lightly. There is an added benefit to early humble pie; there is usually 10–20 percent of the audience that love proving that experts don't know it all. By admitting that early, you end their game before it even gets started.
—TERRY L. PAULSON, PH.D.

I tell people, "Please don't read a big long introduction, my Mother wrote the one you have."
An introduction is supposed to energize the audience, not put them to sleep. Once I had an introducer go on for 20 minutes before I got up—and he was terrible! I laughingly got up and said, "I'm glad I got a chance to talk to you before the break!"
You are good to sit down with the introducer and ask what he has in mind. If it looks like they are going to read some big long thing, give them some quick funny story to say instead. Or ask them to just say, "Here's Ken Blanchard."
—DR. KEN BLANCHARD

Never give an introducer "risky" material that requires comic timing. I also keep it as short as possible. I find no one cares what I did yesterday, they only want to know how good I am today.
—TOM OGDEN

Design your introduction so it is very easy to read. (See Figure 11-2 for a sample.) Use big type and only 5 to 8 words per line. Try to keep it all on one page, one side. Keep it short! Most people are barely listening to the introduction anyway, they want you to get up there and start educating and entertaining them.

Today Lilly Walters, international lecture agent,
  will give us some tips and techniques
of professional speakers

Lilly Walters is the Executive Director
  of Walters International Speakers Bureau,
a professional lecture agency
  with a database of 18,000
speakers and seminar leaders.

She is author of
  ...The book *Secrets of Successful Speakers*
published by McGraw-Hill
  ...and coauthor of the book *Speak and Grow Rich* published by Prentice Hall,
  ...and coauthor of the video training program,
Games Presenters Play.

  Today, we will learn strategies and tips
for our presentations, speeches, and training sessions
  to help get our points across
with the same motivation, captivation, and persuasion
  as professional speakers.

  Help me welcome
Lilly Walters!

After you introduce me, please...

- Turn to face the direction I am coming from and start applauding
- Wait for me at the lectern
- Leave the introduction on the lectern
- Hold out your hand, get ready to greet me at the lectern by shaking my hand
- After we shake, walk in front of me and leave the platform

Thank you for your help in setting the mood of excellence and professionalism that your group is so well known for.

Figure 11-2. Sample of a prepared introduction.

When Your Microphone Acts Up

I want to share some lines you can use to handle your microphone disasters. Memorize the cover-lines you can see yourself using. Then take the time to prepare and practice some of your own.

- Stare cautiously to the left while listening to the microphone buzz; pause and blink your eyes slowly. Then say in hushed concerned tones, "Whatever it is, it's getting closer!"
- "Is this microphone mating season or something?"
- "You know, I'm actually starting to like it."
- When it goes completely silent, say, "How many of you in the back of the room read lips?"
- "1 was going to talk about the myth of perfection, but I guess I've already taken care of that."
- "OK you win!" (looking up as if talking to the sound) "Microphone, you take the parts; I'll take melody."
- "Obviously, someone in the control room has already heard me before."
- "Seriously, most of you know where I was going anyway. While I fix this, go ahead without me."
- Get down on your knees and pray, lifting the microphone to the heavens as for a blessing. "All right God, I'll change the subject!"
- Facing the microphone, say "Prepare to die."
- "These are not tears you see—my eyes are sweating."

Then there are the generics for any cover-up situation:

- "Is this Candid Camera?"
- "Some days you're the bug; some days the windshield."
- "After this program, please keep the razor blades away from me for an hour."
- "This life is a test. It is only a test. If it had been a real life, I would have been given instructions on where to go and what to do."
- "Just my luck—the light at the end of the tunnel was a locomotive."
- "The ability to be cool under fire is such a great skill. I wish I had it."
- Pull out a small retake clapboard from behind the podium and clap together saying, "Cut! Take two!"

As you can see, humor can be a great ally for a frustrated speaker and a concerned audience. No matter what the disaster, you too can prepare to make a hit with a miss.

I've shared what you can say, now let's look at what to avoid. It's tempting in the middle of a microphone disaster to deflect blame to any target you can find. When in pain, we want to find someone to blame. Some speakers rail at the audio people, others glare at the meeting planner or logistics team. Still others pout before the audience in a personalized version of "Poor me!" Avoid the blame frame!

Use your positive energy to pull your audience to you as your support team works to correct the problem. The audio team already feels bad enough; don't add to it. You want them putting their energy into fixing the problem not getting even with you for making them look bad. The pros in any leadership role take more than their share of the blame and less than their share of the credit.

Learn an important lesson early—never blame people from the platform, even if you must confront them privately later. Remember, everyone makes mistakes and some staging problems are no one's fault! They just happened!

Excerpted from "Microphone Man" © reprinted with permission, Terry L. Paulson, Ph.D., CSP, CPAE, psychologist and professional speaker.

Since the government has been caught more than once eavesdropping on me, I like to say, "It's nice to speak into a microphone you can actually see!"
—JACK ANDERSON

Keeping on Schedule and on Track

The classic mark of a beginner is running over the time limit. In case the person preceding you runs over, ask the planner how they want the situation dealt with. You may find your 90-minute presentation cut down to 20 because of a lack of professionalism of the part of the other presenters during the day.

Whenever you are about to begin a talk later than originally scheduled, ask the event coordinator when they now need you to finish, then do it! They may want to postpone the event after you, or they may need you to cut yours short. You don't know their priorities.
—TOM OGDEN

As a timing tip, if you wear a watch, consider wearing it with the face on the inside of your wrist. Try it the normal way and discretely try to check out what time it is. Hard isn't it? Now try it on the inside, you give a discrete glance at your wrist and nobody knows!

How to Stay on Your Topic

Ever realize, 15 minutes too late, that because you allowed yourself to get off the planned agenda, you now don't have time to cover the good stuff you really wanted to cover? It's so easy to blame your audiences. You've only yourself to blame.

I find that people get started down the wrong path for three main reasons.

1. **You don't have clear objectives.** If you develop your mission, a theme to support the mission, and the three or four main points to support the mission, you won't have any problems.

2. **You're not well-prepared.** Rehearse, rehearse, rehearse.

3. **You get irrelevant questions.** You will get asked questions that are totally off the mark. When it happens to me, my first reaction is to say something sarcastic, a fatal error! Luckily, I *usually* manage to bite back my sarcastic retorts. The most brilliant response of successful speakers when they are asked irrelevant questions is to do these two things:

- Answer the question with respect and compassion for your audience. Remember, the audience is your customer. Treat your listeners with care.

- Tie the seemingly irrelevant question back into your topic.

As an example, I'm giving an hour speech on "Speak and Grow Rich," the topic of one of my books. I stop 45 minutes into the speech to get the questions rolling. Some nice woman asks, "Why don't speakers today emphasize the importance of good eating habits in their speeches?"

I looked at her thinking, "why do these people show up in *my* seminars?" My gut reaction was to say, "What on earth does that have to do with my topic?" But, no, no, no, that's not compassionate. Just in time I remember my own advice. Instead I said, "You are right. If speakers could spend a few moments of their time stressing health to their listeners, the world might be a healthier place today." I smiled, quickly turned away from her toward the other side of the room, looked at someone else who I had noticed earlier had their hand up, and said, "Yes, you had a question?"

> When I get pulled off the topic on another tangent, I look at the audience and say, "Now what was I telling you?" they pull me back on track.
>
> **—W MITCHELL**

How Much Time
Will Your Talk Take?

There is only one way to know. Give the talk in a room by yourself and time it.

Prepare twice as much material as you will need to deliver. That's so you are truly an expert on the topic. However, when you are timing it, allow at least 25 percent more time than you think you are going to need. Everything takes longer than you think it will.

> *There are factors in speaking before a live audience that are not present when you time your speech in private. Nervousness may cause you to change your pace, or you may be interrupted—by applause if you are very fortunate, or by heckling if you are not. Even if nothing of this sort happens, very few people are able to estimate time accurately in the absence of such clues as sunrises or sunsets. Even if you are fairly good at it, your modest ability will almost certainly evaporate once you begin a speech which requires you to concentrate on what you're saying and how you're saying it.*
> —STEVE ALLEN, © 1986

Other Time Issues

When your time is cut short at the last minute (and if it hasn't been yet, trust me, it will!), remember the following:

- The professional keeps to schedule

- Make it a point to edit the prepared talk down or quickly write a new one that meets as many of their wants and needs as possible in whatever time is allowed.

- Turn the lemons into lemonade. Say something positive about the situation. Don't say, "I know you are disappointed." Instead, let them tell you later they were disappointed they couldn't have more of you.

> *When time is short, cut a point in its entirety, not just the elaboration. Would you rather eat four scrawny, bony ribs or two with a little meat on 'em?*
> —DIANNA BOOHER

Should you go under the time limit?

> *No one ever complains about a speech being too short!*
> —IRA HAYES

> *One night I was speaking in Portland, Oregon. The meeting promoter said, "Now Norman, this is an important meeting. You've got a big crowd out there. You've got to talk for one hour—sixty minutes—no less! They've paid $20 to get in, and they want their money's worth." I said, "You mean*

quantity will satisfy them, not quality? I've never spoken an hour in my life!" He said, "You've got to speak an hour tonight, no less will be acceptable." Well, I pushed it up to fifty minutes, and walked off the stage. He said, "Boy, you knocked 'em cold! You're wonderful! You gave 'em an hour's talk!" I never told him different!
—DR. NORMAN VINCENT PEALE

Professional speakers often get their talks cut short to make up for the unprofessionals who don't know how to deliver a talk in the time limit.

Entertainers, however, often get asked to "just fill in for an extra 30 minutes." Always prepare for extra, just in case.

The Freeze Factor

What to do when you forget your talk...while you're talking! Don't panic, it happens to just about everyone.

*Easy for you to say, "don't panic!" Panic is **why** I lost my place. I panicked, then I got more confused, which made me panic more, which made my mind even blanker, which....*

I know, I know, I've been there. Here are two tips to help.

Find Something You Do Remember and Just Start Talking About It

When a door closes to you—like your mind is doing on the bit of information you are searching for—go to a window. Just go in another direction. Take any action you can think of and start forward again. Once you do, the block around the information you originally wanted will dissolve and you can go back to it.

I sometimes sing for various events. I often open Celebrity Polo Night at the Los Angeles Equestrian Center with the National Anthem. As I was waiting in the technician's booth for the event to open, I heard Sylvester Stallone, Cloris Leechman, and Jonathan Winters were in the audience that night. I panicked. I could not remember past, "Oh say can you see, by the dawn's early light." My mind was a big blank. The more I thought, the bigger the blank spot got. The two men in the technician's booth had no idea, "Doesn't it go something like 'Oh beautiful for spacious skies'?" "Thanks guys, wrong song." Luckily there was a phone right in the booth and I did the most soothing thing in the world, "Daddy! Help! What are the words...?" He very calmly told them to me.

Having Dad tell me the words again helped. But I'd never really forgotten the words, I was just blocking them. Taking an alternative forward action I could handle—dialing the phone—brought me back in control.

Captain Dave Carey is a wonderful speaker who was a POW in Vietnam for 5½ years. He was tortured often. He says the way to regain control of your mind when it has retreated—as his would do after the Vietnamese would have another go at him—is to grab on to anything you *can* remember. As he was lying on the floor of his cell in a pool of his own blood, hands chained behind him, nothing would come into his mind and stay long enough for him to hold on to. He was desperately trying to remember the lies he had just told the interrogator. But that door was closed. Finally, a window opened, a line emerged and he grabbed it: "Yea though I walk...." He concentrated with all his might on that. Before long another line came along and he could put the two together: "Yea though I walk through the valley of the shadow of death," then the whole verse flooded into his mind:

> I shall fear no evil, for Thou art with me;
> Thy rod and Thy staff, they comfort me.
> Thou preparest a table before me
> in the presence of mine enemies
> Thou anointest my head with oil;
> My cup runneth over.[1]

If it happens to you (not being tortured by the Vietnamese, but going "blank" on the platform), grab on to anything that you do remember. Once in control of something, more will come back. Even if you need to recite some silly poem, just make up an excuse to your audience afterward, "I'll bet you're wondering how that applies to our program today? It doesn't! I just wanted to make sure you were paying attention."

Keep a General Audience Participation Game at the Ready

Get them into a simple audience participation game. A favorite one of mine that is always in my mind is "gather together into groups of three. Discuss which ideas you have learned in the past hour that are most applicable to your work, and how you will use them next week." They will be contented discussing that quite awhile. It will give you time to calm down, look at your notes, and regroup.

I just stutter, stammer, hem an' haw, then take a drink of water. That way I can just blame my forgetfulness on nature!
—Jack Anderson

Forget? I never forget my talk! What was your question?
—Tom Ogden

[1]"Psalm 23," *Old Testament.*

How to Memorize Your Material

Tape yourself giving the speech. Write it out perfectly, the way you hope in your wildest fantasies you will give it. Tape yourself reading it. Then replay the tape over and over—in your car, while you fall asleep, while you are taking a shower. There is something about your own voice talking that makes memorization easier.

Remember also about acronyms and acrostics (see Step 3); in developing a simple memory tool for your audience, you will find you won't forget the material either!

Should you memorize your material?

> *I do not memorize. I find that memorizing takes my attention off of the audience and on to my words. I want to watch the people, connect with them just the way I would if I was talking to each person one-on-one. Would you ever memorize a heart-felt conversation with a loved one?*
> —DANIELLE KENNEDY, M.A.

> *You'll never guess what I'm going to tell you to do if you choose to memorize your speech completely: Don't deliver it exactly as memorized. The remembered form will be in your mind, obviously enough. It's just that it should not become a rigid prison restricting your imagination but should, rather, serve as a strong basis from which you may creatively depart.*
> —STEVE ALLEN, © 1986

Using Food to Create Mood

When you can, try to take control of the type of food your listeners will consume while attending your seminar. Many theorize that foods are directly responsible for a lack of retention.

A study done at the University of Sussex in England showed that heavy intake of food (over 1000 calories) caused inevitable losses of visual perception and reaction time and an afternoon slump occurred. Large meals draw blood away from the brain down to the stomach for digestion.

Some of these ideas may work in your sessions:

- **Feed them three meals.** Because blood sugar drops while they sleep, you need to boost it with breakfast or else drowsiness occurs. Proteins, carbohydrates, and low fats, about 500 to 600 calories, keep them "up" longer.

- **Caffeine.** Wakes them up. Caffeine is addictive—there will be lots of addicts in your audience that need their fix. Keep caffeine available all day—coffee, tea, colas.

- **Fill the mental slumps with food.** Midmorning and midafternoon are the usual mental slump periods for your listeners. Give them a mental and physical breather by doing something unexpected with food. Popcorn is unusual at a meeting, inexpensive, and, if you leave all the butter off, good for you.

- **At breaks.** Avoid pastries which will slow them down. Try chewy rather than filling foods: Peanuts, dried fruit, and sunflower seeds, yogurt, granola, raisins, fruit kabobs, colorful fruit cups, blueberries, strawberries, oranges, grapes. Try mineral water and juices instead of just coffee and tea.

- **Get them moving at lunch.** Get their blood circulating again. Have them do a team-building exercise that takes them on a short hike throughout the building. Serve lunch at a fair distance from the meeting room so they can take a nice brisk walk.
  Get them moving at lunch. If you can have the lunch moved farther away, it gets a little more adrenaline to get there, burns off a few calories, and makes them more attentive when they get back.

- **Serve lunch late.** About 1 o'clock, this makes the afternoon, when they are most tired, shorter.

- **Fighting alcohol.** Alcohol acts as a sedative, dulling the mind and blocking its ability to process information. Heavy alcohol is not being served much at meetings and seminars any more. More often light wine and nonalcoholic drinks are served. High-fat, protein, starch, and B-vitamin snacks such as cheese and crackers help attendees metabolize the alcohol. Drinking makes listeners even more thirsty. Serve tall cool glasses of water with lime or lemon slices close to the bar. They will grab these instead of a second alcoholic drink.

- **Stress relievers.** Physical and mental stress harm the body tissues. High-quality proteins and food rich in vitamin C help relieve the stress.

The following are some meal tips:

- Low-fat, low-calorie, high-protein meals are best. Try broiled, baked, barbecued, or boiled (Not fried.) Trim meats of all fats.

- Serve broth-based soups and avoid chowders and cream-based soups.

- Serve green rather than potato and macaroni salads, which have mayonnaise base that is high in fat.

- Serve the entree on a 9-inch dinner plate so it looks like they are getting more.

What can you eat and drink before a presentation? Everyone's body and reactions to food are different. Make sure you know yours before you go up to present. Here are a few general suggestions.

- Avoid gassy drinks. Belching in front of your audience isn't a good power look. This means no sodas.

- Alcohol? Of course not. You owe your audience every ounce of your best concentration power.

- Coffee? Tea? Unfortunately, they are both diuretics. If you're going to be up there for more than 45 to 60 minutes, you may be asking for problems with Mother Nature and her calls.

- So that leaves you with water. *Bon appetit!*

Deciding what to eat before a presentation is harder. Metabolisms vary greatly. My mother, after 25 years on the platform, still can't eat before a presentation. She says she feels like a runner about to do a marathon, she needs an empty stomach. Usually heavy foods are going to make you more sluggish. But if you're the kind of person who runs extra high and tense emotionally, you may want to try some of the foods that slow you down.

Whatever you decide to eat or drink, use moderation. If you feel terribly hungry or thirsty before you perform, it's probably your nerves. Deal with those first, then try the food or water.

Helpful Tip: Avoid Caffeine*
by Steve Allen

Unless I am overtired, I generally will drink no more than a half cup of coffee if I am scheduled to speak at the close of a dinner program. The reason is that extra adrenaline is already flowing when you're getting ready to perform and the addition of a jolt of caffeine can sometimes make you jumpy for purely chemical reasons, even if you weren't before. Although I'm not the nervous type, I once had what was, for me, a strong case of stage fright; every night for a week while performing at a Las Vegas nightclub. I finally figured out the reason. Because I was tired from overwork at the time, I had gotten into the habit of drinking one or two Cokes or Pepsis before going on stage, for extra energy. It was the caffeine that was making me nervous, not my professional assignment. I switched to no-caffeine beverages—orange soda, root beer, etc.—and the problem vanished.

*Reprinted with permission from *How to Make a Speech,* © 1986, McGraw-Hill Book Company.

When You Notice Misspelled Words in Your Materials

You are happily giving your speech, when suddenly you notice on the overhead you just put up a blatant misspelling. You can be very calm and hope nobody else notices it—after all you missed it the 20 times you proofed the miserable thing!

Or, you can do what Tom Faranda told me he does on occasion. He turns to the audience and says, "To make sure you are paying close attention today, we have hidden many typographical errors throughout the materials, both on the overheads and in the workbook. Each time you see one, *don't tell your neighbor*, just write it down, clearly stating exactly where you found it. Whoever finds the most gets a prize!" (The prize is a copy of his book. This is quite clever as it gives him an opportunity to promote his book in a very subtle way.)

What a great idea! You just hired a room full of cheerful proofreaders at almost no charge!

Keep Calm When Problems Hit

The people who plan a meeting or event have a ton of worries on their mind. Even if you are a mediocre speaker, they will be more than pleased with you if you keep calm when the problems hit. Need more chairs? Go get them. Need another light bulb? Go find the janitor. Be a fixer, not a creator of problems.

My number one rule is don't complain to meeting planners. I make a gentle suggestion to fix staging problems, but I never make an issue of it.
—W Mitchell

If something goes wrong, grin and rise above it—better than a tantrum.
—Hope Mihalap

When it all starts to tumble —KEEP ON GOING! Who's got the power up there anyway?
—Suzie Humphreys

Sincerity is the key. If you are UNFAILINGLY sincere—GENUINELY sincere, then problems and pitfalls merely become situations that endear you to your audience.
—Harvey Diamond

Deal calmly and respectfully with everyone. It's not so much what you say, but how you as a person handle your life and these sometimes potentially embarrassing situations. Use them to assist you in making your point.
—Terry Cole-Whittaker

We Started with You,
We Finish with You
Invest in Yourself

This book is the beginning of a quest. Quests are a journey, not a destination. Keep learning.

> *The only true security in life comes from knowing that every single day you are improving yourself in some way.*
> —ANTHONY ROBBINS

> *The best guarantee that you will be perceived as an expert is for you to be one by continuing to learn and read in your area of expertise. Experts who are done learning are seldom listened to, no matter what their credentials.*
> —TERRY L. PAULSON, PH.D.

> *Success is not a doorway, it's a stairway.*
> —DOTTIE WALTERS

Ethics

If you talk the talk, learn to walk the talk. If you're talking about alcoholism, you'd better not bill your clients for any alcohol or drink in front of them, ever.

That's not fair! A drink once a month hardly constitutes alcoholism.

I understand. But as I discussed in Step 8, you are judged *very unfairly* when you decide to be a presenter. If you decide to talk the talk, then walk the talk. If you don't, it's going to be transparent when you get up there on the platform.

I should say, *try* to walk the talk. I don't know anybody that makes it all the time. Tom Miller, speaker and author of *The Unfair Advantage,* asked an audience of professional speakers how they would feel about having a video camera crew follow them around for the two weeks prior to their next presentation. A video would be prepared with the "highlights" and shown to the presenter's next audience. Every one of us looked terrified. The speaker on "communication" was thinking about how she lost her temper only the day before and screamed at her kids like a fish wife. The person on "personal development" was thinking about the tears she cried the week before because she felt unloved and unliked.

Walking the talk is a quest you enter on when you decide to seriously work on being a good presenter. A quest you may never fulfill, but then that's what quests are about—the striving, not necessarily the arriving.

For I might misunderstand you and the high advice you give,
But there's no misunderstanding how you act and how you live.
—EDGAR A. GUEST, *SERMONS WE SEE*, 1881

As for ethics, I'd say err in favor of being too careful!
—HOPE MIHALAP

In case of doubt, do a little more than you have to do.
—W MITCHELL

Thomas Paine expressed it best: "Reputation is what men and women think about us; Character is what God and angels know of us." I concentrate on character. Reputation follows. I know that ethics in this business consists of many mini-decisions and mini-moments. To the extent that someone else is quoted and not given credit—or we deliver less than promised—we eventually lose our soul and spirit along the way. People "in the know" will turn us off immediately when they hear the uncredited "borrowed" phrase and know we do not own it. The erosion is slow, but the end result can be devastating when our colleagues, who may recognize our talents, look upon us with the disdain reserved for someone who is not a credit to the profession. When we "do the right thing" instead of what is expedient or will serve us best at the moment, eventually, that is recognized, too. The most important aspect of all this ultimately is not what they know or think, but what I know and think.
—ROSITA PEREZ

When it comes to ethics it all begins in the heart.
If your heart is right, all else will be also.
—RALPH ARCHBOLD

You can have a beer with client after the speech, or glass of wine the night before if they are serving. But if drinking can cause a bit of problem for you, you need to realize you are there to do business, you are not there to be at a party. If you don't keep yourself in a business mind set, you are going to get into trouble and perhaps miss some future opportunities.
—W MITCHELL

When the Critics Get You Down

They won't all love you. Even if you motivate, captivate, and change lives, you will still be criticized. It will drive you insane if you try to make all the changes they suggest. Look at their advice from a distance. Measure it against where you are trying to take your audiences. If you follow their advice, will it get the audience there with greater clarity and power? Then do it.

Listen and evaluate, but stay detached. Some people live to be critical. If your ideas are different from someone else's, you are going to get criticized. Don't let it bother you. It's a critic's job to be critical.

There is an adage in the theater world—if you listen to the good reviews, you have to listen to bad ones. Destructive bad reviews are hurtful, and should be dismissed. Constructive bad reviews need to be looked at carefully.

—TOM OGDEN

A drama critic is a man who leaves no turn unstoned.

—GEORGE BERNARD SHAW

It's amazing how you can go through 100 evaluations and two will say you were a real jerk—you can feel all your energy go out. Most of us grew up in environments where we had no history of dealing with praise. We were always caught at doing things wrong rather than doing things right. So now as speakers we turn all our focus to those two people who didn't like us. Even though I talk about it, I do it myself. It's a constant battle. But at least I can catch myself at it now and laugh. Now I try to take the top 10 percent and the bottom 10 percent and throw them out. I worry about the in between. "...you can't please all of the people all of the time."

—DR. KEN BLANCHARD

Arrogance

Arrogance is the disease that makes you an "ugly" speaker.

Arrogance is God's gift to shallow people.

—DENIS WAITLEY

Once I keynoted the National Speakers Association Annual Convention in Dallas. I got all the forms back with the comments: "you were the greatest," "we loved you," "give him a 100," they went on and on. Then I got two: "Why do you move around the platform so much?" and the other said, "no meat." I kept those two to remind me that the reality of speaking is—no matter how good you are, how smart, how perfect you create that moment up there, you are just not going to make everyone happy. Somebody in the audience is not going to find that what you have to say is what they are looking for—at least not that night. As much applause as I get, I need to remember I'm no different than the people in my audience. I'm a wonderful speaker. I'm not a wonderful writer or painter. And it's OK that I realize that I have a talent up there on the platform. But I keep those rating sheets around to remind me that I don't have it all figured out for everybody in the audience.

—W MITCHELL

We are in an industry whose practitioners are often called, motivational, fabulous, awe-inspiring, egotistical, arrogant, and difficult to get along with.

And are we?

All of the above...sometimes. If you decide to tackle the challenge and take the platform, you have a right to feel pride. I think we are called arrogant and difficult because the pressure of the challenge makes us a little crazy.

It is easy to get caught up in the glitter and glamour of the platform and forget the caring and sharing. For the most part, when speakers put on the facade of arrogance, it's because we get scared. We realize we didn't lift and inspire, teach and change, the way we wanted to that day. So we put up a false bravado. Inside, we know the truth.

When I am honest with myself and to others about the pain I feel when I don't do a good job, I am much more attractive. Charles "Tremendous" Jones, a wonderful motivational speaker, tells a story of a young city minister who goes out into the country to give a sermon. The man is excited. These country folk are in for a treat, they will never have heard the like of his message! He swaggers up the steps into the pulpit and lets loose! After a while he realizes he is in trouble, they aren't responding in the right places! They don't laugh at his great lines! He tries harder— nothing works. When he is finally done, he hangs his head and quietly walks off the dais. An old man puts his hand out and whispers in the young man's ear, "Son, if you'd gone up there the way you'd come down, you could have come down the way you'd gone up."

When I get overblown with my own importance my wife has a pin handy.
—JACK ANDERSON

Take your talk seriously, but don't take yourself seriously.
—SOMERS WHITE

The artistic temperament is a disease that afflicts amateurs.
—G. K. CHESTERTON, 1874

I often say at the end of my speech, "I hope you don't think you wish you were as good as Ken Blanchard"—I wish I was that good too! You teach what you need to learn. I was learning a lot while I was talking today. I appreciate your being here listening to me talk to myself.
—DR. KEN BLANCHARD

Imposter Syndrome

There is no more potent leverage in shaping human behavior than identity. We all will act consistently with our view of who we truly are, whether that view is accurate or not.
—ANTHONY ROBBINS

On the surface, people who get into speaking seem very confident and self-assured. We are often teased about having the largest egos in the world. No doubt they are the largest, but they are also the most fragile.

That big smile fades as the last attendee leaves the room and we dive for the rating sheets. Ninety nine out of 100 in the audience may have said, "Great talk! Learned a lot!" "Can't wait to hear her/him again!" Then one says, "This was totally useless. No good information at all." We don't even see the other 99 ratings. For us, that person who was in a rotten mood is all that matters.

Are you that way too? You are not alone. Many of my friends in the speaking industry carry these fears of just being an imposter. "I don't have anything new or unusual to say!" "Tom Peters does it better!" "They can get this out of any book, they won't want to hear it from me!"

Audiences do want to hear you. Typically, my books sell for under $30, the tape album sells for $89, but the people who come to my seminar will pay $299. People learn more and like it better when they can hear it in person.

But I don't have anything new to say!

Do you remember who said, "If you dream it, you can achieve it!" You're thinking Norman Vincent Peale? Actually it is also attributed to Marcus Aurelius, a Roman. I just bet Marcus picked it up from some ancient Babylonian.

You don't have anything new to say? "Dress the old words new." Give credit when it's due. Then touch their hearts. They will reprocess your new version of the old words and apply it to their current problems.

Just last year I was attending a seminar and I was overcome with the meaning and power behind the speaker's message—"Always tell the truth." I have never been very deceitful or dishonest, and the concept is one I have heard all my life, but suddenly the speaker's words blossomed into something that was beautiful and wonderful in my heart. Something I could use to make my journey more joyous.

Your concepts may be old, but *you* are new to your audience.

So my best is dressing old words new.
—SHAKESPEARE, *SONNETS*

I am not a teacher: only a fellow-traveller of whom you asked the way. I pointed ahead—
ahead of myself as well as of you.
—GEORGE BERNARD SHAW, *GETTING MARRIED*

Like a link in the chain from the past to the future....
—ALAN AND MARILYN BERGMAN, FROM THE MOVIE, *YENTL*

Your Presentation Worksheet

- What are you passionate to talk about?
- What topic creates a great compassion in you for your listeners?
- In one sentence, what is the purpose or mission of a specific presentation you want to work on?
- Who wants to hear it?
- If you have no choice in picking the audience or topic, how can you analyze this audience to find their wants, needs, attitudes, and capabilities?
- Once you have made an educated guess about the audience's attitude, will you need to design the presentation using more benefits or humor?
- Are you prepared? What will it take in rehearsal and study to ensure you will not have stage fright and a fear of making changes in your presentation?
- Are you an expert in the topic area you will present on? What else must you do so you will view yourself as a credible expert?
- What overall theme will you use to substantiate your mission?
- What three or four main points must your listeners take home?

1. _____

2. _____

3. _____

4. _____

Do these three or four points meet the four step BAIR test of *b*enefit oriented, *a*dequate, *i*ndependent, *r*elevant?

- How will you organize the material, what format do you like? Analogies? Story telling? Problem, cause, solution? Or any other format?

- What mood does the meeting planner wish to be created with this meeting? Fun? Serious and educational? A special dress theme?

- What image do you want to create of yourself?

- Combining the color of the room, the mood of the event, with the image you wish to project of yourself, what should you wear?

- What title have you given to your presentation?

- What can you do to ensure your listeners will listen?

- What can you do to ensure your listeners will understand?

- What can you do to ensure your listeners will believe?

- What can you do to ensure your listeners will retain?

- What can you do to ensure your listeners will "do"?

- What else can you do to ensure you will have a rapport with your audience?

- Have you checked over the checklist we gave you (see following) so you can make sure you won't have any "warstories" of your own?

Checklist to Save Your Presentation from Disaster

Long Before You Arrive

Get it in writing! All arrangements, agreements, fees, etc. How, when and to whom to make payment.

Take copies. Take copies of your correspondence and the contract with you in your briefcase or purse. If your meeting planner has been fired, you may have been replaced, without notice. Be ready with proof.

Who pays for workbooks, handouts? Will pencils, pads, etc., be paid for by the hotel, the planner, or the presenter?

Who will set the materials out and pay for the labor costs? The hotel, the planner, or the presenter?

Get a deposit in advance. For overseas programs, get full payment in advance.

Who will pick you up at the airport? Have their home and work phone numbers and another emergency number. Be sure to take this information with you in your briefcase, not in your suitcase.

Pack what you absolutely must have with you as a carry on. There are only two kinds of luggage, carry-on and lost!

Dress appropriately for this group. Check with the planner. The theme of the whole convention may be "Western," but you may be speaking at a formal banquet. The presenter should always look businesslike and professional. Plan to dress slightly better dressed than the audience, yet not be out of place. Never dress "down." Look successful, elegant, not "loud" or ostentatious.

Carry a kit of emergency supplies. Tape, scissors, extension cords, chalk.

The mind can only accept what the seat will endure. Find out what is on the program in the 3 hours before and after your presentation. Will the crowd need a stretch or bathroom break before you can begin? Will people slip out before you are finished, because they have another event in a different location? Work with the meeting planner in advance on the flow of the meeting. A receptive audience is easier to give the best you have to offer. Make suggestions on breaks to the planner to help make the meeting a success.

Are you speaking with a meal? Let the planner know it's not effective to have catering serve or clear while the presentation is in progress. Often the planner will forget to inform catering of this ahead of the event.

Tell catering to stop all activities when your program starts. Ask permission of your planner, tell them they will need to plan to stop clearing even if they are not finished yet.

Double-check all details before you leave home. Call your client no more than 4 days before the event to confirm everything. You will be amazed that even the state and date can be different and nobody has let you know. One presenter arrived at the right place and time but the wrong year. Another arrived at the hotel only to be told the meeting (out of country) had been cancelled. Always confirm. Double-check the location of event, addresses, phone numbers at the site, etc. Get a map. Find out about alternate transportation in case the person who is to pick you up does not show up.

Bring props with you. The meeting planner has 1000 details to attend to. Don't ask for difficult or hard to get props. If they must be there, design your presentation in such a way that you carry them on the plane with you.

Who is the contact person when you arrive on site? Where will that person be located? Often the main planner assigns someone else the task of "presenter-sitting" you once you arrive.

Send a copy of your introduction. The planner or the introducer usually wants to practice before the event.

Plan how many assistants you need. Let the planner know. Contact the assistants if needed before you arrive to set up a rehearsal time.

Which room will you be in? Where will the presentation be made at the site?

Submit a seating setup chart to the planner. Do this several weeks before the event for approval.

Submit a seating setup chart to catering. Submit your chart a few days before the event, ask permission of your planner first. Always pack an extra copy or two.

Request location and title of your presentation to be printed in the program.

Request signs be posted outside the presentation room door. Bring signs if your client does not have them. Get easels from the hotel. Attendees choose which break-out session to attend, the presenter is judged by the number who do. Be sure they can find you!

Ship your materials to the bell captain. Call several days ahead of the meeting to check that anything you sent is there. Use a second-day type carrier. It's not as expensive as next day yet still gets there quickly.

Arrange to have your presentation taped. Use a quality reproduction company if possible and affordable. These tapes can be used as demo tapes and products for resale. Only one in ten will be good enough to use, so try to tape all your presentations. If the planner is not taping you, ask the hotel if they have an audiovisual department that can do it. Often the local colleges and universities will send out students to tape you at a low cost. (Murphy's law for presenters is, "You never manage to tape your best presentations.")

Request two mikes, one on you and one on the audience. You want the tape to pick up the audience's laughter.

Is the client taping? You are within your legal rights to refuse to allow planners to tape your presentation. You can require royalties or a re-production fee. If you forget to check with the buyer before you arrive about taping, you can still refuse to perform. Your ethical rights are in question for not being responsible enough to check before the event.

Write articles or press releases for their company publication and in-dustry magazines. This sets you up before the event as an industry authority and helps to promote your image as a celebrity to their group.

Brainstorm with the client's publicity or public relations team.

Negotiate for a publicity day with the client. They arrange interviews with TV, radio, and publications. You are paid an extra fee for the day.

Mention the host organization in all media coverage they help you with. Also mention the event you are speaking at, your name, the location and time of the event, and your presentation title in any PR you do for that buyer or for publications that are distributed to those industries.

What are the buyers' special objectives and needs? What level of person are you addressing? Have they heard someone on your topic before? What were the good and bad aspects of that presenter?

Poll part of or all your audience ahead of the event. Learn their specific needs and problems. Tailor your material to them. For example, if the audience is 90 percent female, do not use football stories. Speak in terms of their interests.

Research current news about their industry. Check the papers, magazines, and the TV. There are services available through the library and the universities that will give you copies of all articles written on a specific topic.

Never use off-color "nightclub" material for business meetings. The audience may laugh, but you won't when the company refuses to pay you. Leave sexual and off-color jokes out of your material. If you wonder if a joke or story is OK, *Don't use it.* Especially watch any racial or male-female material. Once an audience walked out on a presenter who spoke disparagingly about the Japanese during his program. (The company had Japanese owners.) Good rule of thumb is not to disparage any group. Make fun only of yourself.

Emergencies and Delayed Travel

Booking safe travel. It is your obligation when you accept a fee for your speaking services to arrive ready and refreshed at the site. Do not book yourself so tight that you must take "red-eye" flights each night. Plan to arrive at least 4 hours before the event, preferably the day before. If your plane is delayed, you need the leeway to find alternate travel in case of cancellations and weather problems.

If you are delayed. Call ahead to both the hotel and the planner.

Who should you contact if an emergency occurs on the way? If everyone is already at the event and your transportation is delayed, you need at least one other contract with the host organization to help get the message through to the right people.

Compile a list of several other presenters who speak on your subject. Professional presenters say the only reasons for "no-shows" are death (preferably yours) and natural disasters that would stop Sylvester Stallone from reaching the meeting site. So, if either of these situations occur, you (or your next of kin) should be prepared. Some organizations require this "standby" on the contract.

After You Arrive, before the Presentation

Let your contact know at once that you have arrived. Never let your client worry and wonder. You are there to help the meeting planner.

Arrive the night before and check up on your presentation room. If it has not been set up yet, give catering the extra copy of the room setup chart you brought with you, they will no doubt have lost the original. If the room is set up, picture yourself as an audience member. Can the entire audience get the full benefit of your visuals with this seating arrangement? If they don't have it set up correctly, check with the planner. Sometimes it is just impossible to adjust the room to your needs because the next group needs it set up another way. Try for a compromise, and offer to fix it yourself. If it has not been set up yet, give your preapproved room-setup chart to catering.

Ask the hotel people what the emergency procedures are. Each venue has different procedures for fire, earthquake, medical emergencies, etc. Where are the exits and house phones located? Actually walk the fire exit paths to the street.

Assign one of your assistants as the person to call for help in emergencies. Show your assistant where the phones are yourself so you are both clear as to emergency procedures.

Go and meet the telephone switchboard and message center people at the hotel. As soon as you arrive. Say something nice. Let them know you just wanted to say Hi. Let them know you are expecting important calls and you wanted to thank them in advance.

Go to a hall phone and ask to be transferred to yourself. Do this after you have been there 30 minutes. You will be shocked at how many times they don't know you are registered there! Your buyer may call and become panicked, assuming you had plane trouble and are not going to make the meeting!

Check camera angles if videotaping. If a camera tapes your presentation, while you look through the camera lens, have someone stand where you will be speaking from and walk around as you do when you are speaking. Is anything distracting to the viewer's eye in the background? Will the lectern be in the way of the screen? Unneeded chairs in the way? When you write on a flip chart or blackboard is your back to the camera? Where are the dark spots? Stay in the light.

Practice any prop moves, lighting changes, etc. Practice all moves alone or with your assistants, as needed. The light switch people, introducer, projectionist, etc. Appoint someone to each light switch. Practice your signals. Test your visuals in various dimmed lighting.

Get all the electrical equipment up and running. Will you pull too much power when it all goes on and blow a fuse?

Bring *extra* bulbs and batteries. Whatever applies to the equipment you use. Do not leave them in your hotel room.

Safely tape down extension cords.

Write down names and addresses of your assistants. Send thank-you notes and/or bring small gifts to present to them at the meeting. They will never forget you.

Be sure *you* are spotlighted. Never work on stage in the dark. Some presenters carry their own spotlight and extension cords. You are the star, not the slides. Bring the lights up full as soon as possible. The audience needs only a few moments to review each slide. Then they *need* to see your face again, not a dark shadow. Double-check that your slides are in the right order and right side up *before* your presentation.

Check the staging. What will the audience see directly behind you on the stage? A blank wall or drapes are ideal. (Moose heads should be removed unless owned by your client.) Open windows must have sun glare and the view of bikinis at the pool blocked. Find out color of room and coordinate your clothing to complement it.

Make sure your mike is working before the audience enters. Find out where static and squelch sounds occur. Avoid that part of the room. Cordless mikes are great. Many presenters bring their own. These mikes allow the presenter the freedom to move all over the auditorium in an arc as big as a football field. Some are hand held, others fasten on the presenters clothing. But be sure to turn these off when you are finished.

Practice with your introducer. Bring an extra copy of the custom introduction (they usually will have lost it). Give the introducer a gift, just a small remembrance to say thank you for doing a good job of getting the presentation off to a good start.

Ask someone to time your presentation. Wear a watch with very large face, or bring a clock to put just out of sight on the lectern. Don't go over your time limit. If you are forced to start late, check with the meeting planner. Are you to cut your presentation time down, or give them the full time? Adjust to what your client wants.

Get pronunciation of names, titles, and current status with the company correct, if you use stories that involve members or employees of the organization you are addressing. Print them on a card in bold black pen and tape to the lectern where you can glance at them easily.

Distribute your handouts in the quickest manner possible. At meal functions they must be passed out after the dessert. In workshops they can be waiting for attendees on their seats. Include the evaluation forms.

Post signs to divide the room for smoking (with ash trays) and non-smoking. Test air flow. Put the smokers *downwind.*

Know where the facilities person will be at all times. You don't want to hunt if you're in trouble. One presenter discovered an error as she began her presentation. Her mike would not work, and the program from the adjoining room was piped into her room full blast.

Where are the air conditioning controls? Remember, it gets a lot hotter when the room fills up with people. You should feel cool when you are in there alone.

Many people are offended if you drink alcohol. Even if you are drinking a soda, people will often assume it is mixed with alcohol. Consider carrying the bottle or can of your nonalcoholic beverage around with you when you mingle and set it on the table with you at meals.

During the Presentation

Mention emergency procedures. If the Master of Ceremonies or the announcer has not done so, casually mention to the group that "in the unlikely event of a fire, the fire exits are there and there, please notice if anyone next to you needs assistance in leaving the room."

Let the audience stand up to stretch at least every two hours, preferably every hour. Include a participative section in long sessions over an hour and a half where the audience members speak to their neighbors or stand and shake hands, etc.

If catering starts clearing while you are speaking. Don't try to talk over a meal service. Make a joke, and calmly with a smile, ask them to leave. (Make sure the planner knew and agreed to there being no clearing going on during your presentation before you ask catering to leave the room.) One famous presenter began, then was faced with a waitress loudly stacking dishes at the head table. He yelled at the audience, "Let me introduce my wife!" The audience laughed, and the waitress departed.

Remind the attendees several times to fill out the evaluation forms. Allow a few moments at the end of your presentation to fill them out before they must leave for the next event.

If taping, repeat the questions from the audience. They will not pick up well on the tape, even if the audience is miked, unless someone is walking a mike right up to the question askers.

After the Presentation

Send a thank you. Never let your clients forget you. Send them thank you notes, a gift, news of new products and subjects that relate to their interests. Let them know you remember them.

When the show is over and everyone says, "I guess this sort of thing comes easily for you," just smile!

The 10 Percent I Hope You Will Remember About My Book...

1. Know exactly how you want to change the audience's actions and attitudes when they leave you. **Develop a mission.**

2. Realize they won't remember more than a few points anyway, so decide **what three or four points must be remembered.**

3. Speak with **passion for your topic and a compassion for your audience** and the rest will just fall in line!

The very best part of being a speaker is afterwards. People coming up— what they say and what they don't. Looking into their eyes and seeing that they used me as a mirror. Held me up as a mirror and looked inside them- selves and tuned in to some parts of themselves they had turned off for awhile—discovered some things they hadn't been in touch with. Perhaps they discover they no longer had any excuse to hide.

—W MITCHELL

I use one more learning technique at the end of each of my seminars and presentations that once again attempts to illuminate my mission for my audience—"passion and compassion...with a purpose"—a poem! A little corny? Perhaps! Do a few more lights turn on? You bet! Now that you have read this book, you are ready for your own...

Curtain Call
by Lilly Walters

We've shown you the challenge
Many skills to enhance
It's all set before you.
Will you join in the dance?

Your words can bring hope
And joy and new power,
For somebody crying,
In desperate hour.

You stride to the footlights
And the crowd goes so still.
Will they clap and applaud
And stand with the thrill?

Or...
Will glitter and glamour
Cause you to forget
The caring and sharing,
And your mission neglect?

The speech is now over
And gone is the crowd.
Did anyone hear you?
Did you come on...too proud?

Reliving it later
Sadly parked in your car
So much farther to go,
Yet, already *so far*.

Then, some kid at your door,
Says, "'fore you're off to bed,
Would you tell me more?
I *loved* what you said."

"Was unsure of my part.
I was crying today
Then your words touch'd my heart.
Do you mean what you say?"

"Were you talking to me?
I've a race to be run?
Is there power in me?
Did you mean...I'm the one?"

Well...
We've shown you the challenge
Will lives you enhance?
It's all set before you.
Will you join in the dance?

Publications

Sharing Ideas Among Professional Speakers Newsmagazine
Royal Publishing
P.O. Box 1120
Glendora, CA 91740
818-335-8069

Executive Speaker
P.O. Box 292437
Dayton, OH, 45429
513-294-8493

The Toastmaster
P.O. Box 9052
Mission Viejo, CA 92690-7052

Communications Briefings
700 Black Horse Pike, #110
Blackwood, New Jersey, 08012

Training Magazine
50 S. 9th St.
Minneapolis, MN 55402-3165

Educational Materials for Speakers

Speak and Grow Rich by Dottie and Lilly Walters. A book on how to increase your
income in the world of professional speaking. For an autographed copy, contact the authors at:

P.O. Box 1120
Glendora, CA 91740
818-335-8069

Persuasive Platform Presentations—Secrets of Successful Speakers by Lilly Walters. A 4½ hour audio album accompanied by a 70-page workbook. This material taken from an actual seminar.

Royal Publishing
P.O. Box 1120
Glendora, CA 91740
818-335-8069

How to Prepare, Stage, and Deliver Winning Presentations by Thomas Leech.

AMACOM
P. O. Box 319
Saranac Lake, NY 12983
518-891-5510

Games Presenters Play by Lilly Walters and Jeff Dewar. A two-hour training video on designing audience participation exercises.

Royal Publishing
P.O. Box 1120
Glendora, CA 91740
818-335-8069

Games Trainers Play, More Games Trainers Play, and *Still More Games Trainers Play* by Edward Scannell and John Newstrom. Books on training exercises.

McGraw-Hill, Inc.
c/o TAB Books
Blue Ridge Summit, PA 17294- 0701
800-722-4726

Speaking with Magic by Michael Jefferies. A book on using magic in speeches.

Royal Publishing
P.O. Box 1120
Glendora, CA 91740
818-335-8069

Index

About the Author

Lillet "Lilly" Walters is the executive director of Walters International Speakers Bureau, a professional lecture agency with a database of 20,000 professional and celebrity speakers. The speakers in the Speakers Bureau range from world famous celebrities to interesting and entertaining business experts. Lilly sends these speakers all over the world to such companies as ARCO, Shell Oil, Lockheed, Litton, IBM, McDonnell Douglas, and AT&T.

Lilly is the author of the audio program "Persuasive Platform Presentations—Secrets of Successful Speakers" and the video training program "Games Presenters Play." She is also the coauthor of the audio album "How to Enter the World of Paid Speaking" and the anthologies "The Great Communicators" and "FunnyBones! Humor and Health Experts." Her articles on how meeting planners can gain the greatest benefits from speakers have appeared in most major meeting and speaking industry publications, including *Successful Meetings, Meeting Manager* (Meeting Planners International's monthly magazine), *Meeting News, California Meetings, Association Management, Western Association News,* and many others.

Lilly is a frequent keynote and workshop presenter on such topics as "Secrets of Successful Speakers," "Games Presenters Play—How to Develop Audience Involvement Devices," and "How to Organize Meetings, Seminars, Workshops, and Pizzazz!"

Together, Lilly and Dottie, Lilly's world famous presenter mother, publish *Sharing Ideas Among Professional Speakers, Meeting Planners, Bureaus, and Agents,* the largest newsmagazine in the world for professional speakers, covering the tips, news, and trends of professional speaking. Lilly and Dottie are also coauthors of *Speak and Grow Rich,* the handbook of the professional speaking business now in its second printing, published by Prentice-Hall.